Civil Recovery of Criminal Property

OXFORD MONOGRAPHS ON CRIMINAL LAW AND JUSTICE

This series aims to cover all aspects of criminal law and procedure including criminal evidence. The scope of this series is wide, encompassing both practical and theoretical works.

OTHER TITLES IN THIS SERIES

The Insanity Defence
International and Comparative Perspectives
Ronnie Mackay, Warren Brookbanks

Justice In-Between
A Study of Intermediate Criminal Verdicts
Federico Picinali

Criminal Fraud and Election Disinformation
Law and Politics
Jeremy Horder

Policing the Borders Within
Ana Aliverti

Criminalizing Sex
A Unified Liberal Theory
Stuart P. Green

Reasons to Doubt
Wrongful Convictions and the Criminal Cases Review Commission
Carolyn Hoyle and Mai Sato

Fitness to Plead
International and Comparative Perspectives
Ronnie Mackay and Warren Brookbanks

Criminal Misconducts in Office
Law and Politics
Jeremy Horder

The Preventive Turn in Criminal Law
Henrique Carvalho

Criminal Justice and Taxation
Peter Alldridge

In Search of Criminal Responsibility
Ideas, Interests, and Institutions
Nicola Lacey

Preventive Justice
Andrew Ashworth and Lucia Zedner

Character in the Criminal Trial
Mike Redmayne

Homicide and the Politics of Law Reform
Jeremy Horder

The Insecurity State
Vulnerable Autonomy and the Right to Security in the Criminal Law
Peter Ramsay

Manifest Madness
Mental Incapacity in the Criminal Law
Arlie Loughnan

The Ethics of Plea Bargaining
Richard L. Lippke

Prosecuting Domestic Violence
A Philosophical Analysis
Michelle Madden Dempsey

Abuse of Process and Judicial Stays of Criminal Proceedings
Second Edition
Andrew L.-T. Choo

A Philosophy of Evidence Law
Justice in the Search of Truth
H. L. Ho

Civil Recovery of Criminal Property

COLIN KING
University of London
JENNIFER HENDRY
University of Leeds

OXFORD
UNIVERSITY PRESS

OXFORD
UNIVERSITY PRESS

Great Clarendon Street, Oxford, OX2 6DP,
United Kingdom

Oxford University Press is a department of the University of Oxford.
It furthers the University's objective of excellence in research, scholarship,
and education by publishing worldwide. Oxford is a registered trade mark of
Oxford University Press in the UK and in certain other countries

First Edition published in 2023

Published in the United States of America by Oxford University Press
198 Madison Avenue, New York, NY 10016, United States of America

British Library Cataloguing in Publication Data

Data available

Library of Congress Control Number is on file at the Library of Congress

ISBN 978–0–19–882425–1

DOI: 10.1093/oso/9780198824251.001.0001

Printed and bound by
CPI Group (UK) Ltd, Croydon, CR0 4YY

CK: To my mam, Leesa ('Lee'), for her love and support.

JH: To Agnes and Cathie, to whom I owe a great deal.

Foreword

With this timely book, Professor Colin King and Professor Jennifer Hendry have performed a great service to policy debate and legal practice. In many respects it is the book I would have wished to have as a useful corrective to the official narrative, when I was a practitioner in the proceeds of crime list on the respondents' side of the house.

From such a standpoint, this book gives a voice to defending barristers and solicitors that has been largely absent from the celebratory narrative around confiscation of proceeds of crime. One doesn't have to agree with that contrary view to welcome the acknowledgement of those challenging perspectives. Indeed, some of the comments quoted in the book underline the principle that one's views as a citizen and one's views as a legal representative don't have to align (indeed it would probably be a very bad day for the profession if barristers were to be allowed to decide not to take on causes they didn't believe in, such as prosecuting climate activists, for example).

The critique of the somewhat slippery notion of civil recovery as being *in rem*, and thus as having nothing to do with the respondent or their offending, is particularly effective.

The learned authors are to be commended not just for their scholarship and originality of thought, but also for the empirical methodology of their research which gives it a strength and credibility which more abstract work may lack. Some particularly unfortunate writers think that they can definitively lay down the law on intensely practical matters from the comfort of their keyboards, without any significant investigation of, or contact with, what happens "in real life". King and Hendry are a wonderful example of how to avoid that pitfall. The comparative analysis of both England & Wales and Ireland adds a depth and richness to their discussion.

In many respects, this book is a vindication of the techniques of socio-legal studies, blending effortlessly the sociological context, the perspectives of actors in the criminal justice field, and the legal analysis. Jointly authored works can occasionally show the fault-lines of construction, but this is another pitfall the authors have completely avoided. Here, King and Hendry have engaged in a fruitful collaboration that has demonstrated the real explanatory power of setting legal analysis within its social context. As a result, this accessible work will have a wide audience, not just among lawyers, but among a range of professionals, as well as the general reader.

Ultimately the question of how far the law should go in terms of the civil consequences of offending behaviour is largely a policy decision and therefore a political decision. King and Hendry are sceptics, and readers will no doubt make up their own minds about where the balance is to be struck. But wherever it lies, King and Hendry have made an excellent contribution to the debate with this impressive work.

Mr Justice Richard Humphreys
High Court of Ireland
19 June, 2023

Acknowledgements

This book is the culmination of a decade-long collaboration, which was sparked by what at the time appeared to be an innocuous conversation in a Leeds pub. We have been working together on the themes addressed in this book for so long that we have a great many people to thank, not least the six different Oxford University Press editors who tolerated us for the duration. First, we must thank the empirical study's participants—while anonymized in the book, we take this opportunity to acknowledge your specific contribution to this research and to thank you for speaking openly and honestly about your professional experience with civil recovery. We hope that our analysis has done justice to the information you shared with us. Thanks are due to the Arts & Humanities Research Council, whose early-career Leadership Fellowship awards created the necessary space and time for this socio-legal, theoretical, and doctrinal comparative project. We have received support and encouragement from many scholars, all of whom have been influential through their own research as well as being valuable interlocutors for the development of these ideas. We are particularly indebted to Simon Bronitt, Adam Crawford, Andrea Fraser, Clive Walker, Neil Walker, and Simon NM Young, whose work continues to inspire us. Dermot Walsh sparked interest in this topic many years ago at the University of Limerick. Institutionally, we have also been fortunate. We thank colleagues at the University of Sussex, particularly the Crime Research Centre and the Centre for the Study of Corruption, and the Institute of Advanced Legal Studies, University of London. We would also like to thank members of the Centre for Law & Social Justice and the Centre for Criminal Justice Studies at the University of Leeds School of Law. Special mention is due to Alastair Mullis and Carl Stychin for their faith and reassurance; we have relied heavily on both. Our greatest debt of gratitude goes to the friends and colleagues who generously gave their time to read and comment on chapters, frequently across several drafts and often at painfully short notice. To Helen Carr, John Child, Stavros Demetriou, Matt Dyson, Jess Mant, Brad Pomfret, Hannah Quirk, Duncan Sheehan, and Lucy Welsh, thank you so much for sharing your expertise and your time. Your comments and insights were so valuable to us, and really contributed to ensuring the quality of this work. At Oxford University Press we thank Jamie Berezin, Natasha Fleming, Iona Jacob,

Kezia Johnson, Paulina dos Santos Major, and Eve Ryle-Hodges. Thank you all for being patient, and sorry for telling so many fibs about deadlines. Finally, we would like to thank our families and friends, especially Saskia and Alex, who have been living with this book for almost as long as we have, and whose love and support we treasure.

Contents

List of Abbreviations

A1P1	Article 1 of the First Protocol
AML	anti-money laundering
ARO	Asset Recovery Office
Art.	Article
ASBO	Anti-Social Behaviour Order
CAB	Criminal Assets Bureau (Ireland)
CAB Act	Criminal Assets Bureau Act, 1996
cols	columns
CPN	Community Protection Notice
CPO	Civil Preventive Order
CTF	counter terrorist financing
DAPO	Domestic Abuse Prevention Order
ECHR	European Convention on Human Rights
ECtHR	European Court of Human Rights
EU	European Union
FATF	Financial Action Task Force
FBO	Football Banning Order
FIU	financial intelligence unit
GA	General Assembly (of the United Nations)
HL	House of Lords
IRO	interim receiving order
KCPO	Knife Crime Prevention Order
LEA	law enforcement agencies
ML	money laundering
MRO	management receiving order
NCB	non-conviction-based
OECD	Organisation for Economic Co-operation and Development
PEP	politically exposed person
PFO	property freezing order
POC(A)A	Proceeds of Crime (Amendment) Act 2016
POCA	Proceeds of Crime Act (1996, Ireland), (2002, UK)
PSPO	Public Space Protection Order
Rec.	Recital
s.	section
Sch.	Schedule
SCPO	Serious Crime Prevention Order

SCRs	Security Council Resolutions
SOCA	Serious Organised Crime Agency
StAR	Stolen Asset Recovery Initiative
TPIMs	Terrorism Prevention and Investigation Measures
UK	United Kingdom
UNCAC	UN Convention Against Corruption
UNCTOC	UN Convention against Transnational Organised Crime 2000
UNODC	United Nations Office on Drugs and Crime
US	United States
UWO	unexplained wealth order
vol.	volume

1

Introduction

Setting the Scene

Criminal law enforcement procedures have long struggled to cope with the disconnected and cumulative nature of organized criminality, in particular the conundrum of the 'kingpin' career criminal who operates at a remove. Civil recovery, which is the terminology we use to refer to confiscation of the proceeds of crime in the absence of criminal conviction, has thus been presented as a galvanizing measure for criminal justice's blunted weaponry, and a pragmatic answer to the problem of career criminality. In both Ireland and England & Wales,[1] *in rem* proceeds of crime legislation[2] provides that, under a civil standard of proof, an individual may be deprived of property where the court is satisfied that it has been acquired as proceeds of crime.

This impetus to 'make crime pay' can be contextualized within a global trend in the fight against serious and organized crime and corruption towards employing such hybridized 'follow the money' procedures. The motivation behind such indirect measures, compared to direct criminal law enforcement mechanisms, is a straightforward one, namely, to undermine the profit incentive of such criminality. Not only is the confiscation of 'dirty money' and other assets a deterrent in itself but it also impacts negatively against organized crime's animating force, *money*. In targeting the 'dirty assets' of serious and organized crime, therefore, civil recovery purports to represent an advantageous and expedient alternative to the criminal law.

Civil recovery's innovation lies in how it blurs the lines between criminal and civil procedure. Rules of legal procedure determine the steps to be taken and standards to be met in the resolution of issues coming before the law, and

[1] Our focus is on England & Wales, rather than the United Kingdom (UK) more widely given that all our interviewees had experience with the former. An almost identical legal regime exists in Scotland and Northern Ireland, albeit with some slight variations.

[2] Proceeds of Crime Act 1996 (Ireland); Proceeds of Crime Act 2002, Part 5 (UK).

Civil Recovery of Criminal Property. Colin King and Jennifer Hendry, Oxford University Press.
 DOI: 10.1093/oso/9780198824251.003.0001

civil and criminal processes have traditionally been distinguishable on this basis. Processes designated as 'criminal' attract enhanced procedural protections for the accused, while 'civil' processes operate under lesser burdens. The basis for criminal law's elevated protections are liberal values whereby citizens bear rights and state power is limited: those additional safeguards within the criminal process protect the rights of the accused and ensure against the potential misuse of state authority. This is not to say that citizens' rights are not protected in civil proceedings but, rather, that the potential consequences do not necessitate the same degree of mitigation.

Hybrid civil/criminal procedures—of which we argue civil recovery is one—omit the procedural dimensions ordinarily required by their own sort and, in so doing, erode the distinction between the civil law and the criminal law. Discussed in the academic literature under the names *inter alia* punitive sanctions, civil penalties, quasi-criminal measures, and 'civil for criminal processes',[3] such hybrids serve as alternatives to traditional criminal proceedings while displaying increased reliance upon legal techniques situated at the very edges of the civil/criminal distinction. The hybridity of these procedures subsists in how they often omit inbuilt procedural safeguards found respectively in criminal and civil practice. This strategic line-blurring can usually be traced to particular policy goals, such as public security or 'making crime pay', in circumstances where existing—usually criminal justice—measures appear to be inefficient or inadequate.

It is with reference to these two core aspects of civil recovery—'following the money' and procedural hybridity—that our analysis in this book will orient itself. While the former aspect concerns the focus on dirty assets in the context of how Ireland and England & Wales target the proceeds of crime, the latter strand considers the importance of due process and human rights compliance against these legislative goals. In considering the *justifiability* of this particular procedural hybrid, we present this legislative intentionality and due process compliance as countervailing forces that currently skew the balance in civil recovery towards the outcome, that is depriving alleged criminals of proceeds of crime, to the detriment of due process.

[3] See, e.g., Kenneth Mann, 'Punitive Civil Sanctions: The Middleground Between Criminal and Civil Law' (1992) 101 *Yale Law Journal* 1795; Simon Young, 'Enforcing Criminal Law Through Civil Processes: How Does Human Rights Law Treat "Civil for Criminal Processes"?' (2017) 4(2) *Journal of International and Comparative Law* 133; Robin White, '"Civil Penalties": Oxymoron, Chimera and Stealth Sanction' (2010) 126 *Law Quarterly Review* 593.

Arguments

Civil recovery is said to be justified on two counts: the 'failure' of traditional criminal justice process just discussed, and the value-based policy position that crime should not pay. There are four principal and connected arguments that this monograph will lead concerning the hybrid civil/criminal procedure we refer to as civil recovery: (i) the apparent failure of traditional criminal justice approaches has eroded individual procedural protections; (ii) civil recovery is mislabelled as a civil procedure, considering it constitutes a state response to wrongful activity; (iii) it is further mislabelled as an action against the property (*in rem*), as the deprivation of property affects the individual; and (iv) the so-called 'pragmatic' approach downplays the harms of civil recovery, mistakenly justifying these as an acceptable price to pay for its practical benefits.

The first of these is that the introduction of and reliance upon 'follow the money' approaches in general, and civil recovery in particular, are borne from a perceived failure of existing criminal processes effectively and adequately to combat serious and organized crime. The global growth of illegal economic activity, combined with the often diffuse networks and structures of organized criminality, has generated particular difficulties for traditional criminal law enforcement. Primary among the 'obstacles' encountered by traditional approaches are the criminal law's enhanced procedural standards, which not only restrict the exercise of police powers but also complicate the task of prosecutors. These standards, which constitute heightened protections for the individual against the power of the state—for example, the criminal standard of proof, the rule against hearsay, the right to silence, and the presumption of innocence—have been subject to continued and concerted legislative erosion on the grounds that they pose too high an impediment for criminal justice.[4] Instead of being seen as important and necessary protections against abuse, these rights-based protections are presented as the *problem*, as hindrances in the fight against organized crime and to the exercise of criminal justice.[5] We argue that this gradual wearing down of individual procedural rights under the guise of increased efficiency is problematic, and that the notion that this

[4] See generally Antony Duff, Lindsay Farmer, Sandra Marshall, and Victor Tadros, *The Trial on Trial, Volume 3: Towards a Normative Theory of the Criminal Trial* (Hart 2007); Shane Kilcommins, Ian O'Donnell, Eoin O'Sullivan, and Barry Vaughan, *Crime, Punishment and the Search for Order in Ireland* (IPA 2004).

[5] Dáil Éireann, Private Members' Business—Organised Crime (Restraint and Disposal of Illicit Assets) Bill, 1996. Second Stage. 2 July 1996; HL Deb, Proceeds of Crime Bill, 25 June 2002. Cf. Performance and Innovation Unit, *Recovering the Proceeds of Crime* (Cabinet Office 2000).

is either simple pragmatism or a mere 'rebalancing' in favour of state power is disingenuous.

Our second argument draws attention to the normatively motivated political expediency behind civil recovery—and, indeed, other civil/criminal procedural hybrids—and the manner in which that expediency is privileged over considerations of human rights and due process. The seizure of assets that are suspected, on the balance of probabilities, to have resulted from criminal activity is thus vindicated on the grounds that the action is *in rem* (against the property) and not *in personam* (against the person), meaning that no stigma of criminal conviction will attach to the defendant and there is no punishment as such. We argue that, by means of this rhetorical mislabelling of a criminal procedure *as civil*, civil recovery deliberately circumvents individual due process protections in a manner contrary to the rule of law. We further contend that the courts in both Ireland and England & Wales, as well as in Strasbourg, have been problematically lax in scrutinizing this issue.

The third strand of our argument builds on the idea that civil recovery constitutes the mislabelling of a criminal process as civil. We make the case that the procedure's hybridity effectively masks the relevant 'moral harm' caused to a respondent whose assets are wrongly confiscated.[6] Rejecting the premise that civil recovery is a practical and pragmatic *in rem* response to the failure of criminal justice processes adequately to tackle serious and organized crime, we argue that it is erroneous to equate the wrongful seizure of assets with a wrongful civil judgment for the reason that such wrongful seizure *de facto* constitutes the unjust and unjustified *punishment* of that individual *as if they have been engaged in criminal or undesirable* behaviour. The notion that under civil recovery proceedings, it is the property (*in rem*) and not the person (*in personam*) that is liable not only amounts to an unconvincing legal fiction but also belies the illiberal truth: that it is an individual's property rights that are being infringed.

Fourth and finally, informed by empirical data gleaned from practitioner interviews, we interrogate and then reject the prevalent view that civil recovery is a justifiable 'means to an end', where the end is tackling the social problem of organized crime. We lead the argument that practitioners who adopt such a pragmatic approach effectively privilege suspicion over proof and, in doing so, diminish the moral harm of the erroneous deprivation of property.

[6] Ronald Dworkin, *A Matter of Principle* (Harvard University Press 1985) 80–2.

Method

While there is a burgeoning literature on civil recovery powers in Ireland and England & Wales, and further afield, this literature adopts a predominantly doctrinal approach to analyse legislation and subsequent case law.[7] Aside from a few notable and mainly North American exceptions,[8] there has been a distinct lack of empirical engagement with the operation of civil recovery in practice. Our intention is to remedy this deficiency by providing the first theoretically and empirically informed analysis of civil recovery. This approach builds upon the important doctrinal discussions and debates while also contextualizing the respective Proceeds of Crime legislation and judicial reaction within broader trends of procedural hybridization, legislative pragmatism, and 'follow the money' approaches. It further informs these theoretical observations with socio-legal ones by means of semi-structured interviews with practitioners professionally engaged with civil recovery proceedings, both in defence and in enforcement.

The value of practitioner interviews (qualitative methodology) is that they provide valuable insights from those who work at the coalface of the legal system,[9] and into how these provisions operate in practice, insights that facilitate an exploration that goes beyond the mere analysis of legislation and case law. We conducted semi-structured 'elite' interviews with twenty-seven practitioners, each with considerable expertise in civil recovery.[10] In light of the specialized nature of the field,[11] elite interviews were recognized as being the ideal methodological approach to investigate how civil recovery operates in practice.[12]

[7] This literature is explored in detail later in this book.

[8] See M Michelle Gallant, 'An Empirical Glimpse of Civil Forfeiture Actions in Canada' in Colin King, Clive Walker, and Jimmy Gurulé (eds), *The Palgrave Handbook of Criminal and Terrorism Financing Law* (Palgrave 2018); Dick Carpenter, Lisa Knepper, Angela Erickson, and Jennifer McDonald, *Policing for Profit: The Abuse of Civil Asset Forfeiture* (2nd edn, Institute for Justice 2015).

[9] Kate Fitz-Gibbon, 'Overcoming Barriers in the Criminal Court System: Examining the Challenges Faced When Interviewing Legal Stakeholders' in Karen Lumsden and Aaron Winter (eds), *Reflexivity in Criminological Research: Experiences with the Powerless and the Powerful* (Palgrave 2014).

[10] Robert Mikecz, 'Interviewing Elites: Addressing Methodological Issues' (2012) 18(6) *Qualitative Inquiry* 482; William Harvey, 'Strategies for Conducting Elite Interviews' (2011) 11(4) *Qualitative Research* 431.

[11] For example, in Ireland there are fewer than thirty practitioners at the Irish Bar who are actively practising in this area. There are, of course, much more practitioners in this area at the Bar in England & Wales, though it is not possible to suggest precise numbers.

[12] We deliberately explore the views of practitioners and enforcement officials (as opposed to, say, lay individuals) given their professional involvement in civil recovery proceedings. Another avenue of future research is to explore the views of those subject to civil recovery proceedings (i.e. the respondents themselves), which was not possible in this project. For consideration of respondent perspectives in the context of post-conviction confiscation, see Craig Fletcher, 'Social Value or Social Harm? The Impact of the Proceeds of Crime Act 2002 upon the Defendant and their Families' in Katie Benson, Colin King,

Given the expert knowledge of the interviewees, the interviews were presented as 'opportunit[ies] to have an informed discussion'.[13] Participants were identified based on convenience sampling: for example, through their involvement in civil recovery proceedings, by virtue of their position in relevant enforcement agencies, through recommendations from other participants ('snowballing'), or by their attendance at conferences focusing explicitly on proceeds of crime.[14] Interviewees were contacted directly by email and supplied with an information sheet about the study. With a view to retaining a clear emphasis on the operation of civil recovery in practice, this qualitative study was confined to practitioners from both jurisdictions who either were or had been actively involved with such proceedings. Interviews were recorded and transcribed unless specific objections were raised by individual participants, in which case handwritten notes were made.

Interviews were conducted over three time periods. The initial interviews with participants in Ireland (nine in total) were conducted between November 2015 and April 2016. Amendments to the Irish legislation, enacted in July 2016 in response to particular events,[15] necessitated further data collection for completeness, with the result that a tenth interview was conducted in August 2016, while former interviewees still practising actively within this field were contacted to ask if they wished to add further comments in light of the 2016 amendments. In addition, a further three interviews were conducted with Irish participants in May to June 2019. Interviews with Irish practitioners lasted on average ninety-six minutes.

and Clive Walker (eds), *Assets, Crimes, and the State: Innovations in 21st Century Legal Approaches* (Routledge 2020).

[13] Robert Mikecz, 'Interviewing Elites: Addressing Methodological Issues' (2012) 18(6) *Qualitative Inquiry* 482, 485. Relevant themes for interviews were identified from doctrinal and theoretical literature as well as previous discussions with legal practitioners and enforcement officials. Interviews also included scope for participants to identify other issues that have not been prominent in extant literature.

[14] This approach enabled us to ensure a variety of perspectives and, in particular, contrasting views of respondent- and enforcement-focused practitioners. It also ensured that we interviewed individuals with in-depth knowledge of law and practice, as evidenced by their participation in notable civil recovery proceedings. Where recommendations about other potential experts were received from interviewees, we reviewed online profiles (e.g. on Chambers' websites) to confirm that the suggested individual had relevant expertise on civil recovery (as opposed to, for example, post-conviction confiscation proceedings). When seeking recommendations, we also sought suggestions for both respondent-focused and enforcement-focused practitioners. Finally, we drew upon professional connections with enforcement agencies—this allowed a strong representation of views from the Irish Criminal Assets Bureau. By contrast, in England & Wales, professional connections enabled access to former enforcement officials, but—as outlined in n.17—it was more difficult to interview current enforcement officials.

[15] See, e.g., Conor Lally, 'Gang Armed with Assault Rifle Shoot Man Dead at Dublin Hotel', *The Irish Times* (5 February 2016); Ciarán D'Arcy, 'Fears of More Violence After Gangland Shooting in Dublin', *The Irish Times* (22 May 2016).

While the interviews in England & Wales were initially planned for 2017, these were postponed in light of proposals that would amend the legislative framework.[16] These interviews commenced in November 2018 and were concluded by August 2019. Eleven practitioners were interviewed during this period. Initial efforts to interview current enforcement officials were unsuccessful,[17] although two former enforcement officials were interviewed. In October and December 2021, three further interviews were conducted (one with a former enforcement official and two with enforcement officials) to ensure that the enforcement perspective was reflected as best as possible, notwithstanding continued difficulties in securing interviews with current enforcement officials. Interviews with practitioners in England & Wales lasted on average seventy-four minutes.

Interviewees from the two earlier rounds of interviews were contacted by email in August 2021 and given an opportunity to add further comments.[18] The number and length of these twenty-seven expert practitioner interviews, and follow-ups, facilitated greater insight into the 'on the ground' processes of civil recovery and gave a 'voice' to practitioners in their capacity as 'practical' experts.[19] The professional background of interviewees is set out in Tables 1.1 and 1.2.

Our aim in conducting the practitioner interviews was to offer an empirically informed insight into the practical operation of these controversial powers. We were particularly keen to determine whether these views from practice were in keeping with the critical academic position or whether they presented alternatives. This was also the case in terms of central themes: while academic debates tend to coalesce around certain key issues, we were interested as to whether these same issues would be raised as points of central practical concern. We also left scope for interviewees to identify any practice-specific issues that have not been prominent in academic debates thus far. Finally, we

[16] House of Commons, Criminal Finances Bill (First and Second Sittings), 15 November 2016. The Criminal Finances Act 2017 received Royal Assent on 27 April 2017.

[17] As well as contacting enforcement agencies directly, we also emailed personal contacts at these agencies. Some replied indicating willingness, subject to approval, however this was not forthcoming. As one person replied: 'I am sorry for the slow response, ... I have not seen any emails so far regarding the query. I will check the rest of my emails and revert to you.' Another said: 'I would be delighted to assist in whatever way I can with your book. I also have a colleague ... who would have a relevant contribution to make. All of course subject to the caveat that we can get ... approval.' It was noted that such requests had recently been declined due to 'overwhelming operational commitments'.

[18] Only interviewees who were still in active practice were contacted at this stage.

[19] Throughout this book the pronoun 'they' is used when referring to interviewees, to preserve anonymity.

Table 1.1 Interviewee backgrounds—Ireland

Interviewee	Background
IRE1	Criminal defence solicitor
IRE2	Barrister (primarily acts/ acted for respondents in POCA proceedings)
IRE3	Criminal Assets Bureau (CAB) official
IRE4	Barrister (primarily acts/ acted for CAB in POCA proceedings)
IRE5	CAB official
IRE6	Barrister (primarily acts/ acted for CAB in POCA proceedings)
IRE7	Barrister (primarily acts/ acted for CAB in POCA proceedings)
IRE8	Criminal defence solicitor
IRE9	Barrister (primarily acts/ acted for CAB in POCA proceedings)
IRE10	Irish Council for Civil Liberties representative
IRE11	Former CAB official
IRE12	CAB official
IRE13	CAB official

Table 1.2 Interviewee backgrounds—England & Wales

Interviewee	Background
EW1	Criminal defence solicitor
EW2	Criminal defence solicitor
EW3	Barrister (primarily acts/ acted for enforcement authorities in POCA proceedings)
EW4	Barrister (primarily acts/ acted for respondents in POCA proceedings taken by enforcement authorities)
EW5	Barrister (primarily acts/ acted for enforcement authorities in POCA proceedings)
EW6	Criminal defence solicitor
EW7	Barrister (primarily acts/ acted for respondents in POCA proceedings taken by enforcement authorities)
EW8	Criminal defence solicitor
EW9	Barrister (primarily acts/ acted for enforcement authorities in POCA proceedings)
EW10	Former enforcement official
EW11	Former enforcement official
EW12	Former enforcement official
EW13	Enforcement official
EW14	Enforcement official

wanted to chart any clear differences of views expressed, respectively, by interviewees involved in different sides of civil recovery proceedings, as well as salient variations across the two selected jurisdictions. While we distinguish the interviewees along jurisdictional lines here and in our referencing, our critical analysis of civil recovery concerns its central features more than its jurisdictionally specific doctrinal detail, and so draws upon the interview data as a single collection.

It was recognized at the outset that there would be sharply contrasting views on civil recovery in general, as well as on distinct aspects, for example, evidentiary rules and property rights. We do not attempt to find a common ground in these different views; rather, our interviews aimed to draw out these differing views and to explore existing academic criticisms in light of these fresh practitioner insights. The semi-structured interview approach allowed the interviewer to adopt a consistent approach with questions, but also to 'talk back' to the interviewee.[20] The perspective of respondent-focused practitioners was put to enforcement-focused practitioners during interview, and vice versa; this allowed interviewees to engage directly with differing perspectives and offer their own rebuttals or agreement.

All interviews and coding were conducted by the same person to ensure consistency, using a thematic analysis approach.[21] The data was coded manually following the first round of interviews (April 2016). The interpretation of themes was done by reading and rereading interview data, reference to relevant literature, and consultation with colleagues. After the second round of interviews, all data was analysed using nVivo, again coded manually and on a jurisdiction basis—i.e. the Irish data was coded first, followed by the English & Welsh data (March and April 2020). Again here, interpretation of themes involved reading and rereading of data, reference to literature and consultation with colleagues. Subsequently, themes were revised for commonalities or overlaps and, where relevant, themes were combined or grouped together. Finally, the three additional interviews conducted towards the end of this project were coded (December 2021) and the themes identified mapped onto the earlier themes.

[20] Christine Griffin, 'The Researcher Talks Back: Dealing with Power Relations in Studies of Young People's Entry into the Job Market' in William Shaffir and Robert Stebbins (eds), *Experiencing Fieldwork: An Inside View of Qualitative Research* (Sage 1991).

[21] Virginia Braun and Victoria Clarke, 'Using Thematic Analysis in Psychology' (2006) 3(2) *Qualitative Research in Psychology* 77.

Terminology

Setting out the meaning of different terms in the proceeds of crime context is unfortunately not a straightforward task, and this is complicated by the fact that, 'in principle, there is no generally used or accepted terminology in this area'.[22] For example, even just in relation to the non-conviction-based approach to seizing criminal assets, the United States (US) and Ireland use the term 'civil forfeiture',[23] the United Kingdom uses the term 'civil recovery',[24] and continental Europe tends to prefer 'non-conviction-based confiscation'.[25] This awkward lack of terminological consistency makes it important, first, to establish what different terms mean in different jurisdictions, and second, to outline those to be used throughout this book.

In 1984, the Hodgson Committee—established by the Howard League for Penal Reform to report on *Profits of Crime and Their Recovery*—noted that:

> At an early stage we realised that there was no generally accepted terminology to describe the various situations which we should have to examine. To some extent we have had to invent our own vocabulary and we have consequently attributed discrete meaning to terms which in ordinary speech might be treated as synonymous. The four words we use are 'forfeiture', 'compensation', 'restitution', and 'confiscation'.[26]

These terms were then defined by the Committee as follows:

- Forfeiture: 'the power of the Court to take property that is immediately connected with an offence'.
- Compensation: 'financial reparation to a victim by an offender for loss, injury, suffering or damage resulting from an offence'.

[22] Malin Thunberg Schunke, *Extended Confiscation in Criminal Law: National, European and International Perspectives* (Intersentia 2017) 12.

[23] Stefan Cassella, 'The Case for Civil Forfeiture: Why in rem Proceedings Are an Essential Tool for Recovering the Proceeds of Crime' (2008) 11(1) *Journal of Money Laundering Control* 8; Michelle Gallant and Colin King, 'The Seizure of Illicit Assets: Patterns of Civil Forfeiture in Canada and Ireland' (2013) 42 *Common Law World Review* 91.

[24] Anthony Kennedy, 'Justifying the Civil Recovery of Criminal Proceeds' (2004) 12(1) *Journal of Financial Crime* 8; Peter Alldridge, 'Civil Recovery in England and Wales: An Appraisal' in Colin King, Clive Walker, and Jimmy Gurulé (eds), *The Palgrave Handbook of Criminal and Terrorism Financing Law* (Palgrave 2018).

[25] Jon Petter Rui and Ulrich Sieber (eds), *Non-Conviction-Based Confiscation in Europe* (Duncker & Humblot 2015); Michele Simonato, 'Directive 2014/42/EU and Non-Conviction Based Confiscation: A Step Forward on Asset Recovery' (2015) 6 *New Journal of European Criminal Law* 213.

[26] Howard League for Penal Reform, *Profits of Crime and Their Recovery: Report of a Committee Chaired by Sir Derek Hodgson* (Heinemann 1984) 4–5.

- Restitution: 'the return of property or its monetary equivalent to the person from whom it was unlawfully taken'.
- Confiscation: 'the depriving of an offender of the proceeds or the profits of crime'.[27]

Although these definitions appear straightforward, the Scottish Law Commission, in its 1994 Report on confiscation and forfeiture, noted that 'forfeiture' was used within its own terms of reference in two different senses. The first sense is the power of a court to take property used for the purpose of committing, or facilitating the commission of, offences, while the second sense is the power of a court to deprive an offender of the *proceeds* of criminal activity *and of property derived from such proceeds*. In making this observation, the Scottish Law Commission further noted that, in North American usage, forfeiture signifies both of these powers, while in international conventions, including the Convention on Laundering, Search, Seizure and Confiscation of the Proceeds from Crime, the term used to indicate both is 'confiscation'.[28] In the interests of clarity, the Commission expressed a preference that the two terms be distinguished, with 'forfeiture' being used in the first sense, and 'confiscation' in the second.

Frustratingly, however, this terminological schism continues yet today. Barbara Vettori has highlighted the distinction between the understanding of 'forfeiture' within the United Kingdom, Ireland, and the European Union (EU), and the wider coverage of the term in the United States, noting that contemporaneous usage of the two terms—forfeiture and confiscation—is effectively interchangeable, with the result that 'the potential for confusion is high'.[29] The lack of consistency in wording can be illustrated with some examples: EU Directive 2014/42/EU states that confiscation means 'a final deprivation of property ordered by a court in relation to a criminal offence'.[30] The Council of Europe's 2005 Warsaw Convention provides that confiscation means 'a penalty or a measure, ordered by a court following proceedings in relation to a criminal offence or criminal offences resulting in the final deprivation of property'.[31] The global money laundering and terrorist financing watchdog, the

[27] Howard League for Penal Reform, *Profits of Crime and Their Recovery: Report of a Committee Chaired by Sir Derek Hodgson* (Heinemann 1984) 5.

[28] Scottish Law Commission, *Report on Confiscation and Forfeiture. Report on a Reference under Section 3(1)(e) of the Law Commissions Act 1965. Cm 2622* (Stationery Office 1994) 2.

[29] Barbara Vettori, *Tough on Criminal Wealth* (Springer 2006) 2.

[30] Directive 2014/42/EU of the European Parliament and of the Council of 3 April 2014 on the freezing and confiscation of instrumentalities and proceeds of crime in the European Union, Art. 2(4).

[31] Convention on Laundering, Search, Seizure and Confiscation of the Proceeds from Crime and on the Financing of Terrorism, Art. 1(d).

Financial Action Task Force (FATF), sets out yet another definition in its 2012 International Standards, providing that

> The term confiscation, which includes forfeiture where applicable, means the permanent deprivation of funds or other assets by order of a competent authority or a court. Confiscation or forfeiture takes place through a judicial or administrative procedure that transfers the ownership of specified funds or other assets to be transferred to the State... Confiscation or forfeiture orders are usually linked to a criminal conviction or a court decision whereby the confiscated or forfeited property is determined to have been derived from or intended for use in a violation of the law.[32]

And lest anyone believe that the United Nations Office on Drugs and Crime (UNODC) was likely to provide a conclusive definition, in 2012 it outlined that the confiscation of assets or property 'also known in some jurisdictions as "forfeiture", means the permanent deprivation of property by order of a court or other competent authority',[33] then immediately muddied the waters by going on to explain that forfeiture means the 'permanent deprivation of property by order of a court or other competent authority', stating further that 'the term is often used interchangeably with confiscation'.[34]

This terminological confusion continues today, with the effect that, in some instances, the term 'confiscation' is used to represent *all* kinds of confiscation, whereas at other times the term is taken to mean confiscation in relation to *property that is derived from a specific crime for which an individual has been convicted*. Importantly, in this book, and whether that procedure is conviction- or non-conviction-based, we use the term 'confiscation' in the wider sense, that is, to denote a value- or property-based procedure,[35] more about which will be said in the next section.

'Asset recovery' must also be added to the lexicon of relevant terms.[36] Not only does asset recovery denote the legal proceedings to confiscate or forfeit

[32] FATF, *International Standards on Combatting Money Laundering and the Financing of Terrorism and Proliferation* (FATF/OECD 2012, updated in March 2022), Glossary.

[33] UNODC, *Manual on International Cooperation for the Purposes of Confiscation of Proceeds of Crime* (United Nations 2012) 1.

[34] UNODC, *Manual on International Cooperation for the Purposes of Confiscation of Proceeds of Crime* (United Nations 2012) 2.

[35] Johan Boucht, *The Limits of Asset Confiscation: On the Legitimacy of Extended Appropriation of Criminal Proceeds* (Hart Publishing 2017) 16.

[36] See, e.g., Eurojust, *Report on Eurojust's Casework in Asset Recovery* (February 2019). Jean-Pierre Brun et al., *Asset Recovery Handbook: A Guide for Practitioners* (2nd edn, StAR Initiative, World Bank 2020).

property but, according to one European Commission Working Paper, it also encompasses the wider asset tracing phase, such as the work undertaken by national financial intelligence units (FIUs) and Asset Recovery Offices (AROs), *and* the disposal phase, which concerns both the sale of an asset or the re-use of property for public purposes.[37] Furthermore, asset recovery is the term used in the specific context of targeting corruption-related assets of politically exposed persons (PEPs),[38] in which regard a report from the Stolen Asset Recovery Initiative (StAR) has stated that asset recovery is 'defined to include the powers envisaged in article 53–55 of UNCAC and is effectively the process by which proceeds of corruption are recovered and returned to a foreign jurisdiction'.[39] Where 'asset recovery' is used in this book, the term is given its broader meaning, which is to say it is not confined to corruption-related recovery.

Distinguishing Post-Conviction and Non-Conviction-Based Approaches

Additional important distinctions must also be drawn. First, we must distinguish between approaches that are *post*-conviction and those that are *non*-conviction based. We must subsequently also distinguish between criminal and civil non-conviction-based approaches. These will be explained in turn.

Criminal (post-conviction) confiscation

There is legislative provision in Ireland and in England & Wales for the post-conviction confiscation of assets[40] and for the non-conviction-based confiscation of proceeds of crime,[41] the latter of which can be civil or criminal. For a post-conviction confiscation order, all of the criminal process enhanced procedural protections apply at the criminal trial, including the presumption of innocence, the standard of proof beyond reasonable doubt, and exclusionary

[37] European Commission, *Commission Staff Working Paper. Accompanying Document to the Proposal for a Directive of the European Parliament and the Council on the Freezing and Confiscation of Proceeds of Crime in the European Union Impact Assessment* (Brussels, 12 March 2012. SWD (2012) final) para 2.1.1.

[38] For example, Rita Adam, 'Innovation in Asset Recovery: The Swiss Perspective' (2012) *World Bank Legal Review* 253.

[39] Larissa Gray, Kjetil Hansen, Pranvera Recica-Kirkbride, and Linnea Mills, *Few and Far: The Hard Facts on Stolen Asset Recovery* (StAR Initiative, World Bank 2014) 9.

[40] Proceeds of Crime Act 2002, Parts 2 to 4 (E + W); Criminal Justice Act 1994, Parts 2 and 3 (Ireland).

[41] Proceeds of Crime Act 2002, Part 5 (E + W); Proceeds of Crime Act 1996 (Ireland).

rules of evidence, such as the rule against hearsay. At the criminal confiscation hearing, however, the standard of proof employed is the civil standard, which is to say, the balance of probabilities, and the rules of evidence are akin to those in a sentencing hearing.[42]

Within this category of criminal confiscation there are different types. For example, 'ordinary' or 'regular' confiscation is where a link can be established between the property to be confiscated and the specific criminal offence at issue, that is, the criminal offence for which the defendant has been convicted. Given the practical difficulties in establishing such a link, in certain instances confiscation can even be *extended* without one, hence the term 'extended confiscation'.[43] According to the definition provided by the European Commission, extended confiscation is 'the ability to confiscate assets which go beyond the direct proceeds of a crime so that there is no need to establish a connection between suspected criminal assets and a specific criminal conduct'.[44] At this juncture we should also flag the distinction between property-based confiscation, whereby the confiscation is directed at specific property, and value-based confiscation, where the focus is on the value of benefit derived from criminal activity and a monetary penalty imposed that is equal to that value.

Non-conviction-based confiscation

Alongside the expanding criminal confiscation regime, a non-conviction-based regime for the confiscation of proceeds of crime has also emerged in both jurisdictions. Despite being conceived in response to the same basic problem, namely the failure of traditional criminal justice processes that we outlined earlier, this non-conviction-based regime displays considerable

[42] Peter Alldridge, 'Proceeds of Crime since 2003—Two Key Areas' [2014] *Criminal Law Review* 171, 173–4.

[43] Malin Thunberg Schunke, *Extended Confiscation in Criminal Law: National, European and International Perspectives* (Intersentia 2017) 4–5; Michele Simonato, 'Extended Confiscation of Criminal Assets: Limits and Pitfalls of Minimum Harmonisation in the EU' (2016) 41(5) *European Law Review* 727. See also text to n.47 below.

[44] European Commission, *Communication from the Commission to the European Parliament and the Council. The EU Internal Security Strategy in Action: Five steps towards a more secure Europe* (Brussels, 22 November 2010. COM (2010) 673 final) 6. Article 5 (headed 'Extended Confiscation') of Directive 2014/42/EU states: 'Member States shall adopt the necessary measures to enable the confiscation, either in whole or in part, of property belonging to a person convicted of a criminal offence which is liable to give rise, directly or indirectly, to economic benefit, where a court, on the basis of the circumstances of the case, including the specific facts and available evidence, such as that the value of the property is disproportionate to the lawful income of the convicted person, is satisfied that the property in question is derived from criminal conduct.'

variation across countries.[45] The European Commission has acknowledged the complicated nature of the (post-conviction) confiscation process in practice:

> When seeking to deprive criminals of the proceeds deriving from organised criminal activity, law enforcement services are often faced with complex financial flows aimed at hiding the illicit origin of assets as well as structures that distance the offender from the crime. Even if illicit funds are discovered, connecting them to a criminal act and an offender can pose considerable obstacles. In response to this challenge, *legal regimes allowing for the confiscation of property without the need of a prior criminal conviction have been developed in a considerable number of jurisdictions*. ... While the approaches to establish such non-conviction based confiscation regimes in EU Member States differ considerably regarding their design, legal base and application, they were all developed in response to the same problem.[46]

Four typologies of non-conviction-based confiscation are evident in European Union confiscation law.[47] These can be outlined as follows:

> Model 1: Classic non-conviction-based confiscation applies where confiscation is not possible on the basis of a final conviction, on the grounds that the defendant has died, has absconded, or cannot (or is unfit to) be brought before the court (for example, due to immunity, age, or mental state). This model is linked to criminal proceedings.
> Model 2: Extended confiscation allows for the confiscation of assets that are *not connected* to the crime for which the defendant is being prosecuted. The confiscation order is *extended* beyond the assets related to the criminal prosecution at hand to include other assets that the defendant owns.

[45] For consideration of variations in different jurisdictions, see Anthony Kennedy, 'Designing a Civil Forfeiture System: An Issues List for Policymakers and Legislators' (2006) 13(2) *Journal of Financial Crime* 132.

[46] European Commission, *Commission Staff Working Document. Analysis of Non-Conviction Based Confiscation Measures in the European Union* (Brussels, 12 April 2019. SWD (2019)1050 final) 2. (emphasis added)

[47] European Commission, *Commission Staff Working Document. Analysis of Non-Conviction Based Confiscation Measures in the European Union* (Brussels, 12 April 2019. SWD (2019) 1050 final) 3. Note that some countries will provide for more than one model or hybrid versions of these models. Indeed, the European Commission acknowledges this as follows: 'This classification is only meant to help categorise the different approaches taken in Member States. It facilitates mapping the different approaches to this policy area and identifying trends while also providing a useful frame of reference for the reader. The actual legislative regimes in Member States are often of a hybrid nature and the CARIN classification should only be seen as an indication' (3). The models used by the EU were inspired by the Camden Asset Recovery Inter-Agency Network: Camden Asset Recovery Inter-Agency Network, *The History, Statement of Intent, Membership and Functioning of CARIN (CARIN Manual 5th edn)* (Europol 2015).

Model 3: Civil confiscation is an action against the property (*in rem*), not against the person (*in personam*), to confiscate property obtained through unlawful conduct. The process is civil in nature, although with an indirect link to a crime or criminal activity. Known alternatively as 'preventive confiscation' or 'civil recovery', this form of civil non-conviction-based confiscation is our focus in this book.

Model 4: Unexplained wealth involves the comparison of the actual property that a person has acquired against declared income, so as to identify any disparity between the two. Establishing a direct or indirect link to a predicate offence is not necessary.

Our focus in this book is on civil non-conviction-based confiscation, with specific focus on the third typology, which is the model that applies in Ireland,[48] and in England & Wales.[49] Indeed, although English and Welsh law also provides for unexplained wealth orders (UWOs)[50] the effect of such orders is that, where a respondent does not comply with the order, the property in question is to be presumed to be 'recoverable property' for the purposes of civil recovery proceedings—that is, falling within model 3.[51] UWOs in England & Wales can thus be differentiated from unexplained wealth regimes in other jurisdictions, such as Australia (model 4),[52] and further distinguished from the situation in Ireland, where unexplained wealth orders—in either of the senses already discussed—do not apply.[53]

Civil recovery

To minimize confusion, throughout this book we have adopted the term 'civil recovery'—the same term as the one used in the English & Welsh legislation—to denote this third model of non-conviction-based confiscation. We employ

48 Proceeds of Crime Act 1996.

49 Proceeds of Crime Act 2002, Part 5.

50 Proceeds of Crime Act 2002, s. 362A.

51 Proceeds of Crime Act 2002, s. 362C(2).

52 See Parliamentary Joint Committee on Law Enforcement, *Inquiry into Commonwealth Unexplained Wealth Legislation and Arrangements* (March 2012) especially ch.2 ('Overview of Commonwealth Unexplained Wealth Laws'). Cf. Natalie Skead, Hilde Tubex, Sarah Murray, and Tamara Tulich, *Pocketing the Proceeds of Crime: Recommendations for Legislative Reform* (Australian Institute of Criminology 2020).

53 Some literature does refer to the Irish non-conviction-based legislation as an unexplained wealth model, though this is not strictly correct: see Booz Allen Hamilton, *Comparative Evaluation of Unexplained Wealth Orders: Prepared for the US Department of Justice, National Institute of Justice* (October 2011).

this term except when quoting directly from another source that uses different terminology, in which instances we retain the quotation verbatim. This term has been selected in spite of its inherent deficiencies, which Alldridge stresses:

> The procedure is not consistent with normal English usage, 'recovery', and it requires considerable casuistry to call it 'civil'. The primary meaning of the word 'recover' is 'get back, or take back'. Here, civil recovery is not taking back or getting back property that had previously been the State's. It is state appropriation of property. It might be property that the possessor should never have had, or only had because he/she acted illegally, but it was never the State's property, so the State is not getting something back: it is *getting* something, and arguments about the legitimacy of the procedure should start from that basis. These semantic observations matter because the justifications that are offered for 'civil recovery' frequently appeal to ordinary language notions of recovery and return.[54]

While we readily acknowledge and agree with Alldridge's valid criticisms of the term civil recovery, we have nevertheless chosen to use this expression because it emphasizes the purported civil dimension of the proceedings, and prevents any confusion over pre-/post-conviction forfeiture processes. For clarity, we emphasize here some key differences between civil recovery and criminal confiscation.

With civil recovery, no criminal conviction is required; indeed, there is no requirement that criminal proceedings even be initiated. Nor is there a requirement to establish a link between a specific offence and the property subject to confiscation. Civil standards of evidence apply, thus character evidence and hearsay evidence can be admitted, as can improperly obtained evidence, while the standard of proof is the civil standard, *on the balance of probabilities*. Furthermore, while a post-conviction confiscation order operates *in personam*, civil recovery operates *in rem*—that is, against the property itself. Finally, and while a central consideration in relation to all confiscation models is that they should be human rights compliant, thus avoiding controversy in their application, rights and due process concerns are particularly acute in the context of civil recovery.

[54] Peter Alldridge, 'Civil Recovery in England and Wales: An Appraisal' in Colin King, Clive Walker, and Jimmy Gurulé (eds), *The Palgrave Handbook of Criminal and Terrorism Financing Law* (Palgrave 2018) 516.

Before embarking on our dedicated analysis of civil recovery, however, the next chapter introduces and interrogates the idea of civil/criminal hybrid procedures. We then contextualize civil recovery, explaining in consecutive chapters the background, the legal framework, and the judicial reactions in Ireland and England & Wales respectively. Our principal argument throughout these chapters can be stated as follows: hybrid procedures, specifically civil recovery, straddle civil and criminal procedure in a manner that takes advantage of the resultant legal ambiguity, to the detriment of due process and individual rights.

Chapter Outline

In Chapter 2 we elaborate on the idea that civil recovery is a hybrid civil/criminal procedure and further explain this characterization. Pointing to the purported advantages of this type of procedural hybrid, we scrutinize the underlying motivations behind their introduction, including considerations of legislative intentionality, securitization, and preventive justice. We consider civil recovery in terms of procedural rights and protections, first highlighting those features that contribute to its classification as hybrid, and then exploring the civil/criminal distinction. Having presented civil recovery as a process that blurs the lines between the criminal and the civil, we examine its fault lines and elisions both in terms of 'middleground jurisprudence'[55] and in the context of the increasingly pervasive idea that civil recovery is a justifiably pragmatic response to the particular problems posed by serious and organized criminal activity.

In Chapter 3 we contextualize civil recovery in terms of broader national and transnational 'follow the money' approaches to targeting criminal assets, before presenting detailed accounts of how civil recovery has been both enacted and justified, first in Ireland and then in England & Wales. We consider civil recovery's characterization as *inter alia* compensatory, reparative, preventive, non-punitive, and disincentivizing, and then provide a comprehensive account—in each jurisdiction respectively—of the current law governing non-conviction-based actions against the proceeds of crime.

Chapter 4 turns from legislation to the judicial reaction, again considered across both jurisdictions. We take the position, consistent with our earlier work on this issue, that the courts have been too amenable in accepting civil

[55] Kenneth Mann, 'Punitive Civil Sanctions: The Middleground Between Criminal and Civil Law' (1992) 101 *Yale Law Journal* 1795.

recovery as a civil process, with the result that it does not attract the procedural protections usually afforded under the criminal law. To elaborate on this standpoint, we first provide a critical perspective on the judicial reaction in Ireland and England & Wales, before considering whether civil recovery constitutes punishment. We then subject civil recovery to analysis under each of the three *Engel* criteria, as established by the European Court of Human Rights, which determine whether or not proceedings should be considered as criminal.

Chapter 5 commences our dedicated critique of civil recovery as well as introducing our qualitative empirical methodology in the form of semi-structured elite interviews with twenty-seven practitioners in Ireland and England & Wales. Our critical analysis of civil recovery advances in terms of the three key issues identified in the elite interviews, namely, the non-conviction-based approach, the presumption of innocence, and the standard of proof. Until now there has been no dedicated empirical work undertaken in this field, and this blend of practitioner and academic perspectives offers fresh insights into this controversial practice.

Throughout the book we draw attention to how civil recovery is an action *in rem,* that is, against the property. In Chapter 6, we chart the historical development of actions *in rem*, arguing that civil recovery is the latest of these to constitute a legal fiction. Drawing yet further on the practitioner views gleaned from our interviews, we then query the specific-property approach, querying the argument that there is no good title to the property on the part of the respondent, before scrutinizing the characterization of civil recovery as restitutive in character. Our focus on property then shifts to a more theoretical register: with a view to emphasizing how this hybrid civil/criminal procedure effectively downplays the importance of individual rights to estate, compared with those of life and liberty, we consider civil recovery in the context of liberal theories of property.

Chapter 7 takes as its focus another prominent strand within this debate, that is, the recurring theme of pragmatism. More than any other, this issue draws attention to the most prominent 'split' between the academy and practice in relation to civil recovery: while policy-makers and enforcement officials are often criticized for focusing on outcomes over principles, so too are academics maligned for concentrating on fairness and due process rights at the expense of achieving more efficacious and expedient means of tackling organized crime. Drawing on practitioner perspectives, we introduce the important contribution that although proponents acknowledge criticisms about civil recovery, they dismiss these on pragmatic grounds. In light of this, and relying on the Dworkinian distinction between two types of harm, namely bare harm and moral harm, we lead the argument that civil recovery's hybridity serves to *hide* its moral harm.

In the concluding chapter, we draw attention to what we submit are self-legitimation strategies on the part of interviewees, contending that these views reinforce concerns expressed in academic literature as well as evidencing a cognitively dissonant position adopted by proponents of civil recovery, a position aided and abetted by the procedure's perceived hybridity and *in rem* nature. Nonetheless, and notwithstanding ongoing concerns as to this civil/criminal procedural hybrid, it is evident that civil recovery powers are gaining traction internationally. While Ireland and England & Wales are leading jurisdictions in promoting and advancing civil recovery powers, other jurisdictions—both common law and civil law—have also introduced such measures, for example *inter alia* Australia, Canada, Italy, Spain, and there continue to be steps towards an EU model of non-conviction-based confiscation.[56] This leads us to the final section of our book, bringing us back to the opening focus on hybrid proceduralism, and the continued proliferation of this regulatory form both nationally and internationally. This expansion is not just one of scale but of diversification: not only are civil/criminal hybrid measures increasingly identifiable beyond the context of civil recovery but the range and diversity of procedurally hybrid forms continues to expand across jurisdictions.

[56] European Commission, *Proposal for a Directive of the European Parliament and of the Council on asset recovery and confiscation* (Brussels, 25 May 2022. COM(2022) 245 final).

2

Civil Recovery as a Hybrid Civil/Criminal Procedure

Introduction

While there is significant empirical literature on other hybrid procedures, particularly civil preventive orders,[1] civil recovery has not received the same level of attention in the context of preventive justice. This book remedies this lack by providing a comprehensive theoretical and empirically informed critique of civil recovery, starting with its procedural hybridity. Having introduced civil recovery as a civil/criminal hybrid procedure, this chapter elaborates on what is meant by this notion of 'hybridity' and how civil recovery is an example of a hybrid procedure.

Our argument in this chapter proceeds in two parts. First, we explain what we mean by the terms 'procedural hybrid' or 'hybrid procedure', expressions we use interchangeably. We consider the development of such procedures in terms of the challenges they pose to procedural rights, and also in the context of debates on both securitization and prevention. Second, and in light of the proliferation of procedural hybrids over the past two decades, we consider the distinction between civil and criminal procedures, and what benefits—if any—are offered by a more 'middleground' jurisprudence.[2] From the perspective of the state, the attractions of the hybrid approach are obvious, perhaps most evidently the circumvention of procedural protections inherent in the criminal process. These procedural shortcuts are justified on the basis of expediency, that is, on the grounds that they are necessary for the action to be effective. We contend, however, that civil recovery—alongside certain other hybrid procedures—constitutes a securitized and preventive measure that prioritizes

[1] For example, Vicky Heap, Alex Black, and Zoe Rodgers, 'Preventive Justice: Exploring the Coercive Power of Community Protection Notices to Tackle Anti-Social Behaviour' (2022) 24(3) *Punishment & Society* 305; Sam Lewis, Adam Crawford, and Peter Traynor, 'Nipping Crime in the Bud? The Use of Anti-Social Behaviour Interventions with Young People in England and Wales' (2016) 57(5) *British Journal of Criminology* 1230.

[2] Kenneth Mann, 'Punitive Civil Sanctions: The Middleground Between Criminal and Civil Law' (1992) 101(8) *Yale Law Journal* 1795.

Civil Recovery of Criminal Property. Colin King and Jennifer Hendry, Oxford University Press.
 DOI: 10.1093/oso/9780198824251.003.0002

instrumentality and expediency to the detriment of due process and individual rights. Our chapter conclusion presents civil recovery as constituting a damaging legal fiction operationalized as a procedural shortcut.

What is Procedural Hybridity?

Procedural rights and protections

Where an individual is charged with a criminal offence, certain procedural protections become operative. While some of these safeguards cover both criminal and civil proceedings,[3] others only apply in the event of a criminal charge.[4] These elevated protections for the defendant comprise limitations on the exercise of state power and thus militate against any arbitrary or improper conduct on the part of the state and its representatives.[5] As Duff et al. have observed, while the state's 'general claim to legitimate authority over, and responsibility to, its citizens' is expressed by and through the accountability exercise of the trial, the state's very conduct of the trial provides the legitimizing grounds to hold the defendant to account.[6] Inherent in this is the idea of respect for the defendant as a citizen of a liberal polity, as opposed to a mere subject of power.[7]

Three observations can be made here. First, in light of the power asymmetry between the state and the accused, the criminal process' elevated procedural protections are specifically intended to fetter state power and preclude abuse. Second, by imposing these restrictions—in the form of procedural rights—upon the criminal legal process, the state acknowledges the importance of civil liberties and due process. Third, it is only in circumstances where the state has met (or exceeded) all the heightened procedural requirements of the criminal process that it is able to convict, censure, and punish defendants.

Civil/criminal procedural hybrids are designed with the effect of bypassing, circumventing, pre-empting, or otherwise sidestepping the exact procedural protections just discussed. Whether specific hybrid procedures are born out of dissatisfaction with existing criminal justice processes, the perception that law

3 Article 6(1) ECHR—a fair and public hearing; an independent and impartial tribunal; a reasonable time frame; etc.

4 Articles 6(2)–(3) ECHR: such as the presumption of innocence (Art. 6(2)) and the right to confront witnesses (Art. 6(3)(d)).

5 Liz Campbell, Andrew Ashworth, and Mike Redmayne, *The Criminal Process* (5th edn, Oxford University Press 2019) 427.

6 Antony Duff, Lindsay Farmer, Sandra Marshall, and Victor Tadros, *The Trial on Trial, Volume 3: Towards a Normative Theory of the Criminal Trial* (Hart 2007) 287–88.

7 ibid. 288.

enforcement lacks sufficient tools, the desire to weight the system more in the favour of victims, or the pursuit of security, a key feature of procedural hybrids is how they avoid prosecutorial hurdles established by elevated criminal justice procedural standards. In this regard our base definitional view of procedural hybrids aligns with Ashworth and Zedner's characterization of the preventive state's two broad forms: 'its use as a rationale for extending the boundaries of the criminal law, and its use as a rationale for developing various coercive measures designed to sit outside or alongside the criminal process and thereby to avoid the procedural safeguards attached to that process'.[8] Civil recovery provides a perfect illustration in this regard: in both Ireland and England & Wales, post-conviction confiscation powers already existed, although such powers were regarded as failing given their dependence on conventional criminal processes. The alleged 'failure' stems from supposed difficulties in tackling serious and organized criminal activity.[9]

In 'following the money'—that is, targeting the property resulting from organized criminal activity—civil recovery purportedly acts *in rem*, which is to say, against the property itself. The design of civil recovery as an action *in rem* brings with it several advantages, chief among which is the standard of proof employed: because any deprivation is one of property and not liberty, the civil standard of proof on a balance of probabilities is considered acceptable.[10] A further advantage stems from the indirectness of the action: civil recovery provides a different kind of opportunity to impact upon criminal operations where existing criminal law enforcement tools are seen as lacking. By providing for the seizure of criminal assets not only in the absence of criminal conviction but also under the civil standard of proof, the state employs *civil* procedural mechanisms to disrupt organized crime's monetary incentive. This procedural hybridity generates ambiguity as to whether such an action is punitive or non-punitive, corrective or preventive: while the jurisprudence of the Strasbourg Court characterizes civil recovery as non-criminal and non-punitive, this is subject to continued debate.[11]

[8] See Andrew Ashworth and Lucia Zedner, *Preventive Justice* (Oxford University Press 2014) 13. It is worth noting here that key benefits of civil/criminal hybrid procedures lie in how they provide a means of regulating undesirable behaviour by circumventing criminal law's elevated procedural safeguards, as discussed, but also by bringing within the ambit of the criminal law behaviour that is not yet criminal, and then leveraging criminal law consequences against breaches of ostensibly civil law provisions. Civil recovery is representative of the former but not the latter, unlike, for example, preventive hybrids operating on a two-step process.

[9] See Chapter 3.

[10] This is explored further in Chapter 6.

[11] See Simon Young, 'Enforcing Criminal Law Through Civil Processes: How Does Human Rights Law Treat "Civil for Criminal Processes"?' (2017) 4(2) *Journal of International and Comparative Law* 133. See, also, Chapter 4.

Although the disruption of organized crime's monetary incentive is a stated policy aim of the legislation in both Ireland and England & Wales, civil recovery is a *post*-crime measure: it operates on alleged proceeds *of* crime. This approach has two dimensions: one individual and one systemic. While a central feature of civil recovery is ensuring that the individual in question does not benefit from *their* criminal conduct, an important additional aspect is *systemic* incapacity. This concerns less the individualized requirements or restrictions and more the broader impact upon serious and organized crime achieved by affecting the circulation of 'dirty' money. The deprivation of property is thus central to this approach—by taking action directly against property rather than proceeding against the individual concerned, property ceases to be something that incentivizes criminality.[12] This distinction is worth noting because it largely sets civil recovery apart from other civil/criminal procedural hybrids: the disruptive systemic aspect of civil recovery is arguably more prominent than its immediate impact against the individual. The difference here is effectively one of linearity: other civil/criminal hybrid procedures are more direct in how they disincentivize individuals from unwanted and unwelcome behaviour. The example of the Anti-Social Behaviour Order (ASBO)[13] may be useful at this point. The controversial and now-defunct[14] ASBO was expressly conceived as a way of addressing a course of conduct or series of events in a manner that traditional criminal processes—which focus on a singular event—were ill-equipped to do.[15] The ASBO thus impacted directly upon the individual. By contrast, civil recovery was conceived as an alternative to traditional criminal law's perceived ineffectiveness, in this instance against Godfather-style kingpin types. By focusing *directly* on the proceeds of crime, its effect is exerted—at least, in theory—against *money*, the animating medium of organized criminality.[16]

There are two central aspects of hybrid procedures that demand more attention: *security* and *prevention*. Here we discuss each of these aspects in turn.

[12] This *in rem*/*in personam* distinction is considered further in Chapter 6.

[13] Crime & Disorder Act 1998, s. 1.

[14] Albeit not in Scotland. For consideration of the new legal framework, see Stavros Demetriou, 'From the ASBO to the Injunction: A Qualitative Review of the Anti-Social Behaviour Legislation Post-2014' [2019] *Public Law* 343. In Ireland, influenced by the UK ASBO, there is provision in the Criminal Justice Act 2006 for 'civil orders' and 'behaviour orders', to address anti-social behaviour. For a critique, see Dermot Walsh, 'The Criminal Justice Act 2006: A Crushing Defeat for Due Process Values?' [2007] *Judicial Studies Institute Journal* 44, 55–8.

[15] Labour Party, *A Quiet Life: Tough Action on Criminal Neighbours* (1995).

[16] Whether it can be said that civil recovery does not directly impact the individual is questionable, however; we explore this further in Chapter 6.

Security

The role of the state in ensuring security has its roots in Hobbesian political thought but has, over the past two decades, evolved significantly in scope, if not hugely in fundamentals.[17] For Hobbes, the state has a fundamental duty to procure the safety of its people,[18] from which Ashworth and Zedner draw three relevant inferences:

> First, the protective or preventive function is written into the very fabric of state authority and imposes upon the state a duty to promulgate laws and pursue policies in order to provide security for its citizens. Second, citizens owe a *prima facie* duty to the state and to one another to abide by law and to accept state coercion as the necessary price of peace and good order. Third, the state retains the prerogative of exercising executive powers in conditions of emergency outside the normal legal and constitutional limits placed on it.[19]

The emergency prerogative of the state to act in the best interests of public security introduces problematic ambiguities. Whether it is in terms of calibrating the level of magnitude of the threat faced, the necessary duration of such crisis conditions, or the extent to which efficacy demands even the temporary suspension of civil liberties,[20] the qualification of 'no more extensive than required' is insufficiently exacting. Security grounds are relied upon to justify otherwise unthinkable excesses and infractions,[21] whether these are purely instrumental 'greater good' rationalizations or overtly political responses to populist concerns.[22] As Loader and Walker have observed, even employing the term 'security' is:

[17] Klaus Günther, 'World Citizens between Freedom and Security' (2005) 12(3) *Constellations* 379.

[18] 'The office of the Sovereign, (be it a Monarch, or an Assembly,) consists in the end, for which he was trusted with Sovereign Power, namely the procuration of the safety of the people.' Thomas Hobbes, *Leviathan* ([1651] Oxford University Press 2008), ch.XXX 'Of the Office of the Sovereign Representative'.

[19] Andrew Ashworth and Lucia Zedner, *Preventive Justice* (Oxford University Press 2015) 8.

[20] For consideration of emergency powers, see Dermot Walsh, 'Beyond the Ordinary: Criminal Law and Terrorism' in Genevieve Lennon, Colin King, and Carole McCartney (eds), *Counter-terrorism, Constitutionalism and Miscarriages of Justice: A Festschrift for Professor Clive Walker* (Hart 2019); Conor Gearty, 'Terrorist Threats, Antiterrorism, and the Case against the Human Rights Act' in Frederick Cowell (ed), *Critically Examining the Case Against the 1998 Human Rights Act* (Routledge 2018).

[21] Lucia Zedner, *Security* (Routledge 2009) 80: There is a 'growing sense that the "presumption of innocence", "proof beyond reasonable doubt", and the requirement of proportionality in punishment are legal luxuries ill-suited to present perils'.

[22] Peter Ramsey, *The Insecurity State: Vulnerable Autonomy and the Right to Security in the Criminal Law* (Oxford University Press 2012) 4.

> to suggest, and to seek to mobilise audiences behind, the idea that 'we' face an existential threat that calls for immediate, decisive, special measures. It is, in other words, to seek to lift the issue at hand ... out of the realm of normal democratic politics, to claim that as an emergency it demands an urgent, even exceptional response.[23]

The temporal aspect of emergency and exception is salient: while a state of exception might plausibly be generated by emergency conditions, and these might necessitate the restriction of certain liberties or the suspension of other rights and procedures, citizens are entitled to conceive of these limitations as *themselves* time-limited.[24] If they are not temporary, of course, then the state of exception ceases to be exceptional and becomes instead the norm, regardless of whether such a situation is in fact warranted by any real or perceived threat.[25] The expansion in the reach of the criminal law undertaken by means of civil/criminal hybrid procedures constitutes, we submit, such a normalization of exception.[26]

The claim on the part of the state that steps have been taken or measures set in place on grounds of public security is therefore also the claim that these are *de facto* justified for the greater (public) good. The exercise of this prerogative requires a careful balance to be struck between security considerations, on the one hand, and individual human rights and due process safeguards on the other. Throughout this book we argue that—certainly according to a traditional liberal conception of criminal law—such a balance is not currently being achieved in the context of civil recovery. In fact, even recognizing that the state's coercive power makes it both the protector of and a threat to individual security,[27] we contend that civil recovery serves to privilege political expediency in the fight against organized crime, at the expense of due process and individual rights.

[23] Ian Loader and Neil Walker, *Civilising Security* (Cambridge University Press 2007) 11–12.

[24] For wider consideration, see John Ip, 'Sunset Clauses and Counterterrorism Legislation' [2013] *Public Law* 74.

[25] A classic example of this is the Irish Special Criminal Court, an 'emergency' response since 1972. See Alice Harrison, *The Special Criminal Court: Practice and Procedure* (Bloomsbury 2019) and Fergal Davis, *The History and Development of the Special Criminal Court 1922–2014* (2nd edn, Bloomsbury 2014).

[26] Mark Neocleous, *Critique of Security* (Edinburgh University Press 2008) 22. Ramsay would disagree with this; he even goes as far as to argue that the very dialectic of norm/exception is an outdated liberal view, one that the new normal of the 'right to security' has largely demolished. Peter Ramsay, *The Insecurity State: Vulnerable Autonomy and the Right to Security in the Criminal Law* (Oxford University Press 2012) 213–15.

[27] Ian Loader and Neil Walker, *Civilising Security* (Cambridge University Press 2007) 11.

Neither is this asymmetry between considerations of security and individual protections an isolated practice: on the contrary, it can be traced through many, if not most, civil/criminal procedural hybrids, particularly those civil orders that have criminal consequences.[28] Indeed, the increased potential that hybrid procedures provide for earlier interventions, heightened constraints upon civil liberties, and an emphasis on prevention are all indicative of a general 'reconceptualisation of crime as security risk'.[29]

Prevention

The recent focus on mitigating risk and preventing harm, through mechanisms such as civil/criminal hybrid procedures, has been so intense that it is widely accepted as a general 'turn' towards prevention within the criminal law. This is not a newly introduced obligation of the criminal law, of course—alongside its functions of accountability and censure, criminal law's remit has always included the prevention of particular harms and wrongs.[30] Rather, the idea of a 'preventive turn' amounts to recognition that 'the contemporary concern with security appears to have given so much importance to the *need* for criminal law to effectively prevent crime, that this preventive function has been *prioritized* over the promotion and protection of individual justice upheld by liberal legal theory'.[31]

Neither is this a phenomenon isolated to England & Wales and Ireland.[32] Prevention can be seen as a key driver within transnational security architectures,[33] where the preventive use of force—even preventive war—and preventive data sharing across agencies has served to generate both the space and the opportunity for crimefighting. This is most apparent in the realm of serious and organized crime, where military and intelligence services are often brought to bear alongside police.[34] The 'pre-crime' logic of prevention thus

[28] A non-exhaustive list of these includes the ASBO, the Football Banning Order (FBO), the Public Space Protection Order (PSPO), the Knife Crime Prevention Order (KCPO), and the Domestic Abuse Prevention Order (DAPO).

[29] Lucia Zedner, *Security* (Routledge 2009) 71.

[30] Andrew Ashworth and Lucia Zedner, *Preventive Justice* (Oxford University Press 2014) 74.

[31] Henrique Carvalho, *The Preventive Turn in Criminal Law* (Oxford University Press 2017) 3. Emphasis added.

[32] Notably, Irish governments have shown a 'lesser enthusiasm' for such civil preventive orders: Claire Hamilton, 'The Presumption of Innocence in Irish Criminal Law: Recent Trends and Possible Explanations' (2011) 2(1) *Irish Journal of Legal Studies* 3, 21.

[33] See, generally, Klaus Günther, 'World Citizens between Freedom and Security' (2005) 12(3) *Constellations* 379.

[34] ibid., 381.

drives a proactive forestalling of potential insecurities and harms, and this is largely oriented towards combatting behaviour that, if allowed to persist, would cause insecurity or harm. According to this anticipatory logic, punishment is no longer solely reactive or retrospective—in the mode of holding proven wrongdoers to account—but, rather, a viable intervention in advance of certain risky future conduct.

As contended above, civil recovery is a *post*-crime measure that targets the proceeds *of* crime. The extent to which it is in itself preventive is, however, questionable. The courts have focused on its preventive nature, stating that it removes potential working capital from circulation, prevents criminals from benefiting from proceeds of crime, and serves as a form of reparation.[35] None of these arguments is easily reconciled with the more intuitively preventive paradigm, however, whereby risky behaviour is first identified and then pre-empted, by a variety of means, before harm can occur. The preventive paradigm is, in fact, far more prominent in terms of *other* procedural hybrids, notably civil preventive orders (CPOs). Such explicitly preventive civil/criminal hybrid procedures constitute a distinct category, one into which civil recovery does not comfortably fit: for example, an ostensible advantage of these explicitly preventive hybrid procedural forms is that they provide a means of regulating behaviour that would otherwise fall outside the remit of the criminal law by *expanding* this to include behaviour that is minor wrongful activity, conduct adjacent to wrongful activity, or conduct sufficient to constitute wrongful activity only when done repeatedly.[36] The civil/criminal hybrid structure is particularly overt in this regard: the order is made by a civil court according to civil rules of evidence, but its breach constitutes a criminal offence. This built-in escalation has earned this type of preventive hybrid procedure the name 'two-step prohibition',[37] and attracted criticism for, among other things, short-circuiting the distinction between compliance and sanction.[38]

Although there are commonalities across civil/criminal hybrid forms we will not undertake a comparison beyond identifying parallels with and

[35] Relevant jurisprudence is considered in more detail in Chapter 4, 'Punishment'.

[36] Andrew Simester and Andreas von Hirsch, 'Regulating Offensive Conduct through Two-Step Prohibitions' in Andrew Simester and Andreas von Hirsch (eds), *Incivilities: Regulating Offensive Behaviour* (Hart 2006) 176–7.

[37] ibid. 174.

[38] Jennifer Hendry, '"The Usual Suspects"': Knife Crime Prevention Orders and the "Difficult" Regulatory Subject' (2022) 62(2) *The British Journal of Criminology* 378, 387. Additional criticisms of two-step prohibitions include, *inter alia*, their being *ex ante* prohibitions instead of *ex post facto* verdicts, that they grant enormous power to civil courts, and that they create individualized regulatory regimes.

counterexamples to civil recovery, which is our central focus.[39] The innate instrumentality does require further attention, however, specifically that securitized 'needs-must' justification for their design and implementation. The impetus behind the 'follow the money' approach, as we have identified, arose out of a sense of frustration with the limitations of existing criminal justice processes and a sense that those processes and tools were deficient or inefficient.[40] Whether or not such perceptions were in fact accurate, the policy goals of increasing security, prioritizing victims of crime, and making crime pay coalesced in the creation of civil/criminal hybrid procedural forms for the purpose of availing criminal justice of the alleged benefits we have outlined throughout this section. These hybrid forms can thus be said to comprise reliance upon mechanisms of control and legal techniques situated at the very edges of the civil/criminal distinction, and it is to these that our attention will now turn.

The Civil/Criminal Distinction

So far, we have presented the civil/criminal hybridization of procedures as a generally negative development. Such a standpoint demands that we take a clear position in favour of the respective distinctiveness of criminal and civil law and processes. Although the distinctions between the two remain contentious, our justificatory explanation will proceed as follows. First, we outline the generalized features and procedures contributing to this distinction, before demonstrating that it is not so clear-cut. Next, we scrutinize what has come to be known as 'middleground jurisprudence',[41] highlighting those features that distort or challenge the core civil/criminal distinction. Third, we consider the argument that these line-blurring middleground or hybrid approaches are not only more pragmatic but also more forthright than the alternative of relying on prosecutorial ingenuity to stretch or distort existing offences to encompass inconvenient future developments. Perhaps unsurprisingly we reject the argument that this *supposedly* more candid and more practically honest approach is better, and dispute generally the pragmatic label to which such rights- and liberties-infringing procedures so often make claim.

[39] For consideration of different types of hybrid orders, see Rory Kelly, *Behaviour Orders: Preventive and/or Punitive Measures?* (PhD Thesis, University of Oxford, 2019).

[40] This is explored in more depth in Chapter 3.

[41] Kenneth Mann, 'Punitive Civil Sanctions: The Middleground Between Criminal and Civil Law' (1992) 101(8) *Yale Law Journal* 1795.

Drawing the lines

Civil and criminal processes have conventionally been distinguishable on the basis of a variety of factors, including, *inter alia*, culpability of the wrongdoer, harm suffered, the role of state officials, the extent of investigatory powers available to the state, evidential rules, punishment, and stigma. We now consider each of these factors briefly, before outlining doubts as to their ongoing validity. Indeed, we acknowledge, there is a risk of over-simplification of the differences between criminal and civil,[42] and notwithstanding 'obvious differences of objective, the concepts deployed by criminal and tort law have much in common'.[43]

- In terms of culpability, the conventional view is that criminal liability can only be imposed where the wrongdoer is *subjectively* culpable,[44] whereas liability in civil proceedings does not necessarily require culpability.[45] For the former, culpability depends upon morally defective decisions while, for the latter, liability is grounded not in the choices taken but directly in the conduct performed. This dichotomy effectively turns on fault, without which there should be no criminal conviction.[46] An example here would be if D deliberately throws my valuable vase against the wall, breaking it. In that instance, D might be convicted of criminal damage and punished accordingly. If, however, D carelessly drops my vase, breaking it, does D deserve to be punished? In civil proceedings, even if D were blameless, they would still be required to pay compensation.[47]
- Considerations of harm are also central in how conduct is categorized. Harm is generally taken to encompass impairments to an individual's person or property, but can include impairments of collective welfare and of governmental interests.[48] Alongside the conduct element, the harm

[42] Matthew Dyson, 'Challenging the Orthodoxy of Crime's Precedence over Tort: Suspending a Tort Claim Where a Crime May Exist' in Stephen Pitel, Jason Neyers, and Erika Chamberlain (eds), *Tort Law: Challenging Orthodoxy* (Hart 2013).

[43] Graham Virgo, '"We Do This in the Criminal Law and That in the Law of Tort": A New Fusion Debate' in Stephen Pitel, Jason Neyers, and Erika Chamberlain (eds), *Tort Law: Challenging Orthodoxy* (Hart 2013) 95.

[44] *R v G* [2004] 1 AC 1034; *The People (DPP) v Murray* [1977] IR 360.

[45] *Hall v Brooklands Auto Racing Club* [1933] 1 KB 205; *Glasgow Corporation v Muir* [1943] AC 448.

[46] On fault-based crimes, see Grant Lamond, 'What is a Crime?' (2007) 27(4) *Oxford Journal of Legal Studies* 609. For wider discussion on responsibility and blame, see Nicola Lacey and Hanna Pickard, 'From the Consulting Room to the Court Room? Taking the Clinical Model of Responsibility Without Blame into the Legal Realm' (2013) 33(1) *Oxford Journal of Legal Studies* 1.

[47] This example is given in GR Sullivan, 'Wrongs and Responsibility for Wrongs in Crime and Tort' in Matthew Dyson (ed), *Unravelling Tort and Crime* (Cambridge University Press 2014) 88.

[48] Hyman Gross, *A Theory of Criminal Justice* (Oxford University Press 1979) 116.

caused by it is usually key in determining whether it warrants the label of criminal.

- The role of state officials is a further central distinction between civil and criminal proceedings. Police and prosecutors acting on behalf of the state is generally indicative of a criminal matter;[49] given that criminal proceedings are seen as matters of public concern,[50] criminal proceedings are usually instigated either by the state or its representatives on behalf of the public at large. Civil proceedings, on the other hand, are generally raised by private individuals, with any public interest being merely incidental. Being centred on individual interests, civil proceedings usually require damage to have been suffered by a specified individual before any liability for that damage is imposed.
- The focus on 'public' and 'private' wrongs has further consequences, both in investigations and outcomes. First, investigatory powers are a notable difference: in criminal matters state authorities are generally afforded powers that are not usually available in civil matters, for example: powers of arrest, detention, search, and seizure. Such intrusive investigatory powers are balanced by rules of evidence at the trial stage, which are much more restrictive in criminal proceedings than civil ones.[51]
- An investigation—and any subsequent prosecution—is pursued by the state on behalf of society at large. If this results in a conviction, it is followed by punishment, another central consideration to the civil/criminal distinction. The classic dichotomy is that criminal law is concerned with allocating punishment, whereas civil law is concerned with allocating the costs of harm. As Holdsworth points out, 'a suit by a private person sounds in damages, whereas a suit by the king ends in the punishment of the guilty party'.[52]
- Finally, stigma. Henry Hart has argued that only the convicted person will experience 'the moral condemnation of his community'.[53] The

[49] William Blackstone, *Commentaries on the Laws of England* (facsimile edition with introductions by Stanley N Katz, University of Chicago Press 1979), 3. It is also worth noting here the argument made by Malcolm Feeley in his 1979 book *The Process is the Punishment* that simply being subject to such an exercise of state power can be a gruelling experience.

[50] James Fitzjames Stephen, *A History of the Criminal Law of England, Vol. II* (William S Hein reprint 1883) 76.

[51] Abraham S Goldstein, 'The State and the Accused: Balance of Advantage in Criminal Procedure' (1960) 69 *Yale Law Journal* 1149.

[52] William S Holdsworth, *A History of English Law, Vol. II* (4th edn, Sweet and Maxwell 2003) 453.

[53] Henry M Hart Jr, 'The Aims of the Criminal Law' (1958) 23 *Law and Contemporary Problems* 401, 406.

conventional distinction is that an adverse civil judgment does not attract the same censure as a criminal conviction.[54]

These distinguishing features of civil and criminal processes are not uncontested, although they provide a useful starting point to our analysis.[55] There are, however, notable exceptions to these distinctions: for example, in terms of culpability, strict liability offences in criminal law do not require subjective culpability.[56] Such offences might be described as 'an effective means of enforcing certain standards necessary for public protection'; thus by imposing certain standards on, say, a publican to enforce licensing laws, 'strict liability offences also speak to a concern with responding to the results of conduct; to the desire to see that "something must be done" '.[57] The absence of harm also does not mean that a particular action is not criminal. As Sullivan states, '[l]arge swathes of the criminal law are a form of coercive regulation and governance where convictions may be imposed for forms of conduct unconnected to wrongs done to any persons and without any adverse effect on society as a whole'.[58] Thus criminal law might be engaged either where there is harm (e.g. criminal damage to my broken vase, as in the earlier example) or where there is no harm (e.g. preparation offences, where no harm has been realized). In contrast, in cases of civil wrong there tends to be a realized harm.[59]

The public/private distinction is also blurred.[60] In a criminal investigation and subsequent trial, say of a murder, the focus is not so much on the

[54] In the context of 'civil sanctions' under the Regulatory Enforcement and Sanctions Act 2008, Williams contends: 'if stigma and moral signalling is not at issue, then there is no need for those procedural protections to be criminal. There is certainly a need for them to be rigorous, and commensurate with the high cost of potential error, but as long as the necessary high levels of procedural protection are in place they need not be criminal, only public'. Rebecca Williams, 'Criminal Law in England and Wales: Just Another Form of Regulatory Tool?' in Matthew Dyson and Benjamin Vogel (eds), *The Limits of Criminal Law: Anglo-German Concepts and Principles* (Intersentia 2018) 230.

[55] Indeed, it might be that they were never valid. Lindgren, for example, suggests that 'the ancients did not *need* a law of crimes because they often dealt with murder, assault, and theft as private wrongs to be redressed by compensation or more brutal tort substitutes. Because most ancient law systems had such a broad civil system available (both in concept and in remedies), they did not need as extensive a criminal system.' James Lindgren, 'Why the Ancients May Not Have Needed A System of Criminal Law' (1996) 76 *Boston University Law Review* 29, 56.

[56] Alan Norrie, *Crime, Reason and History: A Critical Introduction to Criminal Law* (Cambridge University Press 2014) 104 *et seq.*

[57] Matt Matravers, 'The Criminal Law's Various Persons' in Claes Lernestedt and Matt Matravers (eds), *The Criminal Law's Person* (Hart 2022) 24.

[58] GR Sullivan, 'Wrongs and Responsibility for Wrongs in Crime and Tort' in Matthew Dyson (ed), *Unravelling Tort and Crime* (Cambridge University Press 2014) 98.

[59] See *Watkins v Home Office* [2006] UKHL 17, para 9 where the focus in tort was said to be on 'material damage'.

[60] James Edwards and Andrew Simester, 'What's Public About Crime?' (2017) 37(1) *Oxford Journal of Legal Studies* 105; Ambrose Lee, 'Public Wrongs and the Criminal Law' (2015) 9 *Criminal Law and Philosophy* 155.

wrong against the community, rather it is on the wrong suffered by the *victim*.[61] Moreover, the presence of state officials is not determinative. A state official might instigate civil proceedings on behalf of the state; equally, their absence does not mean that proceedings are not criminal—as is the case where a private prosecution is taken.[62]

As for punishment/compensation as a distinction, while the outcome of civil proceedings might be an award of damages, 'such an award is not the initial point of the process: the initial aim is to determine the alleged wrongdoer's liability, and to hold him accountable for the wrong if it is proved'.[63] Duff gives the example of bereaved parents who sue a hospital for negligence that they claim to have caused the death of their child. In such a situation, the aim is not so much to secure an award of damages but rather to call that hospital to account for its wrong. This aligns, then, with the communicative function of the criminal law in calling offenders to account for their wrongdoing.[64]

Even reliance on stigma as a distinguishing factor is open to criticism. For example, does a conviction for a regulatory offence[65] carry the same stigma as conviction for a 'traditional' crime?[66] Or, is it accurate to say that all criminal convictions carry greater condemnation and stigma than an adverse civil judgment? Contrast the situation of an individual convicted of assault who receives a fine, with another individual who is confronted with civil recovery proceedings and ultimately loses their home. In the latter instance, considering there is both a court case and a deprivation,[67] that individual might be regarded as a ' "criminal", if not in law, then at least in the eyes of his/her fellow citizens'.[68]

[61] For consideration of the role of the victim, see Shane Kilcommins, Susan Leahy, Kathleen Moore Walsh, and Eimear Spain, *The Victim in the Irish Criminal Process* (Manchester University Press 2018); Jonathan Doak, *Victims' Rights, Human Rights and Criminal Justice: Reconceiving the Role of Third Parties* (Hart 2008).

[62] Claire de Than and Jesse Elvin, 'Private Prosecution: A Useful Constitutional Safeguard or Potentially Dangerous Historical Anomaly?' [2019] *Criminal Law Review* 656.

[63] RA Duff, 'Torts, Crimes and Vindication: Whose Wrong Is It?' in Matthew Dyson (ed), *Unravelling Tort and Crime* (Cambridge University Press 2014) 148.

[64] Antony Duff, Lindsay Farmer, Sandra Marshall, and Victor Tadros, *The Trial on Trial, Volume 3: Towards a Normative Theory of the Criminal Trial* (Hart 2007) 119. For a critique, see Abenaa Owusu-Bempah, *Defendant Participation in the Criminal Process* (Routledge 2017) 51–9.

[65] For consideration of 'regulatory offences', see Federico Picinali, 'The Denial of Procedural Safeguards in Trials for Regulatory Offences: A Justification' (2017) 11(4) *Criminal Law and Philosophy* 681.

[66] Ciaran McCullagh, 'Two-Tier Society; Two-Tier Crime; Two Tier Justice' in Shane Kilcommins and Ursula Kilkelly (eds), *Regulatory Crime in Ireland* (First Law 2010).

[67] And assuming that the individual is identified.

[68] Jennifer Hendry and Colin King, 'Expediency, Legitimacy, and the Rule of Law: A Systems Perspective on Civil/ Criminal Procedural Hybrids' (2017) 11(4) *Criminal Law and Philosophy* 733, 749.

Our intention here is not to offer definitive distinctions between criminal and civil processes, if indeed that were possible.[69] Our more modest aim is rather to consider these conventional distinguishing features in light of what Kennedy has referred to as the 'growing homogeneity between criminal and civil procedures', and how 'criminal cases now often involve civil, or quasi-civil, procedures and some civil litigation has become quasi-criminal'.[70] It is to such procedures that our attention will now turn.

Blurring the lines: The 'middleground'

Kenneth Mann's 1992 discussion of 'punitive civil sanctions' as comprising a 'middleground' between civil and criminal law[71] sparked a slew of articles throughout the 1990s.[72] Although not the first to attend to this general issue, having been pre-dated by concerted academic scrutiny of the tort/crime distinction,[73] these articles first charted, then problematized, the marked increase in the prevalence of punitive civil sanctions in the United States and beyond. As the name suggests, punitive civil sanctions have a civil setting but a punitive objective, with the result that they extend the classically compensatory remit of the civil law into issues of blameworthiness.

Mann identified four key factors in this expanding 'middleground jurisprudence': 'a changed philosophy of sanctioning, the general expansion of sanctioning, the growth of the administrative state, and the reforms in procedural rules'.[74] In these pinpointed factors we can identify indications of creeping

[69] For detailed consideration, see the various chapters in Matthew Dyson (ed), *Unravelling Tort and Crime* (Cambridge University Press 2014); Matthew Dyson (ed), *Comparing Tort and Crime: Learning from across and within Legal Systems* (Cambridge University Press 2015).

[70] Anthony Kennedy, 'Justifying the Civil Recovery of Criminal Proceeds' (2004) 12(1) *Journal of Financial Crime* 8, 8. Kennedy refers to injunctions against domestic violence, anti-social behaviour orders, exclusion orders, and football banning orders as examples of multiple strategies being used against criminal conduct.

[71] Kenneth Mann, 'Punitive Civil Sanctions: The Middleground Between Criminal and Civil Law' (1992) 101(8) *Yale Law Journal* 1795.

[72] See, for example, Franklin E Zimring, 'The Multiple Middlegrounds Between Civil and Criminal Law' (1992) 101(8) *Yale Law Journal* 1901; Carol S Steiker, 'Punishment and Procedure: Punishment Theory and the Criminal-Civil Procedural Divide' (1996–1997) 85 *Georgetown Law Journal* 775.

[73] See, for example, Robert W Drane and David J Neal, 'On Moral Justifications for the Tort/ Crime Distinction' (1980) 68 *California Law Review* 398; Jerome Hall, 'Interrelations of Criminal Law and Torts: I' (1943) 6 *Columbia Law Review* 753; Jerome Hall, 'Interrelations of Criminal Law and Torts: II' (1943) 7 *Columbia Law Review* 967.

[74] Kenneth Mann, 'Punitive Civil Sanctions: The Middleground Between Criminal and Civil Law' (1992) 101(8) *Yale Law Journal* 1795, 1844.

criminalization and securitization,[75] increased social control, and the rise of the regulatory state and its associated agencies.[76] All of these continue—contemporaneously—to affect the contested contours of the criminal law, but the unifying element can be identified as one of *control*. It is useful to bear this in mind when considering where and how we draw the civil/criminal distinction, not least because this very generalized policy choice—increased social control—underpins so much of the procedural line blurring that has generated 'middleground jurisprudence'. For example, by creating a viable third option[77] between the traditional options of criminal sanctions and compensatory civil sanctions, *punitive* civil sanctions *necessarily* expand the sanctioning regime of the state by bringing into the ambit of control whole swathes of activity that would otherwise not be covered.[78] This has certainly proven to be the case in terms of hybrid procedures, both for civil recovery and for the preventive hybrid forms that encompass undesirable behaviour by means of two-step prohibition. Indeed, concerning the latter, Ashworth and Zedner have flagged how the UK government has 'seized on the civil preventive order as a model for increasing social control without the need to abide by the protections accorded to defendants in criminal cases'.[79] As we discuss in Chapter 5, the same is very much the case when it comes to civil recovery.

There are at least two points of note here. First, there is an evident openness on the part of governments to experimentation with these new tools, strategies, procedures, and other comparable levers of compliance and control. Second, it does not necessarily follow that a third or 'middleground' option need bypass all of the protections usually afforded by the criminal process: they need not *inevitably* 'weaken ... [the] special normative task of procedure' to protect a 'hierarchy of values'.[80] Indeed, if the central objective behind a 'middleground' option and its resultant sanctioning regime expansion is simply increased social control, correspondingly 'middleground' due

[75] ibid. 1847: 'The general expansion of legal remedies is closely connected to two prominent themes in civic life: the changing perception of what constitutes wrongful conduct and the notion that formal legal process is a vital resource for protecting the public.'

[76] Giandomenico Majone, 'From the Positive to the Regulatory State: Causes and Consequences of Changes in the Mode of Governance' (1997) 17(2) *Journal of Public Policy* 139.

[77] On this viability point, see the 1992 special issue of the *Yale Law Journal* on Mann's middleground, specifically John C Coffee, Jr, 'Paradigms Lost: The Blurring of the Criminal and Civil Law Models And What Can Be Done About It' (1992) 101(8) *Yale Law Journal* 1875.

[78] Kenneth Mann, 'Punitive Civil Sanctions: The Middleground Between Criminal and Civil Law' (1992) 101(8) *Yale Law Journal* 1795, 1861.

[79] Andrew Ashworth and Lucia Zedner 'Just Prevention: Preventive Rationales and the Limits of the Criminal Law' in RA Duff and Stuart Green (eds), *Philosophical Foundations of Criminal Law* (Oxford University Press 2011) 302.

[80] Kenneth Mann, 'Punitive Civil Sanctions: The Middleground Between Criminal and Civil Law' (1992) 101(8) *Yale Law Journal* 1795, 1861 and 1869.

process standards and protections could be established relative to the punitiveness of the sanction, perhaps even on a 'sliding-scale'.[81] As Mann observed, 'our society's normative ideas of procedure strongly suggest that such [severely punitive civil] sanctions should be accompanied by procedural rules that offer extra protection against their erroneous imposition'.[82] This normative point is a strong one, and was echoed by Zimring, albeit from a slightly different angle. He mused: 'if procedural shortcuts are not the major advantage of the civil punitive sanction, [then] rigorous procedural protections can constrain the sanctioning process without sacrificing the central comparative advantage of the civil sanction'.[83] This observation cuts effectively to the heart of the matter and, in terms of the scale of protection, highlights the main source of our unease: the major advantage of the punitive civil sanction appears to be found *in* the procedural shortcuts.

Honest and pragmatic?

One reason given in support of 'middleground' processes and procedural hybrids is the honesty behind their legislative introduction. That argument goes as follows: the motivations behind such hybrids are publicly stated and readily apparent, and these provide sufficient justification for the procedures falling in the middle, so to speak, or relying on a blend of civil and criminal procedural features. Instead of offences being artificially expanded by judges purposefully to encompass activity not initially targeted by the legislation but later seen as problematic, this approach states its instrumental intentions up front—is this not an innately more honest and transparent system? Moreover, is it not preferable for the individual to have the benefits of foreseeability and certainty concerning hybrid procedures instead of the previous situation, where vaguely stated criminal offences combined with prosecutorial discretion have led to inconsistent outcomes?[84] While 'procedural hybrid' has a quality of descriptive accuracy, so the argument goes, the moniker has no practical

[81] Franklin E Zimring, 'The Multiple Middlegrounds Between Civil and Criminal Law' (1992) 101(8) *Yale Law Journal* 1901, 1903

[82] Kenneth Mann, 'Punitive Civil Sanctions: The Middleground Between Criminal and Civil Law' (1992) 101(8) *Yale Law Journal* 1795, 1870.

[83] Franklin E Zimring, 'The Multiple Middlegrounds Between Civil and Criminal Law' (1992) 101(8) *Yale Law Journal* 1901, 1907–8.

[84] Such criticisms have been expressed in relation to, *inter alia*, the Vagrancy Act 1824 (repealed in February 2022) and the Theft Act 1968. See, for example, Simon Parsons, 'Dishonest Appropriation after Gomez and Hinks' (2004) 68(6) *Journal of Criminal Law* 520.

bearing on their real-world operation, meaning that the only ambiguity concerning such procedures is one of categorization, a labelling exercise that can be left to legal academics.

We reject this argument and provide two rebuttals concerning the legislative honesty or otherwise of hybrid procedures: one refutation general to procedural hybrids, and one particular to civil recovery. As discussed earlier, pre-emptive state interventions are justified on the basis of improving and increasing public security; undesirable, dangerous, or risky conduct is first anticipated and then tackled *before it becomes criminal behaviour*.[85] Importantly, however, although they are *ex ante* criminal prohibitions and not *ex post facto* criminal verdicts, as highlighted by Simester and von Hirsch,[86] such preventive orders nonetheless represent a blatant form of creeping criminalization.[87] That this criminalization is also personalized is particularly problematic: such preventive hybrids either explicitly or implicitly identify certain individuals as 'ones to watch', potential enemies, or dangerous 'others', expanding the pre-criminal space of enforcement by means of a problematically asymmetric criminal regulatory regime.[88]

Preventive hybrids thus privilege the 'greater good'—that is, the security of the supposedly non-risky majority—at the expense of other individuals' procedural protections. If this is construed as a balance of rights, then due process rights can be said to be roundly trumped by the right to security,[89] although this is not really the dichotomy that matters. Rather, it is the *bearers* of the respective rights that are salient, as *ad hominem* criminalization differentiates individuals into personalized regulatory regimes. Far from being more forthright and offering greater foreseeability and certainty, the preventive hybrid form facilitates slippage between recalcitrant and thus *risky*, and criminal. Indeed, it is a poor kind of legal certainty that attaches to individual circumstances instead of to general cases.

In the context of civil recovery, the rebuttal to the idea that there are benefits to be found in the legislative candour underpinning such procedures is more

[85] Jude McCulloch and Dean Wilson, *Pre-crime: Pre-emption, Precaution and the Future* (Routledge 2015).

[86] Andrew Simester and Andreas von Hirsch, 'Regulating Offensive Conduct through Two-Step Prohibitions' in Andrew Simester and Andreas von Hirsch (eds), *Incivilities: Regulating Offensive Behaviour* (Hart 2006) 178.

[87] Andrew Ashworth et al., 'Neighbouring on the Oppressive: The Government's "Anti-Social Behaviour Order" Proposals' (1998) 16(1) *Criminal Justice* 7.

[88] Jennifer Hendry, '"The Usual Suspects": Knife Crime Prevention Orders and the "Difficult" Regulatory Subject' (2022) 62(2) *The British Journal of Criminology* 378, 389–90.

[89] On the right to security, see generally Peter Ramsey, *The Insecurity State: Vulnerable Autonomy and the Right to Security in the Criminal Law* (Oxford University Press 2012).

specific. As outlined in the introduction to this book, the term civil recovery takes some semantic and rhetorical liberties. In earlier work we made the argument that civil recovery is mislabelled as a civil process;[90] furthermore, as the confiscated assets are not ones of which the state has been deprived, far from the state *recovering* property, it appropriates it.[91] Further descriptors of civil recovery are similarly misleading: as discussed, the ideas that the process is *inter alia* compensatory, reparative, preventive, non-punitive, or disincentivizing are open to contestation, with the upshot that any claim that civil recovery is fundamentally more forthright or honest than an explicitly criminal law alternative, even one stretched beyond its original remit, is unpersuasive.

This goes beyond mere semantics. Claims to legislative honesty and transparency over the procedure's instrumentality are relied upon to justify not only the slippage in regulatory subjectivity outlined above, but also the securitized *pragmatic* approach to combatting undesirable or criminal activity. Legislative honesty claims are particularly disingenuous; even if we concede that the process is sincere in its calls for action, it is demonstratively *dishonest* in its application. The pragmatic view of civil recovery can be articulated as follows: the problems of serious and organized crime, and the issues these raise for criminal law enforcement, are so significant as to comprise considerations of general welfare, which outweigh *whatever subsequent risk and magnitude of harm* is suffered by individuals whose property is subject to confiscation.[92] We should be under no illusion that this is the ultimate destination of the legislative honesty argument.

In this chapter we have introduced the concept of procedural hybridity, established the contours of the civil/criminal hybrid form of civil recovery, and highlighted our central concerns with this procedure. We revisit these concerns as our analysis continues and as we fold-in our interview data, but it is nonetheless useful to register them here. Civil recovery's purported innovation appears to lie in how its hybrid form is invoked to mask its central functions. Both its characterization as an action against the property (*in rem*), and its allegedly restitutionary nature are relied upon to downplay the severity of confiscation in absence of conviction. Moreover, this process—in a manner so

[90] See Chapter 4 for in-depth engagement with this point.
[91] Peter Alldridge, 'Civil Recovery in England and Wales: An Appraisal' in Colin King, Clive Walker, and Jimmy Gurulé (eds), *The Palgrave Handbook of Criminal and Terrorism Financing Law* (Palgrave 2018) 516. For further discussion, see Chapter 6.
[92] See Chapter 7.

advantageous to the state that it is difficult to construe as anything other than deliberate—first bypasses the due process rights and then dilutes the property rights of individuals merely *suspected* of criminal wrongdoing. In this regard, our rejection of 'we know they did it but just can't prove it' as either a viable or legitimate approach to the problem of serious and organized crime is a recurring theme throughout.

3
Justifications and Legal Framework

Introduction

Civil recovery's non-conviction-based approach, by definition, can result in an individual being permanently deprived of property without having been convicted of any criminal offence. As discussed in the previous chapter, this is emblematic of the trend towards using hybridized approaches within criminal justice, particularly in national and transnational efforts to target organized crime and corruption.[1] The 'follow the money' approach central to civil recovery sees a clear move away from a focus on determination of guilt through criminal proceedings in favour of civil proceedings characterized by a degree of pragmatism about what is either possible or practicable. We will subject this notion of pragmatism to scrutiny in Chapter 7; for now, our concern is charting the background to the enactment of civil recovery powers. In this chapter we also set out the legal framework for non-conviction-based actions against the proceeds of crime in Ireland and England & Wales. Before we do either of these things, however, it is first important to contextualize wider efforts in targeting criminal assets.

'Follow the Money'

The international focus on 'dirty money' is an example of what Andreas and Nadelmann have termed 'global prohibition regimes'.[2] However, the development of such an international anti-money-laundering (AML) regime is, as Joyce observes, no mere 'attempt to codify at the global level existing national or regional norms and standards [but r]ather … a major change in the way

[1] Anthony Kennedy, 'Designing a Civil Forfeiture System: An Issues List for Policymakers and Legislators' (2006) 13(2) *Journal of Financial Crime* 132.

[2] Peter Andreas and Ethan Nadelmann, *Policing the Globe: Criminalization and Crime Control in International Relations* (Oxford University Press 2006) 20. See also Ethan Nadelmann, 'Global Prohibition Regimes: The Evolution of Norms in International Society' (1990) 44(4) *International Organization* 479.

Civil Recovery of Criminal Property. Colin King and Jennifer Hendry, Oxford University Press.
 DOI: 10.1093/oso/9780198824251.003.0003

governments address transnational crime'.[3] While the global AML regime can be traced back to efforts to tackle drug trafficking,[4] its reach extends much further. For example, there is significant contemporary emphasis on corruption, particularly grand corruption.[5] Alongside AML measures, there is emphasis on seizing the proceeds of crime;[6] indeed, Stessens describes confiscation as the 'most important legal tool for depriving offenders of illegal profits'.[7] This section will briefly outline some key developments in the global focus on 'dirty money' and 'following the money'.

Over the past three decades or so, there have been extensive developments in the area of AML and proceeds of crime laws and policies.[8] In 1988 the Vienna Convention[9] embraced the focus on 'following the money' in the context of drug trafficking, although the focus rested specifically on drugs, and the term 'money laundering' was not actually used. In relation to confiscation, Article 5(2) provides: 'Each Party shall also adopt such measures as may be necessary

[3] Elizabeth Joyce, 'Expanding the International Regime on Money Laundering in Response to Transnational Organized Crime, Terrorism, and Corruption' in Philip Reichel (ed.), *Handbook of Transnational Crime and Justice* (Sage 2005) 80.

[4] Peter Andreas and Ethan Nadelmann, *Policing the Globe: Criminalization and Crime Control in International Relations* (Oxford University Press 2006) 147–9. For consideration of the US influence on the global AML regime, see Peter Reuter and Edwin Truman, *Chasing Dirty Money: The Fight Against Money Laundering* (Institute for International Economics 2004), particularly ch.4. For a critical view of AML, see Peter Alldridge, 'Money Laundering and Globalization' (2008) 35(4) *Journal of Law and Society* 437.

[5] FATF, *Laundering the Proceeds of Corruption* (FATF 2011). See also Jason Sharman, *The Despot's Guide to Wealth Management: On the International Campaign against Grand Corruption* (Cornell University Press 2017).

[6] Anna Maria Maugeri, 'The Criminal Sanctions against the Illicit Proceeds of Criminal Organisations' (2012) 3 *New Journal of European Criminal Law* 257; Nicholas Ryder, 'To Confiscate Or Not To Confiscate? A Comparative Analysis of the Confiscation of the Proceeds of Crime Legislation in the United States of America and the United Kingdom' (2013) *Journal of Business Law* 767. Gallant refers to 'the age of the proceeds in crime'. Michelle Gallant, *Money Laundering and the Proceeds of Crime: Economic Crime and Civil Remedies* (Edward Elgar 2005) 1.

[7] Guy Stessens, *Money Laundering: A New International Law Enforcement Model* (Cambridge University Press 2000) 29. Stessens distinguishes between three types of confiscation, namely: (i) Confiscation of instrumentalities of crime (*instrumentum sceleris*), such as the knife used in a murder; (ii) Confiscation of the goods subjected to criminal behaviour (*objectum sceleris*), such as a falsified passport; and (iii) Confiscation of proceeds of crime, that is the financial gains obtained through criminal activities (*fructum sceleris*). Ibid, 30.

[8] A further aspect of 'following the money' is the use of taxation powers. Indeed, there are many avenues in this regard, such as confiscation of proceeds of tax offences (see, e.g., HMIC, *An Inspection of Her Majesty's Revenue and Customs Performance in Addressing the Recovery of the Proceeds of Crime from Tax and Duty Evasion and Benefit Fraud. Revisit 2013* (HMIC 2014)); taxing proceeds of crime (see, e.g., David Lusty, 'Taxing the Untouchables Who Profit from Organised Crime' (2003) 10(3) *Journal of Financial Crime* 209); and prosecuting for tax offences (perhaps the most famous example is that of Al Capone: *Capone v US* 56 F 2d 927 (1931), cert denied, 286 US 553; (1932); *US v Capone* 93 F 2d 840 (1937), cert denied, 303 US 651 (1938); Cf. *DPP v Murphy* [2017] IECA 6). For wider discussion of taxation and crime control, see Peter Alldridge, *Criminal Justice and Taxation* (Oxford University Press 2017).

[9] Convention against Illicit Traffic in Narcotic Drugs and Psychotropic Substances, adopted on 20 December 1988, entered into force on 11 November 1990.

to enable its competent authorities to identify, trace, and freeze or seize proceeds, property, instrumentalities or any other things referred to in paragraph 1 of this article, for the purpose of eventual confiscation.' In 1989 the Financial Action Task Force (FATF) was established by the G7 in Paris,[10] and is, through its International Standards, now regarded as the global standard setter.[11] The original FATF Recommendations provided, in relation to confiscation, that:

> Countries should adopt measures similar to those set forth in the Vienna Convention, as may be necessary, including legislative ones, to enable their competent authorities to confiscate property laundered, proceeds from, instrumentalities used in or intended for use in the commission of any money laundering offense, or property of corresponding value.[12]

In 1990 the Council of Europe's Strasbourg Convention[13] contained detailed provisions on the laundering and confiscation of the proceeds from crime, which influenced subsequent EU laws in this area. The first EU Money Laundering Directive was issued in 1991,[14] with subsequent directives in 2001,

[10] G7, *Economic Declaration*, Paris Summit (16 July 1989), para. 53.

[11] FATF, *International Standards on Combatting Money Laundering and the Financing of Terrorism and Proliferation* (FATF/OECD 2012, updated in March 2022). In 2019 (on FATF's 30th anniversary) FATF was granted an open-ended mandate: FATF, *Mandate* (12 April 2019) para. 16. For further discussion of the FATF, see the 2018 special issue of *Crime, Law and Social Change*; for example, Mark T Nance, 'The Regime that FATF Built: An Introduction to the Financial Action Task Force' (2018) 69(2) *Crime, Law and Social Change* 109.

[12] FATF, *The Forty Recommendations of the Financial Action Task Force on Money Laundering* (FATF 1990), Rec. 8. The current version states: 'Countries should adopt measures similar to those set forth in the Vienna Convention, the Palermo Convention, and the Terrorist Financing Convention, including legislative measures, to enable their competent authorities to freeze or seize and confiscate the following, without prejudicing the rights of bona fide third parties: (a) property laundered, (b) proceeds from, or instrumentalities used in or intended for use in money laundering or predicate offences, (c) property that is the proceeds of, or used in, or intended or allocated for use in, the financing of terrorism, terrorist acts or terrorist organisations, or (d) property of corresponding value.... *Countries should consider adopting measures that allow such proceeds or instrumentalities to be confiscated without requiring a criminal conviction (non-conviction based confiscation), or which require an offender to demonstrate the lawful origin of the property alleged to be liable to confiscation, to the extent that such a requirement is consistent with the principles of their domestic law.*' FATF, *International Standards on Combatting Money Laundering and the Financing of Terrorism and Proliferation* (FATF/OECD 2012, updated in March 2022) Rec. 4 (emphasis added).

[13] Convention on Laundering, Search, Seizure and Confiscation of the Proceeds from Crime, CETS No.141, adopted on 8 November 1990, entered into force on 1 September 1993.

[14] Council Directive of 10 June 1991 on prevention of the use of the financial system for the purpose of money laundering. For consideration of EU developments, see Maria Bergstrom, 'The Global AML Regime and the EU AML Directives—Prevention and Control' in Colin King, Clive Walker, and Jimmy Gurulé (eds), *The Palgrave Handbook of Criminal and Terrorism Financing Law* (Palgrave 2018); Valsamis Mitsilegas and Niovi Vavoula, 'The Evolving EU Anti-Money Laundering Regime: Challenges for Fundamental Rights and the Rule of Law' (2016) 23 *Maastricht Journal of European and Comparative Law* 261.

2005, 2015, and 2018.[15] In 2000, the Palermo Convention[16] expanded upon the focus of the Vienna Convention by requiring states to criminalize 'all crimes' money laundering—not just drugs money laundering—in line with the FATF Recommendations and to implement an appropriate regulatory and supervisory AML regime.[17] Moreover, it also required states to adopt 'to the greatest extent possible' measures to enable the confiscation of proceeds of crime and instrumentalities used or destined to be used in crime.[18]

In 2003, anti-money laundering and confiscation of assets were important aspects of the UN Convention Against Corruption (UNCAC),[19] with provisions relating to *inter alia* establishing a regulatory and supervisory AML regime,[20] money-laundering (ML) offences,[21] and the confiscation of assets.[22] States may also consider enacting an illicit enrichment offence.[23] The return of assets, further, is said to be 'a fundamental principle' of UNCAC.[24] Of particular note for our purposes here is Article 54(1)(c), which requests State Parties to:

> Consider taking such measures as may be necessary to allow confiscation of such [property acquired through or involved in the commission of an offence established in accordance with UNCAC] without a criminal conviction in cases in which the offender cannot be prosecuted by reason of death, flight or absence or in other appropriate cases.

As Rui notes, 'With this endorsement, the UNCAC, for the first time in the text of a global criminal law convention, acknowledges the importance of non-conviction-based forfeiture for the recovery of criminal proceeds'.[25]

[15] The most recent (the Sixth Money Laundering Directive) is Directive (EU) 2018/1673 of the European Parliament and of the Council of 23 October 2018 on combating money laundering by criminal law.

[16] UN Convention against Transnational Organised Crime 2000 (UNCTOC), adopted by GA Res 55/25 of 15 November 2000, entered into force on 29 September 2003.

[17] UNCTOC, Articles 6–7.

[18] UNCTOC, Article 12. There are further provisions in Articles 13 (international cooperation) and 14 (disposal).

[19] UNCAC, adopted by GA Res 58/4 of October 31, 2003, entered into force on December 14, 2005.

[20] UNCAC, Article 14.

[21] UNCAC, Articles 23–24.

[22] UNCAC, Article 31. See also UNCAC, Chapter V.

[23] UNCAC, Article 20.

[24] UNCAC, Article 51. See, generally, Chapter V entitled 'Asset Recovery'. Cf. Anton Moiseienko, 'The Ownership of the Proceeds of Confiscated Proceeds of Corruption Under UNCAC' (2018) 67(3) *International and Comparative Law Quarterly* 669.

[25] Jon Petter Rui, 'Introduction' in Jon Petter Rui and Ulrich Sieber (eds), *Non-Conviction-Based Confiscation in Europe* (Duncker & Humblot 2015) 6. See also *G8 Best Practice Principles on Tracing, Freezing and Confiscation of Assets* (June 2004), para. 26.

The Council of Europe Warsaw Convention[26] was opened for signature in 2005, expanding upon the 1990 Strasbourg Convention particularly in relation to the prevention and control of money laundering and financing of terrorism, as well as provisions on confiscation.[27] Finally, over the past decade and a half, the European Union (EU) has been particularly active in the realm of confiscation, and it is increasingly exploring different forms of confiscation. For example, Article 4(1) of Directive 2014/42/EU[28] provides that:

> Member States shall take the necessary measures to enable the confiscation, either in whole or in part, of instrumentalities and proceeds or property the value of which corresponds to such instrumentalities or proceeds, subject to a final conviction for a criminal offence, which may also result from proceedings in absentia.

Notably, Article 4(2) further provides that:

> Where confiscation on the basis of paragraph 1 is not possible, at least where such impossibility is the result of illness or absconding of the suspected or accused person, Member States shall take the necessary measures to enable the confiscation of instrumentalities and proceeds in cases where criminal proceedings have been initiated regarding a criminal offence which is liable to give rise, directly or indirectly, to economic benefit, and such proceedings could have led to a criminal conviction if the suspected or accused person had been able to stand trial.

There are, moreover, provisions in relation to *inter alia* extended confiscation,[29] third-party confiscation,[30] mutual recognition of orders,[31] establishment of national Asset Recovery Offices and exchange of information between such offices,[32] and access to financial information,[33] to name but a few

[26] Convention on Laundering, Search, Seizure and Confiscation of the Proceeds from Crime and on the Financing of Terrorism, CETS No. 198, adopted on 16 May 2005, entered into force on 1 May 2008.

[27] See Articles 3–8 in relation to confiscation.

[28] Directive 2014/42/EU of the European Parliament and of the Council of 3 April 2014 on the freezing and confiscation of instrumentalities and proceeds of crime in the European Union.

[29] Directive 2014/42/EU, Art. 5.

[30] Directive 2014/42/EU, Art. 5.

[31] Regulation (EU) 2018/1805 of the European Parliament and of the Council of 14 November 2018 on the mutual recognition of freezing orders and confiscation orders.

[32] Council Decision 2007/845/JHA of 6 December 2007 concerning cooperation between Asset Recovery Offices of the Member States in the field of tracing and identification of proceeds from, or other property related to, crime.

[33] Directive (EU) 2019/1153 of the European Parliament and of the Council of 20 June 2019 laying down rules facilitating the use of financial and other information for the prevention, detection,

developments.[34] Non-conviction based confiscation, which is our focus, has proven to be problematic at the EU level, not least given different non-conviction models in the EU, as outlined in Chapter 1, but this form of confiscation remains firmly on the agenda.[35] Indeed, a 2020 report, *Asset Recovery and Confiscation: Ensuring That Crime Does Not Pay*, emphasized: 'The Commission considers that the introduction of further measures in the area of non-conviction based confiscation is feasible and has potential benefits in increasing the levels of freezing and confiscation of proceeds of crime'.[36] Further EU developments in this context are thus to be expected.[37]

Alongside international developments concerning (anti-)money laundering and proceeds of crime, there have been significant developments in relation to counter terrorist financing (CTF). While much of the development in this area has taken place after 11 September 2001 (9/11), efforts to target the finances of terrorists were being undertaken even before 2001:[38] for example, the UN International Convention for the Suppression for the Financing of Terrorism 1999[39] and various UN Security Council Resolutions

investigation or prosecution of certain criminal offences, and repealing Council Decision 2000/642/JHA.

[34] Selvaggi contends that '[t]he state of constant evolution of EU legal framework on freezing and confiscation of criminal assets shows how the adoption and application of property sanctions and measures aimed at countering crime represent a highly controversial issue, which actually affect the asset recovery process in all its phases'. Nicola Selvaggi, 'On Instruments Adopted in the Area of Freezing and Confiscation' (2015) 7 *Diritto Penale Contemporaneo* 1, 1.

[35] For wider discussion of EU developments, see Colin King, 'EU Developments in Non-Conviction-Based Confiscation' in Liz Heffernan (ed.), *Criminal Law and Justice in the European Union* (Clarus Press 2022); Johan Boucht, 'Asset Confiscation in Europe—Past, Present, and Future Challenges' (2019) 26(2) *Journal of Financial Crime* 526; Mihaly Fazekas and Eva Nanopoulos, 'The Effectiveness of EU law: Insights from the EU Legal Framework on Asset Confiscation' (2016) 24(1) *European Journal of Crime, Criminal Law and Criminal Justice* 39; Matthias Borgers, 'Confiscation of the Proceeds of Crime: The European Union Framework' in Colin King and Clive Walker (eds), *Dirty Assets: Emerging Issues in the Regulation of Criminal and Terrorist Assets* (Ashgate 2014); Anna Maria Maugeri, 'The Criminal Sanctions against the Illicit Proceeds of Criminal Organisations' (2012) 3 *New Journal of European Criminal Law* 257.

[36] European Commission, *Report from the Commission to the European Parliament and the Council. Asset Recovery and Confiscation: Ensuring that Crime Does Not Pay* (Brussels, 2 June 2020. COM(2020) 217 final) 15.

[37] See also European Commission, *Commission Staff Working Document. Analysis of non-conviction based confiscation measures in the European Union* (Brussels, 12 April 2019. SWD (2019) 1050 final); European Commission, *EU Strategy to tackle Organised Crime 2021–2025* (Brussels, 14 April 2021 COM(2021) 170 final) 19.

[38] Particularly in countries such as Spain and the United Kingdom who implemented CTF measures in response to Basque and Northern Ireland terrorism, respectively. See, e.g., Thomas Baumert and Mikel Buesa, 'Dismantling Terrorist Economics: The Spanish Experience' in Colin King and Clive Walker (eds), *Dirty Assets: Emerging Issues in the Regulation of Criminal and Terrorist Assets* (Ashgate 2014); Laura Donohue, *The Cost of Counterterrorism: Power, Politics, and Liberty* (Cambridge University Press 2008)ch.3.

[39] Adopted by GA Res 54/109 of 9 December 1999, entered into force on 10 April 2002. Only four states (Botswana, Sri Lanka, the United Kingdom, and Uzbekistan) were signatories to this Convention prior to 9/11, however. Within two years, a further 128 states became signatories.

(SCRs).[40] Unsurprisingly, substantial CTF measures were introduced after 9/11 by both the UN[41] and the FATF,[42] and these measures have subsequently influenced EU developments.[43] As a result, and while many differences subsist between the anti-money laundering/proceeds of crime regimes and the CTF regime,[44] there are also significant overlaps between them.[45]

In this book, we are concerned with one specific aspect of the 'following the money' strategy, namely the seizure of proceeds of crime in the absence of criminal conviction. This chapter now explores the background to the non-conviction-based (NCB) approach introduced in both Ireland and England & Wales, and discusses key underlying and routinely used justifications for this approach.

Enacting Civil Recovery

Prior to their adoption in both Ireland and England & Wales, there had been misgivings about NCB confiscation powers. Indeed, in 1991 the Irish Law Reform Commission rejected a non-conviction-based approach to

[40] See, e.g., UNSCR 1267 of 5 October 1999; UNSCR 1333 of 19 December 2000.

[41] For example, UNSCR 1373 of 28 September 2001; UNSCR 1390 of 16 January 2002; UNSCR 1988 and 1999 of 17 June 2011; UNSCR 2253 of 17 December 2015. For further discussion, see CH Powell, 'The United Nations Security Council Sanctions Regime against the Financing of Terrorism' in Colin King, Clive Walker, and Jimmy Gurulé (eds), *The Palgrave Handbook of Criminal and Terrorism Financing Law* (Palgrave 2018). For wider discussion of CTF efforts, see Jimmy Gurulé, *Unfunding Terror: The Legal Response to the Financing of Global Terrorism* (Edward Elgar 2008); Marieke de Goede, *Speculative Security: The Politics of Pursuing Terrorist Monies* (University of Minnesota Press 2012).

[42] In the aftermath of 9/11, Nine Special Recommendations were adopted, which have now been integrated into the revised FATF International Standards. See: FATF, *FATF IX Special Recommendations October 2001 (Incorporating All Subsequent Amendments until February 2008)* (Financial Action Task Force, n.d) Available at: <https://www.fatf-gafi.org/publications/fatfrecommendations/documents/ixspecialrecommendations.html>.

[43] Council Regulation (EC) No. 2580/2001 of 27 December 2001 on specific restrictive measures directed against certain persons and entities with a view to combating terrorism; Council Regulation (EC) No. 881/2002 of 27 May 2002 imposing certain specific restrictive measures directed against certain persons and entities associated with Usama bin Laden, the Al-Qaida network and the Taliban; Directive 2005/60/EC of the European Parliament and of the Council of 26 October 2005 on the prevention of the use of the financial system for the purpose of money laundering and terrorist financing (the Third Money Laundering Directive). For wider discussion, see Oldrich Bures, 'Ten Years of EU's Fight against Terrorist Financing: A Critical Assessment' (2015) 30 *Intelligence and National Security* 207.

[44] Indeed, it has been said that terrorist financing involves money laundering in reverse in that the aim is not to clean dirty money, rather clean money will be used for illegal purposes. See Stefan Cassella, 'Reverse Money Laundering' (2003) 7(1) *Journal of Money Laundering Control* 92.

[45] For wider discussion, see Mariano-Florentino Cuéllar, 'The Tenuous Relationship between the Fight against Money Laundering and the Disruption of Criminal Finance' (2003) 93 *Journal of Criminal Law and Criminology* 311; Colin King and Clive Walker, 'Counter Terrorism Financing: A Redundant Fragmentation?' (2015) 6(3) *New Journal of European Criminal Law* 372.

confiscating assets, preferring instead the use of post-conviction confiscation. Their reasoning is worth quoting at length:

> While a civil procedure of this nature is not without its attractions, it also presents serious constitutional difficulties. The court would, in effect, be depriving someone of their property on the basis of allegations of criminal activity, in respect of which there had been no conviction or proof. In addition, the procedural safeguards surrounding a criminal trial leading to confiscation are absent in civil proceedings. Hence, it might well be held that legislation of this nature would constitute an 'unjust attack' on property rights in contravention of article 43 of the Constitution.
>
> Unless there was a presumption or a shifting of onus to the defendant, proof even on the balance of probabilities that a particular item represented the proceeds of crime could present almost insuperable difficulties. In a typical case, there would simply not be the evidence necessary to support such an order. One can be reasonably certain that there will be no accounts in financial institutions or securities registered in the suspect's name, nor will there be any business records available. There will indeed be little more than bald information to the effect that a named individual living at a particular address is, for example, dealing in drugs. In the result, in our Discussion Paper, we concluded that a civil procedure would either be ineffective or encounter the risk of a serious constitutional challenge. Our consultations have satisfied us that we are correct in this view and, accordingly, we do not recommend the adoption of such a procedure.[46]

The prospect of adopting US-style civil forfeiture powers was similarly unconscionable in England & Wales, as illustrated by then-Under-Secretary of State for the Home Department David Mellor MP's 1986 statement in relation to the Drug Trafficking Bill:

> The reason why we decided not to adopt the American example of civil proceedings was that we did not think that it could fit readily into the British system. The power is draconian and would have appeared out of sorts with anything that we have hitherto done, because it gives authorities the power to seize property, if they have reasonable suspicion that it has been acquired illegally. Then the individual who claims to be the owner is put to proof.

[46] Law Reform Commission, *Report on the Confiscation of the Proceeds of Crime (LRC 35-1991)* (Law Reform Commission 1991) paras 22–23.

> Without having been convicted of anything, it is up to him to establish that the property was lawfully acquired. If we had proposed that, I suspect that more than Justinian would have spoken of ferocity, and they might have been right.[47]

These views are, however, no longer reflected by contemporary legislation on the proceeds of crime. On the contrary, NCB powers for the civil recovery of criminal assets are today firmly entrenched in both jurisdictions, having been in place now for twenty years.[48] This begs the question: what caused such a marked transformation in both principle and policy?

Shortly before the enactment of the Irish Proceeds of Crime (POCA) legislation in 1996, Deputy Liz O'Donnell explained that, 'given the difficulties experienced in getting convictions, or even gathering evidence, a new power is needed to [restrain] the use of assets outside the context of criminal proceedings'. She concluded with the rhetorical inquiry: 'If we cannot arrest the criminals, why not confiscate their assets?'[49] Similar sentiments were expressed in England & Wales by Lord Goldsmith. During the passage of the POCA Bill in 2002 he elaborated on the motivations behind the legislation:

> Someone at the centre of a criminal organisation may succeed in distancing himself sufficiently from the criminal acts themselves so that there is not sufficient evidence to demonstrate actual criminal participation on his part. Witnesses may decline to come forward because they feel intimidated. Alternatively, there may be strong evidence that the luxury house ... the yachts and the fast motor cars have not been acquired by any lawful activity because none is apparent. It may also be plain from intelligence that the person is someone engaged in criminal activity, but it may not be clear what type of crime. It could be drug trafficking, money laundering or bank robbery. However, the prosecution may not be able to say exactly what is the crime, and thus the person will be entitled to he [*sic*] acquitted of each and every offence. If, in a criminal trial, the prosecution cannot prove that the person before the court is in fact guilty of this bank robbery or that act of

47 HC Deb, Drug Trafficking Offences Bill, 21 January 1986, vol. 90, cols 278–79.

48 Proceeds of Crime Act 1996, as amended (Ire); Proceeds of Crime Act 2002, as amended (E + W).

49 Dáil Éireann, Private Members' Business—Organised Crime (Restraint and Disposal of Illicit Assets) Bill, 1996. Second Stage. 2 July 1996, vol. 467, col. 2435. Similar powers were provided for in the terrorist context under the Offences Against the State (Amendment) Act, 1985, upheld in *Clancy v Ireland* [1988] IR 326.

> money laundering, then he is entitled to be acquitted. Yet it is as plain as a pikestaff that his money has been acquired as the proceeds of crime.[50]

As both of these quotations illustrate, the shared premise underlying the POCA legislation is the idea that the conventional criminal justice process was unsatisfactory and inefficacious in its response to serious crime.[51] In light of these perceived inadequacies, therefore, the power to seize—and retain—'criminal' assets in the absence of criminal conviction was seen as a pragmatic alternative to embarking on processes of arrest and criminal prosecution unlikely to succeed. Far from being draconian, unconscionable, or contrary to principle, shortly after the POCA was enacted in England & Wales, NCB powers were described as 'possibly the most promising provisions in the Act in the fight against crime'.[52]

Justifying Civil Recovery

Alongside the motivations for civil recovery, we must also consider the justifications. Advocates have supplied many reasons vindicating the adoption of civil recovery, most prominent of which concerns the civil nature of such proceedings. Proponents contend that civil recovery falls squarely within the civil paradigm, while critics argue the contrary. The previous chapter provided our critical analysis of the civil/criminal dichotomy in general, while our discussion here concerns civil recovery in particular.

Proponents contend that civil recovery is clearly a civil matter, referring to *inter alia* the nature of proceedings, the venue for the proceedings, the absence of indicia of criminal proceedings, the applicable procedures and rules of evidence, the lack of criminal prosecution and prospect of imprisonment,[53] and the *in rem* nature of the action. The argument that criminal conduct might be alleged against a respondent is considered irrelevant, on the grounds that criminal allegations frequently also arise in civil matters,[54] with the result that not

[50] HL Deb, Proceeds of Crime Bill, 25 June 2002, vol. 636, cols 1270–1271.

[51] Performance and Innovation Unit, *Recovering the Proceeds of Crime* (Cabinet Office 2000) 38–9. See also Anthony Kennedy, 'Designing a Civil Forfeiture System: An Issues List for Policymakers and Legislators' (2006) 13(2) *Journal of Financial Crime* 132; Kenneth Murray, 'A Square Go: Tackling Organised Crime Where It Doesn't Want To Be Tackled' (2013) 16(2) *Journal of Money Laundering Control* 99.

[52] Home Office, *One Step Ahead: A 21st Century Strategy to Defeat Organised Crime* (Cm 6167) (March 2004) 36

[53] Something, it should be flagged, that is not consistent across all procedurally hybrid forms, notably civil preventive orders (CPOs), many of which have a custodial sentence as a result of breach.

[54] See, e.g., *Bank St Petersburg PJSC v Arkhangelsky* [2020] EWCA Civ 408.

only are civil recovery proceedings deemed civil in nature but there is also no requirement for the enhanced procedural protections that would apply within criminal proceedings.[55] This position has been upheld in the courts; our next chapter provides a critical analysis of this jurisprudence.[56]

Amidst concern as to the growth of serious crime, particularly organized crime concerning drugs, the traditional criminal law approach of investigation, prosecution, conviction, and imprisonment was seen either as inadequate or failing. The pre-POCA era was captured succinctly by one former enforcement official in England & Wales: 'The reality in 2002 was all criminals kept all the money'.[57] The Working Group on Confiscation, in its Third Report, illustrated this situation through several examples, referring *inter alia* to a middle-aged man, who had never had any settled employment and who purchased—for cash—a farm in the Surrey stockbroker belt. This same man had access to both a helicopter and a private jet, and had assets totalling in excess of £8 million. It was believed that this man was the custodian of funds for several criminal families but was too far removed from criminal operations to be a viable target for criminal prosecution. Another example was a male in his early sixties who, having previously lived in a council flat, not only moved into a £1 million house without a mortgage but also purchased outright yet further properties abroad. Although the police had strong circumstantial evidence that these real estate purchases were funded by the proceeds of drug trafficking, there was insufficient evidence to sustain a criminal prosecution.[58]

Political discourse in both Ireland and England & Wales has stressed the untouchability of these so-called 'Mr Bigs' of organized crime groups, individuals in these groups' upper tiers who are effectively insulated against viable criminal prosecution. In England & Wales, as the then-Minister for the Home Office, John Denham MP, stated, 'many major criminal figures have become untouchable by criminal prosecution. They organize or finance the criminal activity of others and profit from the results, but remain remote from the commission of particular crimes. That often makes it impossible for law enforcement authorities to build a case against them'.[59] In Ireland, similarly, politicians referred

[55] Felix J McKenna and Kate Egan, 'Ireland: A Multi-Disciplinary Approach to Proceeds of Crime' in Simon NM Young (ed.), *Civil Forfeiture of Criminal Property: Legal Measures for Targeting the Proceeds of Crime* (Edward Elgar 2009).

[56] Similarly, jurisprudence from Strasbourg endorses the NCB approach, for example: *M v Italy*, App. No. 12386/86, 15 April 1991; *Air Canada v UK* [1995] 20 EHRR 150; *Dassa Foundation v Liechtenstein*, App. No. 696/05, 10 July 2007; *Gogitidze v Georgia* [2015] ECHR 475.

[57] EW11.

[58] Working Group on Confiscation *Third Report: Criminal Assets* (Home Office 1998) para. 4.13.

[59] HC Deb, 30 October 2001, vol. 373, col. 760, per Mr Denham MP (Minister for Police, Courts and Drugs).

to a 'home-grown Mafia',[60] the 'godfathers of crime',[61] and 'drug super criminals', who 'live in big houses, have expensive lifestyles, frequently fly abroad and cannot be touched by the State forces of law and order'.[62] In *Gilligan*, McGuinness J described these individuals as:

> an entirely new type of professional criminal who organises, rather than commits, crime and who thereby renders himself virtually immune to the ordinary procedures of criminal investigation and prosecution. Such persons are able to operate a reign of terror so as effectively to prevent the passing on of information to the Gardaí. At the same time their obvious wealth and power causes them to be respected by lesser criminals or would be criminals.[63]

Civil recovery is thus presented as 'a method of attacking a certain form of criminality'.[64] By divesting major players within criminal organizations of assets resulting from criminal activity, the hope is that their power and influence will be diminished, which in turn will 'render them more vulnerable to arrest, trial and conviction'.[65] It appears to be somewhat different in practice, however, with civil recovery developing effectively as a default for when an offence cannot be proven.[66] As one former enforcement official outlined: 'In the operational environment, if you were investigating somebody and you found assets, that there had been money laundering, but you couldn't prove the crime what we would then do is we would put it forward for civil recovery'.[67] Much of this impetus has been taken from the idea that criminal bosses operate at a remove from the criminal activity,[68] with the distance making it difficult for law enforcement to bring an effective prosecution against such individuals. However, while the Godfather figure of cinema has long dominated the imagery of

[60] Dáil Éireann, Private Members' Business—Organised Crime (Restraint and Disposal of Illicit Assets) Bill, 1996, Second Stage, 2 July 1996 vol. 467, col. 2442, per Deputy Alan Shatter.

[61] Dáil Éireann, Private Members' Business—Measures Against Crime: Motion, 2 July 1996, vol. 467, col. 2396, per Deputy Mary Harney.

[62] Seanad Éireann, Proceeds of Crime Bill, 1996, Second Stage, 26 July 1996, vol. 148, col. 1377, per Senator Neville

[63] *Gilligan v CAB* [1998] 3 IR 185, para. 152.

[64] *Gilligan v CAB* [1998] 3 IR 185, para. 86.

[65] *Gilligan v CAB* [1998] 3 IR 185, para. 86.

[66] EW10.

[67] EW10. A similar point was made by another former enforcement official, who stated that where a criminal offence could not be proven the adoption of civil recovery 'does something to address that in part'. EW11.

[68] As Simser explains, 'where organized crime insulates itself from culpability through the use of foot soldiers, civil forfeiture can still effectively get at the lifeblood of the organization—its money'. See Jeffry Simser, 'Perspectives on Civil Forfeiture' in Simon NM Young (ed.), *Civil Forfeiture of Criminal Property: Legal Measures for Targeting the Proceeds of Crime* (Edward Elgar 2009) 20.

organized crime, there has been increasing recognition that the nature of organized crime groups is evolving. Indeed, the rising prominence of the *business* side of organized crime has been a central driver behind the development of responsive new law enforcement strategies;[69] as one interviewee explained:

> It is much easier to argue that civil recovery is recognising the reality of the occupational criminal, which the criminal justice system is simply unsuited to do because the criminal justice system is geared towards people who are on the straight and narrow and have strayed off it once or twice.[70]

Further to this, and with *post*-conviction confiscation supposedly nullified due to difficulties in obtaining a criminal conviction required in order to confiscate property,[71] there is now an identifiable and arguably global trend towards using stand-alone civil proceedings as a means of recovering the proceeds of crime. Such proceedings are undertaken on the grounds that they are likely to be 'more effective than proceedings which are ancillary to, and dependent on, a criminal prosecution'.[72] Even where criminal convictions have been secured, deficiencies in post-conviction confiscation regimes have often meant that criminals have still been in a position *after punishment* to enjoy their criminal gains, and to use them for further criminal activity, even to the extent of directing criminal activity while incarcerated.[73] 'Almost from the off', stressed one enforcement official, 'while [post-conviction confiscation under the Irish Criminal Justice Act 1994] was very helpful in many respects, it had inherent weaknesses within it, which became obvious and, to some extent, they're still there'.[74] It was this official's view that civil recovery was *supplementary* to

[69] R.E. Bell, 'Prosecuting the Money Launderers Who Act for Organised Crime' (1999) 3(2) *Journal of Money Laundering Control* 104.

[70] EW11.

[71] Mike Levi and Lisa Osofsky, *Investigating, Seizing and Confiscating the Proceeds of Crime* (Home Office 1995).

[72] Anthony Kennedy, 'Justifying the Civil Recovery of Criminal Proceeds' (2004) 12(1) *Journal of Financial Crime* 8, 9.

[73] Performance and Innovation Unit *Recovering the Proceeds of Crime* (Cabinet Office 2000) para. 2.4. In *Gilligan v The Special Criminal Court* [2005] IESC 86 the Irish Supreme Court upheld the decision that the Special Criminal Court did not have jurisdiction to impose a post-conviction confiscation order under the Criminal Justice Act 1994. In *R v Cuthbertson* [1981] AC 470 the defendants had pleaded guilty and been sentenced to imprisonment for conspiracy to manufacture and supply Class A drugs; an appeal against forfeiture orders made under the Misuse of Drugs Act 1971, s. 27 was successful (albeit 'with considerable regret' on the part of the House of Lords (p. 479)) as conspiracy was not an offence under the 1971 Act.

[74] IRE03. An enforcement barrister made a similar point: 'And part of the thinking ... was that they wanted to avoid a situation where they had to prove that the person had committed the crimes, I mean that's more the Criminal Justice Act 1994 type approach, confiscation orders following conviction where it can be demonstrated that particular property was acquired as a result of the crimes

post-conviction confiscation,[75] a position supported by an enforcement barrister who articulated this underpinning rationale: 'Hit them in the pockets. If you send them to prison, they'll get out of prison, but they'll come back to their properties.'[76]

The gravity of the threat posed by serious, organized criminal activity is a further central motivation behind the adoption of the non-conviction-based approach. Indeed, it is the seriousness of this criminal activity that has justified this approach as both necessary and proportionate. In *M v D*, Moriarty J stated:

> It seems to me that I am clearly entitled to take notice of the international phenomenon, far from peculiar to Ireland, that significant numbers of persons who engage as principals in lucrative professional crime, particularly that referable to the illicit supply of controlled drugs, are alert and effectively able to insulate themselves against the risk of successful criminal prosecution through deployment of intermediaries, and that the Act of 1996 is designed to enable the lower probative requirements of civil law to be utilised in appropriate cases, not to achieve penal sanctions, but to effectively deprive such persons of such illicit financial fruits of their labours as can be shown to be proceeds of crime.[77]

According to McKenna and Egan, these newly introduced civil measures 'were intended to provide a remedy for the situation where persons involved in drug trafficking and serious crime were openly enjoying the proceeds of their crimes due to insufficient evidence being available for prosecution.'[78] The scale of organized crime was stressed in our study,[79] particularly in the Irish context: it was said, for example, that organized crime issues were 'getting over us, too many cases',[80] that certain criminals were seen as being 'untouchable'[81] and as 'acting with impunity',[82] and that reliance on the criminal law was seen as 'a

for which the person was convicted. But, as you know, there are real limitations in the utility of that in truth.' IRE09.

[75] IRE03. They stressed, though, that '[t]hey're two separate and distinct pieces of legislation, in my view, which are not really strongly connected'.

[76] EW03.

[77] [1998] 3 IR 175, 178.

[78] Felix J McKenna and Kate Egan, 'Ireland: A Multi-Disciplinary Approach to Proceeds of Crime' in Simon NM Young (ed.), *Civil Forfeiture of Criminal Property: Legal Measures for Targeting the Proceeds of Crime* (Edward Elgar 2009) 66.

[79] For a comprehensive overview of the empirical study, see Chapter 1.

[80] IRE11.

[81] IRE12.

[82] IRE03.

joke'.[83] The high-profile murders of journalist Veronica Guerin and Detective Garda Jerry McCabe[84] were, as one interviewee put it, 'the catalysts that prompted the swift introduction of the legislation'. This same interviewee also acknowledged that, while the legislation had 'already been in contemplation at the time ... people—policy makers and legislators—for the first time realized that this thing couldn't be postponed any further'.[85] As another interviewee stated, 'It was essential. It was absolutely essential'.[86]

Supporters of the non-conviction-based approach have lauded it as both efficient and cost-effective, and as compliant with human rights norms, in pursuit of a legitimate goal.[87] Kennedy encapsulates this position as follows: 'Justice in the civil courts, delivered on the balance of probabilities, cannot be criticised as somehow lesser in quality than the justice delivered by the criminal courts. To do so would logically call into question the standard of justice in all civil cases as somehow deficient'.[88] A key argument is that the confiscation of property using the civil standard of proof is both pragmatic and entirely proportionate: depriving an individual of property on the civil standard does not constitute an allegation of criminality against that individual, and so the presumption of innocence is not affected. Moreover, so the argument goes, this presumption remains unaffected by reverse onus provisions requiring 'persons to demonstrate that their property was lawfully acquired in order to avoid

[83] IRE12.

[84] For consideration of these murders, see John Meade, 'Organised Crime, Moral Panic and Law Reform: The Irish Adoption of Civil Forfeiture' (2000) 10(1) *Irish Criminal Law Journal* 11.

[85] IRE03.

[86] IRE07. In contrast to such views, however, a defence solicitor had a more circumspect view: 'Well it was all in the making a long time before the murder of Veronica Guerin. Organised crime in Ireland has a very very short life. It's only going back 25 years cos I mean there were minor players by international standards; ... But very few people were making huge amounts of money out of it until the early-mid 90s and, at that point, it had become a bit of a problem... the north of our city, Inner Dublin, in the late 80s and early 90s was like a war zone. It was really rife with heroin-addicted acquisitive violent criminality. It was very very bad... But it was a very confined problem, you know... it was really confined to Dublin for the most part and really confined to the sectors of the city where heroin addiction was an issue... and I don't think anybody was getting hugely rich out of it. Then Veronica Guerin started talking about Gilligan and talking him up and all that sort of stuff. There became a generalised impetus that we needed to do something about crime. And the Bureau was set up. The Act was 96...... The Bureau didn't appear out of nothing. The Bureau had obviously been in the making in the Department of Justice for a couple of years and, you might say, the murder of Veronica Guerin and the shooting of Jerry McCabe came along at very opportune times for the Bureau because, after that, it was no holds barred for organised crimes—or against organised crime more correctly'. IRE08.

[87] Anthony Kennedy, 'Justifying the Civil Recovery of Criminal Proceeds' (2004) 12(1) *Journal of Financial Crime* 8, 14.

[88] Ibid, 18. This book examines the NCB approach in Ireland and England & Wales. However, according to the World Bank's *Asset Recovery Handbook*, 'Other jurisdictions, mainly civil law ones, require the same higher standard of proof used for criminal conviction: "intimate conviction of the truth"'. Jean-Pierre Brun et al., *Asset Recovery Handbook: A Guide for Practitioners* (2nd edn, World Bank 2020) 16.

confiscation', provisions that are considered 'necessary in practice [and] justifiable in principle'.[89]

In light of these apparent benefits and justifications, it is unsurprising that the non-conviction approach has grown in prominence in recent decades. This increased significance has exemplified a shift from proceeds of crime being seen as a reactive or ancillary option to the main event of prosecution and conviction, to becoming *in its own right* a proactive crime control strategy, independent of other proceedings.[90] In terms of additional descriptors for civil recovery, however, there are several, often-competing possibilities. One option is to consider the non-conviction-based approach as fundamentally compensatory: 'rather than imposing a criminal sanction, it provides a civil remedy to society to compensate for the harm caused to the community by crime and redress the unjust enrichment of those who profit at society's expense'.[91] As Newman J stated in *Ashton*, by enacting civil recovery, Parliament 'is seeking to make a recovery for the state and in the public interest of the state, so that the proceeds of crime should not be at large in society for the benefit of those who happen to be in possession of them at the time'.[92] Another—although arguably similar—potential descriptor for civil recovery is as reparative in that it removes property from those who have no lawful entitlement to it: there is no 'right' to hold property that constitutes proceeds of crime.[93] Thus, in *Gilligan*, it was stated that 'the State has a legitimate interest in the forfeiture of the proceeds of crime',[94] and that '[t]he right to private ownership cannot hold a place so high in the hierarchy of rights that it protects the position of assets illegally acquired and held'.[95] A third option for describing civil recovery is preventive in that it deprives individuals engaged in criminal activity of the proceeds of

[89] David Lusty, 'Civil Forfeiture of Proceeds of Crime in Australia' (2002) 5(4) *Journal of Money Laundering Control* 345, 357.

[90] Felix J McKenna and Kate Egan, 'Ireland: A Multi-Disciplinary Approach to Proceeds of Crime' in Simon NM Young (ed.), *Civil Forfeiture of Criminal Property: Legal Measures for Targeting the Proceeds of Crime* (Edward Elgar 2009).

[91] David Lusty, 'Civil Forfeiture of Proceeds of Crime in Australia' (2002) *Journal of Money Laundering Control* 345, 357.

[92] *R (Director of the Assets Recovery Agency) v Ashton* [2006] EWHC 1064 (Admin), para. 41. In the context of compensating a victim of crime, Newman J stated: 'Crime, when it is committed, is not simply a crime against a victim who may be the individual victim of the crime. Crime, when it occurs, is an offence against the good order of the state and, apart from the victim, it puts the state to enormous expense to resolve questions in connection with crime. I see force in the suggestion that, because, underlying this legislation, there is a plain intention that the state should benefit by recovery from somebody in possession of the proceeds of crime, the legislation has to be regarded as having no compensatory element' (para. 42).

[93] Jeffrey Simser, 'Perspectives on Civil Forfeiture', in Simon NM Young (ed.), *Civil Forfeiture of Criminal Property: Legal Measures for Targeting the Proceeds of Crime* (Edward Elgar 2009).

[94] *Gilligan v CAB* [1998] 3 IR 185, para. 134.

[95] *Gilligan v CAB* [1998] 3 IR 185, para. 136.

that criminal activity, thus precluding future reliance on these as working capital. As Lord Dyson stated in *Gale*: 'The purpose of Part 5 proceedings is not to determine or punish for any particular offence. Rather it is to ensure that property derived from criminal conduct is taken out of circulation.'[96] Similarly, in *Walsh*, it was said that '[t]he recovery of assets may more readily be described as a preventative measure ... After all, the person who is required to yield up the assets does no more than return what he obtained illegally'.[97] The next descriptive option for civil recovery is as non-punitive, on the grounds that the action is taken against the *property* and not against the individual. Prior to the enactment of POCA in England & Wales, it was stressed that:

> [t]he action will concern the property, not the individual. Civil recovery is a matter not of finding a person guilty of a crime but of recovering the proceeds of crime, if that can be established to the satisfaction of the courts and according to the tests laid out in the Bill.[98]

The stance taken in this quotation is that the focus rests on the property and not the individual, with the upshot that civil recovery imposes no sanction on an individual. Furthermore, and contrary to suggestions that the property is *guilty*, civil recovery is 'viewed simply as a procedural device for resolving all objections to the forfeiture of the property at one time in a single proceeding, after giving everyone with an interest in the property notice and a full opportunity to be heard'.[99] A final descriptive option for civil recovery is as disincentivizing, which builds on the underpinning idea that crime should not pay.[100] The limitations of the conviction-based approach have done little to counter the idea that crime *does* pay, with the result that civil recovery has become an appealing alternative: in the words of one enforcement barrister, 'the best way in which to make somebody feel that they have paid for their crimes is actually to take their money away'.[101] Kennedy underscores this point, stating that 'there is a moral imperative on governments to take action to remove the proceeds of crime

[96] *Gale v SOCA* [2011] UKSC 49, para. 123.

[97] *Walsh v Director of the Assets Recovery Agency* [2005] NICA 6, para. 38. See also *R (Director of the Assets Recovery Agency) v Ashton* [2006] EWHC 1064 (Admin), para. 43.

[98] HC Deb 30 October 2001, vol. 373, col. 761, per Mr Denham (Minister for Police, Courts and Drugs).

[99] Stefan D Cassella, 'The Case for Civil Forfeiture: Why *in rem* Proceedings Are an Essential Tool for Recovering the Proceeds of Crime' (2008) 11(1) *Journal of Money Laundering Control* 8, 9.

[100] Jeffrey Simser, 'Perspectives on Civil Forfeiture' in Simon NM Young (ed.), *Civil Forfeiture of Criminal Property: Legal Measures for Targeting the Proceeds of Crime* (Edward Elgar 2009).

[101] EW03.

from the hands of those who possess them'.[102] In terms of civil recovery's disincentivizing effect, these words from another enforcement barrister provide useful insight:

> For criminals, doing a spell in prison is seen by them as an occupational hazard or as something that they should take on the chin when it happens as it is recognised as a risk that they run. When it comes to civil recovery, the impression I get is that there is a real shock that their 'stuff' can be taken by the state in a way in which they have very little to do as an alternative (in contrast to, say, confiscation where they can choose to go to prison if they don't want to pay up), but with civil recovery the action is in respect of the property itself so that will be forfeited. In a way, that really gets to criminals. And, I think, *it really has a disruptive effect on their ability to do business.*[103]

These descriptors of civil recovery—as compensatory, reparative, preventive, non-punitive, and/or disincentivizing—will be discussed and challenged throughout this book. Prior to this, however, and now that the justifications underpinning civil recovery's adoption in Ireland and England & Wales have been outlined, we turn to the legal framework.

Law: Ireland

The primary legislation governing civil recovery in Ireland is the Proceeds of Crime Acts 1996–2016.[104] The long title provides that it is '[a]n Act to enable the High Court, as respects the proceeds of crime, to make orders for the preservation and, where appropriate, the disposal of the property concerned and to provide for related matters'. 'Proceeds of crime' is defined as 'any property obtained or received at any time (whether before or after the passing of this Act) by or as a result of or in connection with criminal conduct'.[105] 'Criminal conduct' is defined as

[102] Anthony Kennedy, 'Justifying the Civil Recovery of Criminal Proceeds' (2004) 12(1) *Journal of Financial Crime* 8, 14.

[103] EW05. Emphasis added.

[104] The 1996 Act was amended by the Proceeds of Crime (Amendment) Act 2005 and the Proceeds of Crime (Amendment) Act 2016. It is now specified that the Acts are together to be known as the Proceeds of Crime Acts 1996–2016. POC(A)A 2016, s. 7(2).

[105] POCA 1996, s. 1(1), as substituted by POC(A)A 2005, s. 3.

any conduct:

(a) which constitutes an offence or more than one offence, or

(b) which occurs outside the State and which would constitute an offence or more than one offence—

(i) if it occurred within the State,

(ii) if it constituted an offence under the law of the state or territory concerned, and

(iii) if, at the time when an application is being made for an interim or interlocutory order, any property obtained or received at any time (whether before or after the passing of this Act) by or as a result of or in connection with the conduct is situated within the State.[106]

Significantly, in proceedings under the Act it is not necessary for an application to relate particular proceeds to a particular crime.[107]

Section 2 of POCA makes provision for an interim order- a pre-trial restraint order.[108] The application for an interim order can be brought by a senior police officer, an authorized officer of the Revenue Commissioners, or by the Criminal Assets Bureau (CAB). If granted, this order prohibits disposal of, or otherwise dealing with, or diminishing the value of specified property.[109] Applications for an interim order are usually brought on an *ex parte* basis, the rationale being to ensure that assets cannot be dissipated or removed from the jurisdiction pending a full *inter partes* hearing.[110] An interim order can only be granted where the Court is satisfied that a person is in possession or control of specified property that constitutes, or was acquired with, proceeds of crime and is of a certain minimum value (€5,000).[111] The civil standard of proof applies[112] and belief evidence is admissible.[113] The Court may also direct the respondent

[106] POCA 1996, s 1(1), as inserted by POC(A)A 2005, s. 3.

[107] *FMcK v AF; FMcK v EH* [2005] IESC 6.

[108] Proceedings shall be held otherwise than in public: POCA 1996, s. 8(3).

[109] POCA 1996, s. 2(1), as amended by POC(A)A 2005, s. 4.

[110] While the risk of dissipation may be one consideration, such a risk is not a formal requirement under the Act: *FMcK v DC* [2006] IEHC 185. Jurisprudence relating to Mareva and Anton Pillar orders in the commercial field applies to *ex parte* applications under the Proceeds of Crime Act, thus there is an obligation of full disclosure on the part of the applicant: *FMcK v DC* [2006] IEHC 185. For an example of where a s. 2 order was lifted for lack of full disclosure, see *CAB v Base Garage Supplies Ltd* [2013] IEHC 302.

[111] POCA 1996, s. 2(1), as amended by POC(A)A 2016, s. 4. Initially, the minimum value was IR£10,000, which was subsequently changed to €13,000 with the adoption of the Euro. See Euro Changeover (Amounts) Act 2001. The minimum value was reduced to its current level, €5,000, by the Act of 2016.

[112] POCA 1996, s. 8(2).

[113] POCA 1996, s. 8(1). To briefly explain: the legislation permits a senior police officer or revenue official to state their 'belief' that a person is in possession or control of specified property that constitutes or stems from proceeds of crime and that the value of that property is not less than €5,000. If the court is satisfied that there are reasonable grounds for that belief, then it shall be admitted as evidence.

to file an affidavit specifying the property that he is in possession or control of, or his income and sources of income for a specified period (not exceeding ten years up to the date of application of the order), or both.[114] Documentary evidence is also admissible.[115] An interim order lasts for twenty-one days and then lapses unless an application for an interlocutory order is brought during that period.[116]

Section 3 of POCA provides for an interlocutory order—whilst this is described as an 'interlocutory order', the section 3 hearing is to be regarded as the trial of the action.[117] An application for an interlocutory order can be brought by a senior police officer, an authorized officer of the Revenue Commissioners, or by the Criminal Assets Bureau. Where it appears to the Court that a person is in possession or control of specified property that constitutes, or was acquired with, proceeds of crime and is of a certain minimum value (€5,000) the Court shall grant an interlocutory order.[118] Where an interlocutory order is granted, that order prohibits disposal of, or otherwise dealing with, or diminishing the value of specified property.[119] Here again, the civil standard of proof applies[120] and belief evidence is admissible.[121] So too may the Court direct the respondent to file an affidavit specifying the property that he is in possession or control of, or his income and sources of income for a specified period (not exceeding ten years up to the date of application of the order), or both.[122] Documentary evidence is also

[114] POCA 1996, s. 9(1), as renumbered by POC(A)A 2005, s. 11. Such an affidavit is not admissible in criminal proceedings against that person or spouse, except where such proceedings relate to perjury arising from statements in the affidavit: POCA 1996, s. 9(2), as inserted by POC(A) 2005, s. 11.

[115] POCA 1996, s. 16A, as inserted by POC(A)A 2005, s. 12.

[116] POCA 1996, s. 2(5). This does not require that the application be actually moved in court within the twenty-one-day period: *FMcK v AF; FMcK v EH* [2005] IESC 6.

[117] *FJMcK v AF and JF* [2002] 1 IR 242; *FJMcK v FC, PL, and MAC; FJMcK v MJG, T Ltd, and E Ltd* [2001] 4 IR 521.

[118] Since 2005 there is provision for a consent disposal order to be granted at this stage where all parties agree to such an order, in which case s. 4A applies: POCA 1996, s. 3(1A), as inserted by POC(A)A 2005, s. 5.

[119] POCA 1996, s. 3(1). By virtue of POCA 1996, s. 8(3), a hearing under section 3 may be held *in camera*: see *CAB v MacAviation Ltd* [2010] IEHC 121.

[120] POCA 1996, s. 8(2).

[121] POCA 1996, s. 8(1). In *McK v D* [2004] 2 IR 470 McCracken J set out a step-by-step approach to be followed in proceedings under POCA. The application of this seven-step approach can be seen in, e.g., *CAB v W* [2010] IEHC 166. See also *P.B. v A.F.* [2012] IEHC 428, where the court declined to admit belief evidence under s. 8(1). In *CAB v McCarthy* [2019] IECA 140, para. 56 the Court of Appeal cautioned against an 'over-slavish or strict adherence to the seven separate steps'. It continued: 'The guidance should not be elevated to the status of a mandatory direction such that any failure to adhere to any one of the steps leads to the invalidation of the order. It is compliance with the Act which is required. The trial judge's judgment must be seen "in the round" so to speak in order to ascertain whether the requirements of s.3, in conjunction with s.8 of the Act have been satisfied.'

[122] POCA 1996, s. 9(1), as renumbered by POC(A)A 2005, s. 11. Such an affidavit is not admissible in criminal proceedings against that person or spouse, except where such proceedings relate to perjury arising from statements in the affidavit: POCA 1996, s. 9(2), as inserted by POC(A)A 2005, s. 11.

admissible.[123] The legislation explicitly provides a safeguard that 'the Court shall not make the order if it is satisfied that there would be a serious risk of injustice'.[124] A further safeguard is that, at any time when an interlocutory order is in force, the respondent or any other person claiming ownership of any of the property concerned can apply to the Court to have the order varied or discharged.[125] Subject to being discharged, an interlocutory order normally continues until (a) the determination of an application for a disposal order in relation to the property concerned, (b) the expiration of the ordinary time for bringing an appeal from that determination, or (c) if an appeal is brought the determination or abandonment of that appeal or any further appeal or expiration of the ordinary time for bringing any further appeal.[126]

At any time while an interim or interlocutory order is in force, an application can be made to the Court to enable the discharge of reasonable living and other necessary expenses (including legal expenses in relation to proceedings under POCA) or to enable the carrying on of a business, trade, profession, or other occupation to which the property concerned relates.[127]

At any point when an interim order or an interlocutory order is in force, the court may appoint a receiver to take possession of any property to which the order relates. Subject to the court's directions, the receiver will manage, keep possession of, dispose of, or otherwise deal with any property over which they are appointed.[128] In practice, where a receiver is to be appointed, the Bureau Legal Officer will usually be appointed to this role.

Section 4 provides for a disposal order: after an interlocutory order has been in force for seven years, the court, on application, may grant a disposal order directing that the property be transferred (subject to any terms and conditions

[123] POCA 1996, s. 16A, as inserted by POC(A)A 2005, s. 12.

[124] POCA 1996, s. 3(1). There are different perspectives on this safeguard: for example Ashe and Reid describe it as 'an important safeguard' whereas O'Higgins is more critical, describing it as 'a vague and intangible yardstick'. See Michael Ashe and Paula Reid, 'Ireland: The Celtic Tiger bites—The Attack on the Proceeds of Crime' (2001) 4(3) *Journal of Money Laundering Control* 253, 259; Michael O'Higgins, 'The Proceeds of Crime Act 1996' (1996) 2(1) *Bar Review* 12, 12. For an example of where it was argued (unsuccessfully) that the making of a s. 3 order would result in a serious risk of injustice, see *CAB v O'Brien* [2010] IEHC 12. For consideration of the approach to be adopted where property is seized illegally or in breach of constitutional rights, see *CAB v Murphy* [2018] 3 IR 640, para. 134 et seq.

[125] POCA 1996, s. 3(3). In practice, this opens the possibility for victims of crime to apply to court to have their rights recognized. For an in-depth consideration of an application under s. 3(3), see *Murphy v Gilligan* [2011] IEHC 62. The Supreme Court declined to re-open this issue in *Murphy v Gilligan* [2014] IESC 43. Cf. *CAB v Kelly* [2012] IEHC 595. For further consideration, see *Murphy v Gilligan* [2017] IESC 3.

[126] POCA 1996, s. 3(5).

[127] POCA 1996, s. 6(1), as amended by POC(A)A 2005, s. 8. See, e.g., *MFM v MB* [1998] IEHC 174.

[128] POCA 1996, s. 7(1). For consideration, see *Murphy v J.G.* [2008] IEHC 33; *CAB v Russell* [2020] IECA 61.

specified by the court) to the Minister for Public Expenditure and Reform[129] or to such other person as the court may determine.[130] While it would appear that the court has a discretion under section 4(1), section 4(2) explicitly states that the court '*shall* make a disposal order ... unless it is shown to its satisfaction that that particular property does not constitute, directly or indirectly, proceeds of crime and was not acquired, in whole or in part, with or in connection with property that, directly or indirectly, constitutes proceeds of crime'.[131] The civil standard of proof continues to apply at this stage.[132] The effect of a disposal order is to deprive the respondent of their rights (if any) in the property concerned and, upon the order being made, the property shall stand transferred to the Minister for Public Expenditure and Reform or other specified person.[133] Similar to section 3, here too there is a safeguard in that the court shall not grant a disposal order if it is satisfied that there would be a serious risk of injustice.[134] Post-2005, there is provision for a disposal order to be granted before the seven year period has elapsed where an application is made with the consent of all the parties concerned. The effect of such a consent disposal order is the same as an order under section 4.[135]

An interim, interlocutory, or disposal order can apply to 'any profit or gain or interest, dividend or other payment or any other property payable or arising, after the making of the order, in connection with any other property to which the order relates'.[136]

Two final points are worth mentioning: first, section 11(7) of the Statute of Limitations does not apply in relation to proceedings under the Act.[137] Second, compensation provisions in relation to interim, interlocutory, and disposal orders are set out in section 16.[138]

[129] See SI No. 418/2011: Finance (Transfer of Departmental Administration and Ministerial Functions) Order 2011.

[130] POCA 1996, s. 4(1). The hearing under s. 4(1) may be adjourned for up to two years: POCA 1996, s. 4(7). A hearing under s. 4 may be held in camera: POCA 1996, s. 8(3). For an example of s. 4 in practice, see *Murphy v Gilligan* [2011] IEHC 464.

[131] POCA 1996, s. 4(2). Emphasis added. The s. 4 hearing is not intended to re-litigate matters that have already been determined: *Murphy v Gilligan* [2014] IESC 43.

[132] POCA 1996, s. 8(2).

[133] POCA 1996, s. 4(4). The Minister may sell or otherwise dispose of any such property. Any money realized under this section shall be paid into or disposed of for the benefit of the Exchequer: POCA 1996, s. 4(5). Contrast this with the Asset Recovery Incentivisation Scheme (ARIS) in England & Wales.

[134] POCA 1996, s. 4(8). For consideration in the context of the 'family home' see *CAB v Kelly* [2012] IESC 64.

[135] POCA 1996, s. 4A, as inserted by POC(A)A 2005, s. 7.

[136] POCA 1996, s. 5(3).

[137] POC(A)A 2005, s. 10.

[138] POCA 1996, s. 16.

A new section 16B was inserted by the Proceeds of Crime (Amendment) Act 2005, making provision for a corrupt enrichment order. A person is corruptly enriched if he 'derives a pecuniary or other advantage or benefit as a result of or in connection with corrupt conduct, wherever the conduct occurred'.[139] Where the court is satisfied that a defendant has been corruptly enriched, the court may grant a corrupt enrichment order directing the defendant to pay to the Minister for Public Expenditure and Reform, or such other person as specified by the court, an amount equivalent to the amount by which it determines that the defendant has been so enriched.[140] The standard of proof under this section is that applicable to civil proceedings.[141] Belief evidence is admissible.[142] The court may also direct the defendant to file an affidavit specifying the property owned by him, his income and sources of income, or both.[143] Unlike the affidavit that can be required in proceedings under section 2 (interim order) and section 3 (interlocutory order), there is no time restriction here. An *ex parte* application can be brought to the court for an order prohibiting the defendant, or any other person having notice of the order, from disposing of, otherwise dealing with, or diminishing the value of the property during a specified period.[144]

In 2016, new provisions were inserted into POCA enabling administrative seizure and detention of property by a bureau officer. Certain conditions must be satisfied before property may be seized, namely that a bureau officer has reasonable grounds for suspecting that certain property, in whole or in part, constitutes proceeds of crime and is of a value not less than €5,000.[145] The Chief Bureau Officer of CAB can authorize detention for a period not exceeding twenty-one days.[146] Again here, there are provisions for payment of compensation where appropriate.[147]

[139] POCA 1996, s. 16B(1)(a), as inserted by POC(A)A 2005, s. 12. 'Corrupt conduct' is defined as 'any conduct which at the time it occurred was an offence under the Prevention of Corruption Acts 1889 to 2001, the Official Secrets Act 1963 or the Ethics in Public Office Act 1995': POCA 1996, s. 16B(1)(b), as inserted by POC(A)A 2005, s. 12.

[140] POCA 1996, s. 16B(2), as inserted by POC(A)A 2005, s. 12.

[141] POCA 1996, s. 16B(8), as inserted by POC(A)A 2005, s. 12.

[142] POCA 1996, s. 16B(5), as inserted by POC(A)A 2005, s. 12.

[143] POCA 1996, s. 16B(6)(a), as inserted by POC(A)A 2005, s. 12. Such an affidavit is not admissible in criminal proceedings against that person or spouse, except where such proceedings relate to perjury arising from statements in the affidavit: POCA 1996, s. 16B(6)(b), as inserted by POC(A)A 2005, s. 12.

[144] POCA 1996, s. 16B(4), as inserted by POC(A)A 2005, s. 12.

[145] POCA 1996, s. 1A(1), as inserted by POC(A)A 2016, s. 3.

[146] POCA 1996, s. 1A(2), as inserted by POC(A)A 2016, s. 3. An application can be brought to the court to vary or revoke such an authorization: POCA, s. 1B(1).

[147] POCA 1996, s. 1C(1), as inserted by POC(A)A 2016, s. 3.

The agency tasked with implementing POCA is the CAB.[148] Indeed, the establishment of such a specialized agency was described as 'a necessary adjunct to [the] assets' freezing Bill and is somewhat consequential to it'.[149] The multi-agency approach[150] facilitates greater cooperation and collaboration between officials from different agencies,[151] sharing of powers and duties,[152] greater admissibility of evidence,[153] and sharing of information.[154] The CAB Act contains a number of provisions in relation to investigatory powers, including provision for anonymity of non-Garda bureau officers,[155] search warrants,[156] an 'Order to make material available',[157] a 'tipping-off' offence in relation to such an order,[158] and an order in relation to obtaining information regarding any property held in trust.[159]

A number of offences are also set out in the CAB Act. It is an offence to publish or cause to be published the fact that a person is, or was, a bureau officer[160] or member of staff at the bureau, or is a member of the family of such a person, or the address of any such person.[161] It is an offence to delay, obstruct, impede, interfere with, or resist either a bureau officer in the exercise or performance of his powers or duties or a member of staff of the bureau who is accompanying or assisting such a bureau officer.[162] It is an offence to utter or send threats to, or in any way intimidate or menace, a bureau officer or member of staff of the bureau, or the family or either such person.[163] It is an offence to assault or

[148] Criminal Assets Bureau Act, 1996 (herein CAB Act). As well as its civil forfeiture powers, CAB also has significant taxation and social welfare powers.

[149] Dáil Éireann, Criminal Assets Bureau Bill, 1996, Second Stage, 25 July 1996, vol. 4668, col. 1031, per Deputy McCreevy. The objectives and functions of the Bureau are set out in CAB Act, ss 4 and 5.

[150] CAB Act, s. 8. For consideration of the multi-agency approach—with officials from An Garda Síochána (Irish police), Revenue Commissioners (taxation), and Department of Social Protection (social welfare), see Patrick Ryan, *An examination of how the methods employed by the Criminal Assets Bureau move Ireland in a new direction of crime control* (PhD Thesis, University of Limerick, 2019); Colin King, 'Civil Forfeiture in Ireland—Two Decades of the Proceeds of Crime Act and the Criminal Assets Bureau' in Katalin Ligeti and Michele Simonato (eds), *Chasing Criminal Money in the EU* (Hart 2017).

[151] CAB Act, s. 8(5).

[152] CAB Act, s. 8(6)(c).

[153] CAB Act, s. 8(6)(d).

[154] CAB Act, s. 8(5) and (7). In *CAB v Craft* [2001] 1 IR 121, 133 O'Sullivan J stated: 'The members of the Criminal Assets Bureau are entitled to exchange information amongst themselves and clearly they would be in dereliction of duty if they failed to do this in an appropriate case.'

[155] CAB Act, s. 10.

[156] CAB Act, s. 14.

[157] CAB Act, s. 14A, as inserted by POC(A)A 2005, s. 18.

[158] CAB Act, s. 14B, as inserted by POC(A)A 2005, s. 18.

[159] CAB Act, s. 14C, as inserted by POC(A)A 2005, s. 18.

[160] As defined in CAB Act, s. 8.

[161] CAB Act, s. 11(1).

[162] CAB Act, s. 12(1).

[163] CAB Act, s. 13(1).

attempt to assault a bureau officer, a member of staff of the bureau, or a family member of either such person.[164]

Law: England & Wales

The purpose of Part 5 of the Proceeds of Crime Act 2002 (POCA)[165] is to enable the enforcement authority[166] to recover, in civil proceedings, property which is, or represents, property obtained through unlawful conduct.[167] The focus is 'on the fruits of crime themselves'.[168] As Newman J noted in *Ashton*, in enacting Part 5 of POCA, Parliament was 'seeking to make a recovery for the state and in the public interest of the state, so that the proceeds of crime should not be at large in society for the benefit of those who happen to be in possession of them at the time'.[169] The powers under Part 5 'are exercisable in relation to any property (including cash) whether or not any proceedings have been brought for an offence in connection with the property'.[170] 'Unlawful conduct' is defined as conduct occurring in any part of the United Kingdom that is unlawful under the criminal law of that part of the United Kingdom.[171] 'Unlawful conduct' extends to conduct occurring outside the United Kingdom that is unlawful in that foreign jurisdiction and that would, if it occurred in a part of the

164 CAB Act, s. 15(1).

165 The civil recovery provisions came into force on 24 February 2003: SI 2003/120 The Proceeds of Crime Act 2002 (Commencement No. 4, Transitional Provisions and Savings) Order 2003. For an overview of the scheme as originally enacted see Home Office Circular 016/2003 *Guidance on the new civil recovery scheme and powers to disclose information to and from the Assets Recovery Agency*.

166 In Part 5 of POCA, 'enforcement authority' means HM Revenue and Customs, the Financial Conduct Authority, the National Crime Agency, the Director of Public Prosecutions, the Director of the Serious Fraud Office, the Scottish Ministers, or the Director of Public Prosecutions for Northern Ireland. POCA, s. 316(1).

167 POCA, s. 240(1)(a). In relation to cash forfeiture, s. 240(1)(b) goes further, providing that cash may be forfeited not only where it has been obtained through unlawful conduct but also where the cash is intended to be used in such conduct.

168 *Gale v SOCA* [2011] UKSC 49, para. 2.

169 *R (Director of the Assets Recovery Agency) v Ashton* [2006] EWHC 1064 (Admin), para. 41.

170 POCA, s. 240(2). According to the Explanatory Notes, cases where criminal proceedings have not been brought would include those cases where there are insufficient grounds for prosecution, where the person suspected of an offence is outside the jurisdiction, or where that person has died. Cases where criminal proceedings have been brought would include those where a defendant was acquitted in the criminal proceedings or where the person was convicted but a confiscation order was not made. *Explanatory Notes to the Proceeds of Crime Act 2002*, para. 290. There is a twenty-year limitation period under Part 5: POCA, s. 288.

171 POCA, s. 241(1). In *The Queen (Director of the Assets Recovery Agency) v E & B* [2007] EWHC 3245 (Admin) Mitting J ruled that a claim for civil recovery was not an abuse where it was based on unlawful conduct (keeping a brothel), notwithstanding the fact that the unlawful conduct appeared to have been tolerated by senior police officers, leading to the stay of criminal proceedings.

United Kingdom, be unlawful under the criminal law of that part.[172] 'Unlawful conduct' also extends to conduct which (a) occurs in a country or territory outside the United Kingdom, (b) constitutes, or is connected with, the commission of a gross human rights abuse or violation, and (c) if it occurred in a part of the United Kingdom, would be an offence triable under the criminal law of that part on indictment only or either on indictment or summarily.[173] Civil recovery proceedings are brought in the High Court or (in Scotland) the Court of Session 'against any person who the [enforcement] authority thinks holds recoverable property'.[174] Also: 'For the purpose of deciding whether or not property was recoverable at any time (including times before commencement), it is to be assumed that this Part was in force at that and any other relevant time.'[175]

The legislation explicitly provides that the standard of proof is the balance of probabilities: the court must decide on a balance of probabilities whether it is proved that any matters alleged to constitute unlawful conduct have occurred.[176] It has been suggested that, by explicitly stating that the balance of probabilities is to be applied, 'POCA is thus proactively encouraging the courts to apply a 51/49 per cent "more likely than not" balance of probabilities test'.[177]

A person obtains property[178] through unlawful conduct if he obtains property by or in return for that conduct. And the unlawful conduct in question might be his own or that of another person.[179] Thus POCA covers situations where a person, say, obtains money as a result of committing robbery or where

[172] POCA, s. 241(2). For consideration of a foreign conviction, see *Assets Recovery Agency v Virtosu* [2008] EWHC 149 (QB).

[173] POCA, s. 241(2A). The conditions that must be satisfied for conduct to constitute 'the commission of a gross human rights abuse or violation', or connected thereto, are specified in s. 241A(2)–(5).

[174] POCA, s. 243(1) and s. 244(1). For illustration, see *NCA v Odewale* [2020] EWHC 1609 (Admin). In appropriate circumstances, summary judgment is permitted: *Director of ARA v Woodstock* [2006] EWCA Civ 741. Section 304(1) provides that: '[p]roperty obtained through unlawful conduct is recoverable property'. Note that property may cease to be 'recoverable property' where another person claims that she was deprived of the property (or of property which it represents) by unlawful conduct; that the property was not recoverable property immediately before she was deprived of it; and the property belongs to her: s. 281. Thus, the legislation 'gives the claims of a true owner precedence over those of the enforcement authority'. *Explanatory Notes to the Proceeds of Crime Act 2002*, para. 386. See *NCA v Robb* [2014] EWHC 4384 (Ch) para. 32 et seq. The minimum threshold for an order under Part 5 is £10,000: SI 2003/175 The Proceeds of Crime Act 2002 (Financial Threshold for Civil Recovery) Order 2003. See also POCA, s. 287.

[175] POCA, s. 316(3).

[176] POCA, s. 241(3).

[177] Mark Sutherland Williams, Michael Hopmeier, and Rupert Jones, *Millington and Sutherland Williams on The Proceeds of Crime* (5th edn, Oxford University Press 2018) 313.

[178] 'Property' includes money; all forms of property, real or personal, heritable or moveable; and things in action and other intangible or incorporeal property. POCA, s. 316(4).

[179] POCA, s. 242(1). In *Perry v Serious Organised Crime Agency* [2012] UKSC 35, para. 39, Lord Phillips stated: 'The focus is not on a particular defendant but upon property that is the product of criminal conduct . . . It is not necessary that the person who holds or owns the property should be the person guilty of the criminal conduct.' See, e.g., *Sanam v NCA* [2015] EWCA Civ 1234.

she obtains money having accepted a bribe from another person to award a contract. In deciding whether a person has obtained property through unlawful conduct 'it is immaterial whether or not any money, goods or services were provided in order to put the person in question in a position to carry out the conduct'.[180] This puts the focus on the proceeds, not just the profits, of unlawful conduct. An example here is of a person buying illicit drugs with honestly held money and selling those drugs at a profit: the entire proceeds of sale will count as property obtained by unlawful conduct, not just the profit.[181] Further, it is not necessary to show that the conduct 'was of a particular kind', so long as it is shown that the property 'was obtained through conduct of one of a number of kinds, each of which would have been unlawful conduct'.[182]

Moreover, an application[183] for an order under Part 5 can be made 'in respect of any property or person, whether or not the property or person is (or is domiciled, resident or present) in' any part of the United Kingdom.[184]

POCA provides for situations where recoverable property is disposed of 'into the hands of [another] person'[185] and for tracing of property.[186] A claim for civil recovery is said to 'follow[] the property so that recovery cannot be thwarted by simply converting the recoverable property into something else or by granting an interest in it'.[187] So, where the original property has been disposed of then a 'pick and mix' approach is available: the enforcement authority may opt to trace the original property itself through various hands or it may

[180] POCA, s. 242(2)(a).

[181] *Explanatory Notes to the Proceeds of Crime Act 2002*, para. 295.

[182] POCA, s. 242(2)(b). See *R (Director of the Assets Recovery Agency) v Green* [2005] EWHC 3168 (Admin). See also *Director of the Assets Recovery Agency v Szepietowski* [2007] EWCA Civ 766; *Olupitan v Director of the Assets Recovery Agency* [2008] EWCA Civ 104; *SOCA v Gale* [2009] EWHC 1015 (QB); *SOCA v Pelekanos* [2009] EWHC 2307 (QB); *SOCA v Hymans* [2011] EWHC 3332 (QB). According to the *Explanatory Notes to the Proceeds of Crime Act 2002*, para. 296, 'it will not matter, for example, that it cannot be established whether certain funds are attributable to drug dealing, money laundering, brothel-keeping or other unlawful activities, provided it can be shown that they are attributable to one or other of these in the alternative, or perhaps some combination'.

[183] See Practice Direction—Civil Recovery Proceedings, para. 4 et seq.

[184] POCA, s. 316(8B). Section 282A provides that an order may be made in respect of property wherever situated and in respect of a person wherever domiciled, resident, or present, subject to specified exceptions (s. 282A(1)). An order may not be made in respect of property outside the United Kingdom or property in the United Kingdom, but outside the relevant part of the United Kingdom, 'unless there is or has been a connection between the case and the relevant part of the United Kingdom.' (s. 282A(2)). See POCA, Sch. 7A in relation to where property has 'Connection with relevant part of United Kingdom' (for application, see *NCA v Khan* [2017] EWHC 27 (QB), para. 94). The provisions thereby addressed the decision in *Perry v Serious Organised Crime Agency* [2012] UKSC 35, which confined Part 5 of POCA to property within the UK. In relation to enforcement of orders abroad, see sections 282B–F.

[185] POCA, s. 304.

[186] POCA, s. 305.

[187] Edward Rees, Richard Fisher, and Richard Thomas, *Blackstone's Guide to The Proceeds of Crime Act 2002* (5th edn, Oxford University Press 2015) 176.

recover the property which now represents the original property.[188] For example, if a person robs a jewellery store the items stolen will be recoverable property. If the stolen jewellery is then disposed[189] of, such as by gifting it or selling it to another person, the jewellery remains recoverable property.[190] If the money received in exchange for the jewellery is subsequently used to buy a house then the house becomes recoverable property. The enforcement authority thus can either target the jewellery (the 'original property') or the house (which 'represents the original property').[191] In *Szepietowski* Moore-Bick LJ emphasized the need 'to bear in mind that the right to recover property does not depend on the commission of unlawful conduct by the current holder. All that is required is that the property itself be tainted because it, or other property which it represents, was obtained by unlawful conduct'.[192]

Where recoverable property is mixed with other property, then the portion of that property that is attributable to the recoverable property will be taken to represent the property obtained through unlawful conduct.[193] And if profits accrue in respect of recoverable property, that 'further property' will also be treated as representing property obtained through unlawful conduct.[194] An example here might be a house that is recoverable property: if that house increases in value then that increase in value will also be treated as having been obtained through unlawful conduct.[195] Where a person grants an interest in his recoverable property that interest can also be treated as having been obtained by, or representing, unlawful conduct.[196]

[188] Edward Rees, Richard Fisher, and Richard Thomas, *Blackstone's Guide to The Proceeds of Crime Act 2002* (5th edn, Oxford University Press 2015) 176.

[189] 'Disposing' includes disposing of part of property, granting an interest in it, making a payment to another, and the passing of property under a will or intestacy rules. POCA, s. 314.

[190] Note though POCA s. 308: where a person obtains recoverable property 'in good faith, for value and without notice that it was recoverable property', then 'the property may not be followed into that person's hands and, accordingly, it ceases to be recoverable'. But see *SOCA v Lundon* [2010] EWHC 353 (QB). There are further exceptions whereby property ceases to be recoverable including *inter alia* following a payment to a claimant in civil proceedings or in pursuance of a compensation order, a slavery and trafficking reparation order, or a restitution order. See POCA, ss 308–309.

[191] POCA, ss 304–305. See *SOCA v Lundon* [2010] EWHC 353 (QB). In *Re Warnock* [2005] NIQB 16, para. 15 the entitlement of the deceased's estate under a life assurance policy was held to be recoverable property where the court determined that the monthly premiums were the proceeds of crime.

[192] *Director of the Assets Recovery Agency v Szepietowski* [2007] EWCA Civ 766, para. 106.

[193] POCA, s. 306. See *Olupitan v Director of the Assets Recovery Agency* [2008] EWCA Civ 104.

[194] POCA, s. 307. See *NCA v Namli and Topinvest Holding International Ltd* [2014] EWCA Civ 411. In *SOCA v Pelekanos* [2009] EWHC 2307 (QB), para. 14 it was said that s. 307 'provides for the recovery of rental income received from a property which is, of itself, recoverable property'.

[195] In *SOCA v Olden* [2009] EWHC 610 (QB), para. 89 Holroyde J gave the example of a person taking a cash sum out of the proceeds of crime, using that money to place a bet, and successfully doubling his money: 'it seems to me that the increased sum is caught by POCA 2002 s. 307 and all of it is recoverable property'.

[196] POCA, s. 310.

POCA makes provision for property freezing orders (PFO).[197] Such an order will specify or describe the property to which it applies and, subject to any exclusions, prohibit any person to whose property the order applies from in any way dealing with the property.[198] An application for a PFO can be made without notice 'if the circumstances are such that notice of the application would prejudice any right of the enforcement authority to obtain a recovery order in respect of any property'.[199] The option of applying for a PFO without notice is designed to safeguard against the risk that a respondent might attempt to transfer, or otherwise dissipate, his assets.[200] Before the court can grant a PFO it must be satisfied that there is a good arguable case[201] that the application concerns recoverable property, or if the property, or part thereof, is not recoverable property that it is 'associated property'.[202]

POCA also contains provision for management receiving orders (MROs) in relation to property to which a PFO applies.[203] In practice, few MROs are now being made: 'The risk-averse authorities, wary of cost implications, are simply

[197] The equivalent in Scotland is the Prohibitory Property Order: see POCA, s. 255A-I. For an example of where a PFO was granted, see *NCA v Grubisic* [2019] EWHC 2622 (Admin). See also *NCA v Leahy* [2020] EWHC 1242 (QB), where an application to discharge a PFO was rejected.

[198] POCA, s. 245A(2). The exclusions are provided for in s. 245C.

[199] POCA, s. 245A(3). See also *National Crime Agency (NCA) v Simkus & Ors* [2016] EWHC 255 (Admin).

[200] For consideration of the obligation to make full and fair disclosure of all material facts in a without notice application, see *Re Keenan* [2005] NIQB 67; *NCA v Davies* [2016] EWHC 899 (Admin). See also *Director of the Assets Recovery Agency v Kean* [2007] EWHC 112 (Admin), paras 54–55. In *National Crime Agency (NCA) v Simkus & Ors* [2016] EWHC 255 (Admin), para. 114 et seq, Edis J concluded that there was a non-disclosure of a material fact however refused the application to discharge the PFO. See also *Faerman v Director of the SFO* [2020] EWHC 1849 (Admin).

[201] In *Director of the Assets Recovery Agency v Szepietowski* [2007] EWCA Civ 766, para. 28 Waller LJ stated: 'In this case, in considering whether a good arguable case has been established, it will be necessary to examine first whether it is arguable on the evidence that unlawful conduct of the kind asserted by the ARA has taken place, i.e. mortgage fraud. Next needs to be considered whether it is arguable that the property sought to be frozen represents property originally obtained through such unlawful conduct, but not necessarily through specific examples of that conduct; and finally, if there is some evidence that property was obtained though unlawful conduct, consideration needs to be given to any untruthful explanation or a lack of explanation where opportunity has been given to provide it. An untruthful explanation or a failure to offer an explanation may add strength to the arguability of the case.' See, e.g., *SOCA v Khan* [2012] EWHC 3235 (Admin).

[202] POCA, s. 245A(4)–(5). If the court decides that property to which a PFO applies is no longer 'recoverable property' nor 'associated property', then it must vary the PFO so as to exclude that property: *SOCA v O'Docherty* [2013] EWCA Civ 518. If the application for a PFO concerns associated property the court must be satisfied that if the enforcement authority has not established the identity of the person who holds it that the enforcement authority has taken all reasonable steps to do so. POCA, s. 245A(6). 'Associated property' is defined in s. 245(1). The legislation contains further detail in relation to varying and setting aside a PFO (s. 245B), exclusions (s. 245C), and restrictions on proceedings and remedies (s. 245D). For example, provision can be made in relation to reasonable living expenses (s. 245C(3)(a)) and legal expenses (s. 245C(5)–(6)). In Scotland, however, s. 255C(5) provides: '[a]n exclusion may not be made for the purpose of enabling any person to meet any legal expenses in respect of proceedings under this Part.'

[203] POCA, s. 245E. Powers of management receivers are dealt with under s. 245F, while s. 245G deals with supervision and variation of orders.

not promoting or using them in the way the [Serious Crime Act 2007] had contemplated.'[204]

Where the enforcement authority may take proceedings for a recovery order, it can apply to the court for an interim receiving order (IRO).[205] An IRO provides for the detention, custody or preservation of property, and the appointment of an interim receiver.[206] As with a PFO, an application for an IRO can be made without notice 'if the circumstances are such that notice of the application would prejudice any right of the enforcement authority to obtain a recovery order in respect of any property'.[207] The court may grant an IRO where it is satisfied that there is a good arguable case that the relevant property is, or includes, recoverable property, or if the property, or part thereof, is not recoverable property that it is associated property.[208] Unlike an MRO, the person nominated as interim receiver may not be a member of staff of the enforcement authority.[209] This reflects the fact that an interim receiver is seen as an independent officer of the court.[210]

When an IRO is made, the relevant director is deemed to no longer be carrying out a civil recovery investigation.[211] As such, the powers under Part 8 of POCA will no longer be available (these powers are outlined later).[212] Rather, alongside its management role, an interim receiver fulfils an investigative role:

> An interim receiving order must require the interim receiver to take any steps which the court thinks necessary to establish—
>
> (a) whether or not the property to which the order applies is recoverable property or associated property,

[204] Mark Sutherland Williams, Michael Hopmeier, and Rupert Jones, *Millington and Sutherland Williams on The Proceeds of Crime* (5th edn, Oxford University Press 2018) 329. It was suggested that this, at least in part, follows on from the decision in *Barnes v The Eastenders Group* [2014] UKSC 26.

[205] POCA, s. 246(1). The equivalent in Scotland is the interim administration order: see POCA, s. 256–265.

[206] POCA, s. 246(2).

[207] POCA, s. 246(3). See *Director of the Assets Recovery Agency v Satnam Singh* [2004] EWHC 2335 (Admin) para. 42 et seq for consideration of the obligation to make full and fair disclosure of all material facts.

[208] POCA, s. 246(4)–(5). See, e.g., *R (Director of the Assets Recovery Agency) v He and Chen* [2004] EWHC 3021 (Admin), para. 80. If the application for an IRO concerns associated property the court must be satisfied that if the enforcement authority has not established the identity of the person who holds it that the enforcement authority has taken all reasonable steps to do so. POCA, s. 246(6).

[209] POCA, s. 246(7).

[210] *Director of the Assets Recovery Agency v Jackson* [2007] EWHC 2553 (QB), para. 29. See also *Explanatory Notes to the Proceeds of Crime Act 2002*, para. 309.

[211] POCA, s. 341(3)(b).

[212] See text associated with n.235.

(b) whether or not any other property is recoverable property (in relation to the same unlawful conduct) and, if it is, who holds it.[213]

In *Wilson*, the court stated:

> The role of Interim Receiver is that of a court-appointed expert to investigate the origin and owner of assets and to report to the court on those assets. In the absence of evidence to the contrary such a report will be compelling evidence in any application based upon it. Its detailed contents relating to accountancy matters are accepted as fact unless shown otherwise.[214]

It has been said that:

> The imposition of the investigative function upon the interim receiver confers a unique role amongst receivers in UK jurisprudence. A vital aspect of the scheme is that the interim receiver is not a witness for the enforcement authority and is not supervised by the enforcement authority. He is the court's investigator and it can be expected that the report will be used to determine which issues can be agreed and which remain in dispute.[215]

An interim receiver has considerable powers under POCA, Schedule 6 including: power to seize property to which the order applies;[216] power to obtain information or to require a person to answer any question;[217] powers of entry, search, inspection, and removal;[218] and power to manage any property to which the order applies.[219] An IRO must—subject to any

[213] POCA, s. 247(2). POCA also contains specific provisions on duties of respondents (s. 250), supervision of the interim receiver and variation of an order (s. 251), restrictions on proceedings and remedies (s. 253), exclusion of property which is not recoverable (s. 254), and reporting (s. 255).

[214] *Director of the Asset Recovery Agency v Wilson* [2007] NIQB 49, para. 10. In *Director of the Assets Recovery Agency v Jackson* [2007] EWHC 2553 (QB), para. 30, the court accepted 'that the Receiver's findings of recoverable property are not binding on the court, that it is the primary evidential material underlying her findings and said by her to justify them, which is of crucial importance together with any additional evidence called before the court, and that it is the duty of the court in determining any area of dispute between the parties carefully to scrutinise and weigh that evidence in order to determine whether the claim to recoverable property is made out'.

[215] Mark Sutherland Williams, Michael Hopmeier, and Rupert Jones, *Millington and Sutherland Williams on The Proceeds of Crime* (5th edn, Oxford University Press 2018) 333.

[216] POCA, Sch. 6, para. 1.

[217] POCA, Sch. 6, para. 2(1). Paragraph 2(3) provides that an answer given under para. 2(1) may not be used in evidence against that person in criminal proceedings.

[218] POCA, Sch. 6, para. 3.

[219] POCA, Sch. 6, para. 5(1). This includes selling or otherwise disposing of assets; carrying on, or arranging for another to carry on, a trade or business; or incurring capital expenditure in respect of the property: para. 5(2).

exclusions[220]—'prohibit any person to whose property the order applies from dealing with the property.'[221] In practice though, '[l]ike MROs ... the reality in 2017 is that IROs are not being utilised in the way the legislation originally contemplated. Prosecuting authorities remain risk averse, particularly in relation to costs, and as a result the number of IROs are few and far between.'[222]

Provision for the making of a recovery order is contained in section 266: 'If in proceedings under this Chapter the court is satisfied that any property is recoverable, the court must make a recovery order'.[223] This is subject to the exception, however, that a court may not make in a recovery order any provision in respect of any recoverable property where certain conditions are met and it would not be just and equitable to do so.[224] These conditions are:

(a) the respondent obtained the recoverable property in good faith,
(b) he took steps after obtaining the property which he would not have taken if he had not obtained it or he took steps before obtaining the property which he would not have taken if he had not believed he was going to obtain it,
(c) when he took the steps, he had no notice that the property was recoverable,
(d) if a recovery order were made in respect of the property, it would, by reason of the steps, be detrimental to him.[225]

[220] For example, to make provision for reasonable living expenses, the carrying on of any trade, business, profession, or occupation, or incurring reasonable legal expenses: see POCA, s. 252(3)–(4).

[221] POCA, s. 252(1). There is a need for expedition: in *R (Director of the Assets Recovery Agency) v He and Chen* [2004] EWHC 3021 (Admin), para. 81 it was said: 'it is plain that there is a need for expedition. The receiver has an obligation to report as soon as practicable and there is a serious interference with Mr He's property and his ability to carry on business if the reality is that he is not in any way involved in criminal conduct and this is not to be regarded as recoverable property. The matters which the receiver has to investigate are of some complexity, and it is not surprising that she is taking some time to resolve them. But the time is nigh when enquiries must be brought to a conclusion.'

[222] Mark Sutherland Williams, Michael Hopmeier, and Rupert Jones, *Millington and Sutherland Williams on The Proceeds of Crime* (5th edn, Oxford University Press 2018) 333.

[223] POCA, s. 266(1). Summary judgment is possible, but see *NCA v Nuttall* [2019] EWHC 10 QB) where there was factual dispute between the parties. The recovery order must vest the recoverable property in the trustee for civil recovery: s. 266(2). The functions of the trustee are set out in s. 267. Under s. 276, the court may make a consent order 'staying ... any proceedings for a recovery order on terms agreed by the parties for the disposal of the proceedings if each person to whose property the proceedings, or the agreement, relates is a party both to the proceedings and the agreement'. The court cannot make a recovery order if it thinks that the enforcement authority's right to recover the 'original property' has been satisfied by a previous recovery order (under s. 266) or consent order (under s. 276): s. 278(3).

[224] POCA, s. 266(3)(a).

[225] POCA, s. 266(4). The conditions that apply if a recovery order is sought in Scotland are set out in s. 266(5).

In deciding whether it would be 'just and equitable' to make a provision in a recovery order, the court must have regard to '(a) the degree of detriment that would be suffered by the respondent if the provision were made, (b) the enforcement authority's interest in receiving the realised proceeds of the recoverable property'.[226] Neither may the court make in a recovery order any provision which is incompatible with Convention rights (within the meaning of the Human Rights Act).[227] Certain material may be withheld from the respondent where a public interest immunity certificate is granted.[228]

Where an IRO or a PFO[229] under Part 5 has been made, and the court subsequently does not decide that the property concerned is recoverable property or associated property, then an application for compensation can be made.[230]

POCA also contains provisions for the recovery of cash[231] and listed assets[232] in summary proceedings.[233] There is also provision for the forfeiture of money held in bank and building society accounts.[234] The authorities have extensive powers[235] available for the purposes of a civil recovery investigation,[236] including: production orders;[237] orders to grant entry;[238] search and seizure warrants;[239] disclosure orders;[240] unexplained wealth orders;[241] customer

226 POCA, s. 266(6).
227 POCA, s. 266(3)(b).
228 In *Director of the Assets Recovery Agency v Personal Representatives of Daly (deceased)* [2006] NIQB 36, Coghlin J declined to recuse himself from the substantive civil recovery proceedings where he had previously seen withheld intelligence material: 'I am quite satisfied that I can exclude from my consideration those reports/ observations the entire contents of which have been withheld from the defendants. I propose to conduct the substantive hearing solely on the basis of the disclosed material' (para. 16).
229 Or, in Scotland, a prohibitory property order or an interim administration order: see POCA, ss 255A and 256.
230 POCA, s. 283.
231 Defined in POCA, s. 289(6).
232 Defined in POCA, s. 303B(1).
233 POCA, Part 5, Chapters 3 and 3A.
234 POCA, Part 5, Chapter 3B.
235 The equivalent powers in Scotland are set out in Chapter 3 of Part 8, POCA. The powers are available to the enforcement authority up until an interim receiving order has been made or a claim form has been issued: POCA, s. 341(3).
236 Defined as an 'investigation for the purpose of identifying recoverable property or associated property and includes investigation into (a) whether property is or has been recoverable property, (b) who holds or has held property, (c) what property a person holds or has held, or (d) the nature, extent or whereabouts of property' POCA, s. 341(2).
237 POCA, s. 345. In *R (Director of the Assets Recovery Agency) v He and Chen* [2004] EWHC 3021 (Admin), para. 8 Collins J stated: 'Production Orders are usually made against financial institutions such as banks or building societies, or sometimes against solicitors who have dealt with property transactions of one sort or another, and is an obviously important and useful means of obtaining information for the Director to see whether there is a good arguable case which would justify, if that is thought necessary, the request for an interim receiver'.
238 POCA, s. 347.
239 POCA, s. 352.
240 POCA, s. 357.
241 POCA, s. 362A. For consideration of whether a disclosure order or an UWO ought to be used, see *NCA v Hussain* [2020] EWHC 432 (Admin).

information orders;[242] account monitoring orders;[243] and requesting assistance if it is thought that there is relevant evidence in a country or territory outside the United Kingdom.[244] There is provision for the use of pseudonyms by relevant state officials.[245] It is an offence to make a disclosure which is likely to prejudice a civil recovery investigation, or to falsify, conceal, destroy, or otherwise dispose of, or cause or permit the same, of documents which are relevant to the investigation.[246]

Now that the background to the adoption of civil recovery in Ireland and England & Wales has been detailed, alongside the respective legislative frameworks, the next chapter will review the judicial reaction in both countries before querying the judicial deference to describing civil recovery as non-punitive and as a civil process.

242 POCA, s. 363.
243 POCA, s. 370.
244 POCA, s. 375A.
245 POCA, s. 449 and 449A.
246 POCA, s. 342(2).

4
Judicial Responses

Introduction

Proceeds of crime legislation, considering the extent to which it operates on the edge of the civil/criminal distinction, was always going to be subject to significant legal challenge. Indeed, civil recovery's characterization as civil proceedings is the most prominent point of disagreement, with the second being that the action is *in rem* (against the property) and thus supposedly does not infringe an individual's property rights. While we discuss actions against the property and property rights in Chapter 6, our focus in this chapter is the judicial reaction to the introduction of civil recovery.

The role of the courts to regulate the exercise of state power within the established parameters of the rule of law is a vital one within a democratic society. The law, as Raz argues, 'inevitably creates a great deal of arbitrary power [and] the rule of law is designed to minimize [this] danger'.[1] The rule of law can be said to operate as a curb on governmental over-reaching or excess: it is intended to prevent abuse on the part of the executive and legislative branches of government, with the task of oversight and holding to account falling to the judicial branch. In this regard, a procedural understanding of the rule of law requires the courts not only to give effect to legislation as set out but also, as Waldron notes, that they apply the rules contained therein 'with all the care and attention to fairness that is signaled [sic] by ideals such as "natural justice" and "procedural due process" '.[2]

It is our contention, both in this chapter and in earlier work, that the courts have been 'overly acquiescent' in accepting claims that civil recovery does not attract criminal procedural protections due to being a civil process. We also contend that the courts have been similarly accommodating in their conclusions that civil recovery operates—in practice—against the property instead of against the individual, and that it is an efficacious, essential, proportionate,

[1] Joseph Raz, 'The Rule of Law and its Virtue' (1977) 93 *Law Quarterly Review* 195, 206.
[2] Jeremy Waldron, 'The Concept and the Rule of Law' (2008) 43(1) *Georgia Law Review* 1, 8.

Civil Recovery of Criminal Property. Colin King and Jennifer Hendry, Oxford University Press.
 DOI: 10.1093/oso/9780198824251.003.0004

and justifiable response to a rise in serious and organized criminal activity.[3] In this readiness—even willingness—to accept the legislative label 'civil' as determinative in their characterization and categorization of civil recovery, we argue that the judiciary in both Ireland and in England & Wales have seemed disinclined to bring important rule of law considerations to bear against the non-conviction-based approach.

This chapter proceeds in three parts. We provide an account of the judicial reaction to civil recovery, first in Ireland and then in England & Wales. We then turn our attention to the issue of punishment: specifically, whether the courts are justified in their repeated assertion that civil recovery is not punitive but rather preventive, reparative, and/or compensatory. Next, we reinforce our contention that the courts have been overly deferential to legislative intention at the expense of due process, and reiterate our call for civil recovery proceedings to be regarded as *criminal*, and thus deserving of the criminal law's elevated procedural protections. In making this argument we employ the *Engel* criteria, according to which the European Court of Human Rights (ECtHR) determines whether or not a particular matter ought to be accepted as criminal.

Judicial Reaction—Ireland

Over the past two decades, the Irish courts have consistently upheld the constitutionality of the Proceeds of Crime Act (POCA). The leading decision is the joined case of *Murphy v GM, PB, PC Ltd, GH and Gilligan v CAB*[4] (herein referred to as *GM/Gilligan*). In that case, the Supreme Court not only upheld the constitutionality of the Act but also dismissed a number of challenges on non-constitutional points. The arguments advanced are therefore worth dedicated attention. Most prominently, it was argued that POCA formed part of the criminal law, not the civil law, and that persons affected by this legislation were deprived of traditional criminal law safeguards.[5] It was further alleged that the Act permitted oppressive delays; the maxim *audi alteram partem* was violated; the privilege against self-incrimination was contravened; the Act was overbroad and vague; the Act violated the guarantee of private property; there was

[3] Jennifer Hendry and Colin King, 'Expediency, Legitimacy, and the Rule of Law: A Systems Perspective on Civil/ Criminal Procedural Hybrids' (2017) 11(4) *Criminal Law and Philosophy* 733, 743.

[4] [2001] 4 IR 113. This case was an appeal from separate High Court decisions in *Gilligan v CAB* [1998] 3 IR 185 and *Murphy v GM, PB, PC Ltd* [1999] IEHC 5.

[5] The specific safeguards mentioned were the presumption of innocence, the standard of proof, trial by jury, and the rule against double jeopardy.

an impermissible interference with the judicial function; the Act purported to allow, or at least recognize, the possibility of an appeal from the Supreme Court to a non-specified court or authority; and, finally, that the Act had retrospective effect contrary to Article 15.5, and extraterritorial effect contrary to Article 29.3 and 29.8 of the Constitution.

These arguments were dismissed by the Supreme Court. The Court first noted that the legislation enjoys a presumption of constitutionality,[6] before addressing each of the listed arguments in turn. In relation to the criminal nature of the proceedings, the Court began by stating:

> It is almost beyond argument that, if the procedures under ss. 2, 3 and 4 of the Act of 1996 constituted in substance, albeit not in form, the trial of persons on criminal charges, they would be invalid having regard to the provisions of the Constitution. The virtual absence of the presumption of innocence, the provision that the standard of proof is to be on the balance of probabilities and the admissibility of hearsay evidence taken together are inconsistent with the requirement in Article 38.1 of the Constitution that: 'No person shall be tried in any criminal charge save in due course of law.' It is also clear that, if these procedures constitute the trial of a person on a criminal charge, which, depending on the value of the property, might or might not constitute a minor offence, the absence of any provision for a trial by jury of such a charge in the Act would clearly be in violation of Article 38.5 of the Constitution.[7]

The key question for the court was whether the procedures under POCA are criminal in character. After reviewing several authorities,[8] the court stated that in the present case the indicia of crime are 'conspicuously absent',[9] continuing to say that:

> in proceedings under ss. 3 and 4 of the Act of 1996, there is no provision for the arrest or detention of any person, for the admission of persons to bail, for the imprisonment of a person in default of payment of a penalty, for a form of

[6] See *McDonald v Bord na gCon (no.2)* [1965] IR 217; *East Donegal Co-Operative Livestock Mart Ltd v Attorney General* [1970] IR 317.

[7] [2001] 4 IR 113, 135.

[8] Including *Attorney General v Southern Industrial Trust Ltd* (1957) 94 ILTR 161; *Melling v O'Mathghamhna* [1962] IR 1; *Clancy v Ireland* [1988] IR 326; *McLoughlin v Tuite* [1989] IR 82; and *O'Keeffe v Ferris* [1993] 3 IR 165 (HC) and [1997] 3 IR 463 (SC). The court also referred to the US decision in *United States v Ursery* (1996) 518 US 267.

[9] [2001] 4 IR 113, 147.

> criminal trial initiated by summons or indictment, for the recording of a conviction in any form or for the entering of a *nolle prosequi* at any stage.[10]

The court further rejected the contention that the presence of *mens rea* is a prerequisite to an order under either section 3 or 4, observing that such 'orders can be made even though it has not been shown to the satisfaction of the court that there was *mens rea* on the part of the person in possession or control of the property'.[11] It then went on to state that forfeiture of property which represents the proceeds of crime 'is not a punishment and its operation does not require criminal procedures'.[12]

The next argument, that the Act permitted oppressive delays, was then swiftly dismissed by the court on the grounds that, since:

> the procedure under the Act is perfectly capable of being operated in such a manner as to ensure that no unreasonable delay elapses between the making of the interim order and the interlocutory order: that indeed is clearly what the Act envisaged.[13]

In relation to the seven-year period between the making of an interlocutory order and a disposal order, the contention that the delay is unduly oppressive was rejected as it 'rests on the misconception' that the application for a disposal order equates to the trial of the action. A person affected by an interlocutory order under section 3 can apply, at any point when such an order is in force, to have it either varied or discharged.[14]

The Court was also quick in dealing with the complaint regarding the maxim *audi alteram partem*. After reiterating the presumption that, in enacting legislation, the Oireachtas intended that procedures established under such would

[10] [2001] 4 IR 113, 147.

[11] [2001] 4 IR 113, 148. See also *Murphy v Gilligan* [2011] IEHC 62, para. 8 et seq.

[12] [2001] 4 IR 113, 153.

[13] [2001] 4 IR 113, 154.

[14] [2001] 4 IR 113, 154. This reasoning was applied in *Murphy v Gilligan* [2011] IEHC 62, para. 12 et seq. It was said: 'Insofar as the first-named respondent's contention in relation to delay is based upon a claim that the 1996 Act mandates a seven year delay prior to a disposal application being brought and that the present proceedings have lasted for nearly seven more years and such delay is excessive, the court is satisfied that the first-named respondent cannot rely upon this contention as it was open to him at any time since the making of the s. 3 order, including during the seven year period provided for in s. 4, to bring an application under s. 3(3). It is the first-named respondent himself who chose not to commence such an application until 2009 and in those circumstances the legal authorities relied upon by the first-named respondent in relation to delay in criminal trials have no application. In criminal trials it is for the prosecution to bring matters before the court whilst in s. 3(3) applications it is for persons, such as the first-named respondent, who are affected by s. 3 orders to commence such applications. If they delay in commencing such applications they cannot seek to rely on such delay' (para. 14).

be applied according to the principles of constitutional justice and that any departure therefrom would 'be restrained or corrected by the courts',[15] the Supreme Court then declared its satisfaction that:

> in any case brought under the procedures laid down by the Act, the affidavits grounding the interim and interlocutory application of necessity will indicate to the respondents the nature of the case being made on behalf of the applicant. Nor is the provision for the admission of hearsay of itself unconstitutional: it was a matter for the court hearing the application to decide what weight should be given to such evidence. The court is satisfied that there is no substance in these grounds of challenge to the constitutionality of the legislation.[16]

The next ground of challenge was that there was no equality of arms, given that the applicant could rely on opinion evidence whereas the respondent could not. Again, the Court categorically rejected this argument: 'the respondents to an application under s. 2 or s. 3 will normally be the persons in possession or control of the property and should be in a position to give evidence to the court as to its provenance without calling in aid opinion evidence'.[17] The argument that the Act contravenes the privilege against self-incrimination was also unceremoniously dismissed:

> Parties to civil proceedings, whatever their nature, may find themselves in a position where they are reluctant to adduce evidence beneficial to them because it might also expose them to the risk of a criminal prosecution. That factual position, however, cannot be equated to a statutory provision obliging a person to give evidence, even in circumstances where his or her evidence might be incriminating. Similarly, the fact that a person can be required to file an affidavit specifying his or her property and income cannot, on any view, be equated to a statutory provision requiring a person to adduce evidence which may incriminate him or her. The court is satisfied that these grounds of challenge are also without foundation.[18]

[15] [2001] 4 IR 113, 154.
[16] [2001] 4 IR 113, 155. For further consideration of hearsay, see *CAB v McCarthy* [2019] IECA 140.
[17] [2001] 4 IR 113, 155.
[18] [2001] 4 IR 113, 156. In *CAB v Connors* [2018] IECA 371 the possibility of parallel civil and criminal proceedings was considered: 'it is clear from the Proceeds of Crime Act, 1996 that it is envisaged that there will be both civil and criminal proceedings relating to the same activities in existence at the same time. Accordingly, there are significant public policy reasons, in my view, as to why the civil proceedings, such as those which emanate from s. 3 of the act, should not be postponed until the determination of any criminal proceedings concerning the same activities' (para. 26).

The next argument addressed by the Court was whether the Act was overly-broad and vague, specifically as regards the term 'proceeds of crime', and the Court's power not to grant an order where there is 'a serious risk of injustice'. In terms of the former, the Court outlined its position as follows: 'in every case before an order can be made, the court must be satisfied on the balance of probabilities that on the evidence adduced to it in that particular case the property in respect of which the freezing order is sought was the proceeds of crime'.[19] In relation to the latter challenge, which the Court also rejected, it was said that, while this power 'is undoubtedly wide in its scope, that can only be in ease of the individuals whose rights may be affected and the court, in applying these provisions, will be obliged to act in accordance with the requirements of constitutional justice'.[20]

Neither did the Court dwell on the argument that the Act violated the guarantee of property rights under the Constitution. Adopting the decision of Barrington J in *Clancy v Ireland*, concerning the Offences Against the State (Amendment) Act 1985, where it was held that that legislation was 'a permissible delimitation of property rights in the interests of the common good',[21] the Court rejected this challenge to POCA on this ground. The next argument to be rejected was the challenge on the ground of interference with judicial function. The contention here was that the legislation impermissibly requires the High Court to make an order in certain circumstances, but the Court disagreed, stating that 'it is perfectly permissible for the legislature to provide that, where certain conditions are met, the making of an order of a particular nature by a court may be mandatory rather than discretionary'.[22]

The Court also rejected the challenge to the legislation based on the grounds of retrospective effect and extraterritorial effect:

> The Act does not offend in any way the prohibition in Article 15.5 against declaring acts to be infringements of the law which were not so at the date of their commission. The fact that it enables the court to make orders in respect of property constituting the proceeds of crimes committed before the coming into force of the legislation is not in any sense a contravention of that prohibition.[23]

[19] [2001] 4 IR 113, 156.
[20] [2001] 4 IR 113, 156.
[21] *Clancy v Ireland* [1988] IR 326, 336.
[22] [2001] 4 IR 113, 156.
[23] [2001] 4 IR 113, 157. See also *Murphy v Gilligan* [2011] IEHC 62, para. 6.2.

It continued:

> Nor was the fact that the legislation may be operated so as to require the compliance of citizens within the jurisdiction with orders of the court directing the transfer of property in their possession or control to a receiver appointed by the court in circumstances where the property is in another jurisdiction constitute in any way a breach of the principles of international law which the State accepts under Article 29 of the Constitution.[24]

Yet another argument advanced was that the Act impermissibly authorized and/or recognized the possibility of an appeal from the Supreme Court to a non-specified court or authority. This argument was also rejected:

> The court is satisfied that the words 'or if any further appeal' in s. 2(5)(c) are, at worst, surplusage and, in accordance with well established principles of statutory construction, can be disregarded where the result would otherwise be unconstitutional or would, as in this case, produce an absurd or anomalous result.[25]

Finally, the Court declined to consider whether POCA conflicted with the European Convention on Human Rights, on the ground that the Convention was not then part of domestic law. The Supreme Court then, accordingly, upheld the constitutionality of POCA.

Judicial Reaction—England & Wales

Similar to the Irish courts, the courts in England & Wales have determined that civil recovery is not of a criminal character, notwithstanding its 'potential for use as an uneasy and unsatisfactory substitute for the criminal process'.[26] As Leveson P succinctly put it in *Robb*, 'For the purposes of Article 6 civil proceedings such as these under Part 5 of POCA only engage article 6(1). A criminal charge will engage Articles 6(1), 6(2) and 6(3)'.[27] In considering whether such proceedings are criminal for the purposes of Article 6 of the ECHR, in

[24] [2001] 4 IR 113, 157.
[25] [2001] 4 IR 113, 157.
[26] Edward Rees, Richard Fisher, and Richard Thomas, *Blackstone's Guide to The Proceeds of Crime Act 2002* (5th edn, Oxford University Press 2015) 171.
[27] *Robb v NCA* [2014] EWCA Civ 171, para. 43.

Walsh both Coghlin J[28] and the Court of Appeal[29] concluded that civil recovery under Part 5 of POCA should be classified as civil proceedings.[30] Central to this finding were the tripartite criteria established by the Strasbourg Court in *Engel*, namely: the domestic classification of the proceedings at issue, the nature of the offence in question, and the nature and severity of the penalty that may be imposed.[31]

In relation to the first *Engel* criterion, in *Walsh* it was held that:

> [A]ll the available indicators point strongly to this case being classified in the national law as a form of civil proceeding. The appellant is not charged with a crime. Although it must be shown that he was guilty of unlawful conduct in the sense that he has acted contrary to the criminal law, this is not for the purpose of making him amenable as he would be if he had been convicted of crime. He is not liable to imprisonment or fine if the recovery action succeeds. There is no indictment and no verdict. The primary purpose of the legislation is restitutionary rather than penal.[32]

That Part 5 is classed as civil in domestic law is not determinative, however. As Lord Phillips stated in *Gale*, 'the fact that POCA unequivocally designates recovery proceedings as "civil recovery" does not establish conclusively that they do not involve the charge of a criminal offence'.[33] This reflects that 'the classification under national law is only a starting point and the essential nature of the proceedings is of greater importance'.[34]

[28] *Re Walsh* [2004] NIQB 21.

[29] *Walsh v Director of the Assets Recovery Agency* [2005] NICA 6. While *Walsh* was, of course, a Northern Ireland decision, its reach extends much further: the Supreme Court in *Gale v SOCA* [2011] UKSC 49 applied it; it was followed also by the Privy Council in *Williams v Supervisory Authority* [2020] UKPC 15.

[30] A subsequent application to the European Court of Human Rights was declared inadmissible: *Walsh v UK* (dec.), App. No. 43384/05 (21 November 2006).

[31] *Engel v Netherlands* [1976] 1 EHRR 647. This application of the *Engel* criteria to Part 5 of POCA has been followed in subsequent cases, including: *R (Director of the Assets Recovery Agency) v He and Chen* [2004] EWHC 3021 (Admin). See also *Scottish Ministers v Doig* [2009] CSIH 34.

[32] *Walsh v Director of the Assets Recovery Agency* [2005] NICA 6, para. 27. In considering the first *Engel* criterion, Kerr LCJ was influenced by decisions related to post-conviction confiscation provisions yet there are significant differences between those provisions and Part 5 of POCA. For criticism of the 'supposed analogy' that influenced Kerr LCJ, see Peter Alldridge, 'Civil Recovery in England and Wales: An Appraisal' in Colin King, Clive Walker, and Jimmy Gurulé (eds), *The Palgrave Handbook of Criminal and Terrorism Financing Law* (Palgrave 2018) 525–6. For further discussion on the issue of civil recovery's allegedly restitutionary character, see Chapter 6.

[33] *Gale v SOCA* [2011] UKSC 49, para. 16.

[34] *Gale v SOCA* [2011] UKSC 49, para. 121, per Lord Dyson. See also *R (Mudie) v Dover Magistrates' Court* [2003] EWCA Civ 237, para. 36.

In relation to the second *Engel* criterion, similar considerations applied as with the first, with Kerr LCJ stating that:

> The allegation made against the appellant does not impute guilt of a specific offence; the proceedings do not seek to impose a penalty other than the recovery of assets acquired through criminal conduct; and they are initiated by the director of an agency, which, although it is a public authority, has no prosecutorial function or competence.[35]

The final criterion was also dealt with rather brusquely:

> [R]ecovery may only be ordered in relation to assets that have been acquired by proven unlawful conduct. The recovery of assets may more readily be described as a preventative measure, therefore. After all, the person who is required to yield up the assets does no more than return what he obtained illegally.[36]

Although Kerr LCJ noted that 'a provision will not be classified as non-penal solely because it partakes of a preventative character', he ultimately did not have to express any final view on whether civil recovery should be regarded as penal.[37] It was said, however, that even if such proceedings were to be regarded as imposing a penalty, that alone would not suffice to cause them to be classified as 'criminal' for the purposes of Article 6.[38] Kerr LCJ thus concluded that 'the predominant character of recovery action is that of civil proceedings. *The primary purpose is to recover proceeds of crime; it is not to punish the appellant in the sense normally entailed in a criminal sanction*'.[39]

Kerr LCJ also dismissed the argument that, viewed cumulatively, the *Engel* criteria ought to result in civil recovery being held as criminal in character:

> The essence of Art 6 in its criminal dimension is the charging of a person with a criminal offence for the purpose of securing a conviction with a view to exposing that person to criminal sanction. These proceedings are obviously and significantly different from that type of application. They are not directed

[35] *Walsh v Director of the Assets Recovery Agency* [2005] NICA 6, para. 29. In considering the second criterion, Kerr LCJ again referred to decisions concerning post-conviction proceedings (paras 30–35).
[36] *Walsh v Director of the Assets Recovery Agency* [2005] NICA 6, para. 38. Here, Kerr LCJ drew a distinction between post-conviction confiscation and civil recovery (para. 38).
[37] *Walsh v Director of the Assets Recovery Agency* [2005] NICA 6, para. 38.
[38] *Walsh v Director of the Assets Recovery Agency* [2005] NICA 6, para. 39.
[39] *Walsh v Director of the Assets Recovery Agency* [2005] NICA 6, para. 39. Emphasis added.

> towards him in the sense that they seek to inflict punishment beyond the recovery of assets that do not lawfully belong to him. As such, while they will obviously have an impact on the appellant, these are predominantly proceedings in rem. They are designed to recover the proceeds of crime, rather than to establish, in the context of criminal proceedings, guilt of specific offences. The cumulative effect of the application of the tests in Engel is to identify these clearly as civil proceedings.[40]

When civil recovery powers were challenged in the Supreme Court, it was said that:

> The essential nature of the proceedings is civil. The respondent to the proceedings is not charged with any offence. He does not acquire a criminal conviction if he is required to deliver up property at the conclusion of the Part 5 proceedings. None of the domestic criminal processes are in play. On the contrary, as Kerr LCJ put it in *Walsh v Director of the Assets Recovery Agency* ... 'all the trappings of the proceedings are those normally associated with a civil claim'. These include the express provision that the standard of proof is on the balance of probabilities. The nature of the proceedings is essentially different from that of criminal proceedings. The claim can be brought whether a respondent has been convicted or acquitted, and irrespective of whether any criminal proceedings have been brought at all... The purpose of Part 5 proceedings is not to determine or punish for any particular offence. Rather it is to ensure that property derived from criminal conduct is taken out of circulation. It is also of importance that Part 5 proceedings operate *in rem*. The governing concept is that of "recoverable property" which represents both property obtained directly by unlawful conduct and also property which represents the original property.[41]

The courts have also rejected arguments[42] that the presumption of innocence ought to apply in civil recovery proceedings:

40 *Walsh v Director of the Assets Recovery Agency* [2005] NICA 6, para. 41.

41 *Gale v SOCA* [2011] UKSC 49, para. 123, per Lord Dyson.

42 Such arguments have been based on, for example, the contention that an essential step in establishing that property is 'recoverable property' is proof that the respondents had been guilty of criminal conduct. As such, so the argument goes, Article 6(2) of the ECHR ought to apply and the standard of proof ought to be the criminal standard: see, e.g., the arguments summarized in *Gale v SOCA* [2011] UKSC 49, para. 14.

> [T]here is no sufficient link between civil recovery proceedings under Part 5 of POCA and any criminal proceedings to justify the application of article 6(2) to the Part 5 proceedings. Indeed, there is no link at all. The Part 5 proceedings are not a 'direct sequel' or 'a consequence and the concomitant' of any criminal proceedings. They are free-standing proceedings instituted whether or not there have been criminal proceedings against the respondent or indeed anyone at all.[43]

The conclusion by the English & Welsh courts that civil recovery constitutes a civil process is important also for Article 7 of the ECHR.[44] The courts have rejected the argument that Article 7 applies to Part 5 of POCA. Dealing with such submissions rather briskly, in *He and Chen*, Collins J stated the following:

> [T]here is no question of any penalty involved in these proceedings. Furthermore, there has been no conviction of a criminal offence leading to a penalty. Of course, property cannot be recoverable unless, at the time it was acquired, it was obtained through unlawful conduct. That conduct must have been criminal at that time. To that extent, the prohibition against retrospectivity will apply, but only because the Act says that the property must be property which was obtained by criminal conduct. In those circumstances, it is quite clear that Article 7 has no application.[45]

The courts have also rejected challenges based on property rights under Article 1 of the First Protocol (A1P1), which provides the following:

> Every natural or legal person is entitled to the peaceful enjoyment of his possessions. No one shall be deprived of his possessions except in the public interest and subject to the conditions provided for by law and by the general principles of international law.
>
> The preceding provisions shall not, however, in any way impair the right of a State to enforce such laws as it deems necessary to control the use of property in accordance with the general interest or to secure the payment of taxes or other contributions or penalties.

[43] *Gale v SOCA* [2011] UKSC 49, para. 133.

[44] *Director of the Assets Recovery Agency V Commissioners of Customs and Excise* [2005] EWCA Civ 334.

[45] *R (Director of the Assets Recovery Agency) v He and Chen* [2004] EWHC 3021 (Admin), para. 69 referring to, *inter alia*, *M v Italy* App. No. 12386/86, 15 April 1991. A similar conclusion was also reached by Newman J in *R (Director of the Assets Recovery Agency) v Ashton* [2006] EWHC 1064 (Admin). Cf. *Scottish Ministers v McGuffie* [2006] CSIH 54.

The courts have concluded that civil recovery 'represents a significant inroad into traditional property rights, not depending on proof of a criminal offence'.[46] While a criminal conviction is not a prerequisite, the focus is nonetheless on *proceeds of crime*. In *Green*, it was said that 'Part 5 proceedings are not concerned with any property, however obtained. They are concerned only with property which has been obtained through conduct which is unlawful under the criminal law'.[47] In *He and Chen*, Collins J referred to relevant European Convention on Human Rights (ECHR) jurisprudence[48] and said that 'Parliament has quite clearly decided that these measures are necessary in order to fight crime, and in particular to ensure, as far as possible, that those involved in crime should be unable to enjoy the fruits of their criminal activities'.[49] He continued: 'it seems to me that it would be quite wrong for me to strike these provisions down, in effect, when I know that Parliament has decided that they are indeed necessary. In my judgment, therefore, the provisions in question are indeed proportionate'.[50] Similarly, in *Jackson*, King J stated:

> I however see nothing unfair in the balance here being struck given the legitimate public interest in the prevention of crime by ensuring that crime does not pay and my findings against the Respondent that his assets the subject of this claim are all in effect the product of criminal conduct.[51]

The courts have also rejected challenges brought in relation to the right to respect for private and family life under Article 8: for example, in *He and Chen*, it was said: 'it seems to me that, even assuming it applies, it adds nothing, and the question of proportionality applies equally to it as it does to Article 1'.[52] In *Wilson*, it was said that even if Article 8 were held to apply, any interference

[46] *Olupitan v Director of the Assets Recovery Agency* [2008] EWCA Civ 104, para. 41.

[47] *R (Director of the Assets Recovery Agency) v Green* [2005] EWHC 3168 (Admin), para. 25.

[48] *M v Italy*, App. No. 12386/86, 15 April 1991; *Arcuri v Italy*, App. No. 52024/99, 5 July 2001.

[49] *R (Director of the Assets Recovery Agency) v He and Chen* [2004] EWHC 3021 (Admin), para. 74. In *R (Director of the Assets Recovery Agency) v Ashton* [2006] EWHC 1064 (Admin), para. 43, Newman J stated: 'the person who is in possession of the proceeds of crime has, in accordance with the purpose and intention of Parliament, no right to hold that property. It is not a deprivation of anything. Parliament has said that such proceeds are not the entitlement of anyone. That is not to deprive anybody of anything.'

[50] *R (Director of the Assets Recovery Agency) v He and Chen* [2004] EWHC 3021 (Admin), para. 74.

[51] *Director of the Assets Recovery Agency v Jackson* [2007] EWHC 2553 (QB), para. 220. For consideration of A1P1 and the matrimonial home, see *Sanam v NCA* [2015] EWCA Civ 1234.

[52] *R (Director of the Assets Recovery Agency) v He and Chen* [2004] EWHC 3021 (Admin), para. 75. See also *Director of the Assets Recovery Agency v Jackson* [2007] EWHC 2553 (QB), para. 221.

with such property rights is 'justified by the need to control the misuse of drugs and other unlawful activity, in a democratic society'.[53]

Now that the judicial response in both Ireland and England & Wales has been outlined, we turn our focus to two key questions that go to the heart of civil recovery: whether such proceedings impose punishment, and whether they are criminal proceedings acting under a civil guise.

Punishment

There is significant academic commentary on the issue of punishment in this context. Campbell, for example, has observed that '[c]ivil forfeiture promotes punishment's traditional aims of condemnation, retribution and deterrence',[54] while King has noted that, '[a]s with a criminal fine, civil forfeiture might be seen as akin to criminal punishment'.[55] In the same vein, Naylor has asserted that '[i]t is impossible for seizure of property to be anything but punitive'.[56] Punishment is not only a key issue for academics, however, but also plays a central role in judicial decisions, where the point has been stressed, repeatedly and strenuously, that civil recovery *does not* constitute punishment. Instead of reflecting the stance of the academy, therefore, the courts have consistently taken the position that civil recovery is a *preventive*, *reparative*, and/or *compensatory* measure.

In *Gale*, for instance, Lord Dyson noted that the purpose of civil recovery proceedings 'is not to determine or punish for any particular offence. Rather it is to ensure that property derived from criminal conduct is taken out of circulation'.[57] Similarly, in *Walsh*, on the reasoning that the individual being required to forfeit the assets is merely returning property obtained by unlawful conduct, it was said that the recovery of assets 'may more readily be described as *a preventative measure*'.[58] The court continued: 'the person who is required to yield up the assets does no more than *return* what he obtained illegally'.[59]

[53] *Director of the Asset Recovery Agency v Wilson* [2007] NIQB 49, para. 42. See also *NCA v Khan* [2017] EWHC 27 (QB).

[54] Liz Campbell, 'The Recovery of "Criminal" Assets in New Zealand, Ireland and England: Fighting Organised and Serious Crime in the Civil Realm' (2010) 41 *Victoria University Wellington Law Review* 15, 26.

[55] Colin King, 'Civil Forfeiture and Article 6 of the ECHR: Due Process Implications for England & Wales and Ireland' (2014) 34(3) *Legal Studies* 371, 374.

[56] RT Naylor, 'Wash-out: A Critique of Follow-the-Money Methods in Crime Control Policy' (1999) *Crime, Law and Social Change* 1, 41.

[57] *Gale v SOCA* [2011] UKSC 49, para. 123.

[58] *Walsh v Director of the Assets Recovery Agency* [2005] NICA 6, para. 38. Emphasis added. See also *R (Director of the Assets Recovery Agency) v Ashton* [2006] EWHC 1064 (Admin), para. 43.

[59] *Walsh v Director of the Assets Recovery Agency* [2005] NICA 6, para. 38. Emphasis added.

In *Williams*, the Privy Council stated that 'the relevant characterisation of the regime is as *preventive in nature*, rather than involving the imposition of a criminal penalty'.[60] In Ireland, in *Gilligan v Murphy*, it was said that '[t]he legislation was enacted to establish a prompt and effective method to *prevent* criminals benefiting from the proceeds of crime'.[61] In *Gilligan v CAB*, McGuinness J stated that 'if this money or property can be shown to the satisfaction of the Court to be the proceeds of crime, its removal could well be viewed in the light of *reparation* rather than punishment or penalty'.[62] Similar conclusions on the part of the Strasbourg Court are also evident. In *Gogitidze v Georgia*, for example, the court held that 'the forfeiture of property ordered as a result of civil proceedings *in rem*, without involving the determination of a criminal charge, is not of a punitive but of *a preventive and/or compensatory nature*'.[63]

In this regard it is undeniable that the courts' stance on the issue of punishment has been robust, not to mention clearly reminiscent of the policy rationales underpinning civil recovery.[64] It is yet further apparent that the courts have distinguished civil recovery proceedings from post-conviction ones in circumstances where there is a direct relationship between conviction and the imposition of a confiscation order.[65] Notwithstanding the consistency across the courts in England & Wales, Ireland, and Strasbourg, we do not find this judicial position convincing. On the contrary, it is our position that the judicial stance— that civil recovery is preventive, reparative, and/or compensatory, and *thus not punitive*—merits further scrutiny.[66]

[60] *Williams v Supervisory Authority* [2020] UKPC 15, para. 81. Emphasis added. The Privy Council continued: 'in the context of the combined regime there is no equivalent direct relationship between a civil forfeiture order and the conviction of a defendant on a criminal charge; *the preventive aspect of the regime is predominant*; and the operation of the regime, the concepts it employs and the relevant standard of proof on issues which may arise are all in the civil sphere or civil in nature. Accordingly, the Board feels able to be more definite than the court in *Walsh*. In the Board's view, as explained above, it is not appropriate to describe the effect of the combined regime as involving the imposition of a penalty' para. 81. Emphasis added.

[61] *Gilligan v Murphy* [2011] IEHC 465, para. 4.8. Emphasis added.

[62] *Gilligan v CAB* [1998] 3 IR 185, para. 86. Emphasis added.

[63] [2015] ECHR 475, App. No. 36862/05, para. 126. Emphasis added. In the same judgment, the court reiterated 'its well-established case-law to the effect that proceedings for confiscation such as the civil proceedings in rem in the present case, which do not stem from a criminal conviction or sentencing proceedings and thus do not qualify as a penalty but rather represent a measure of control of the use of property within the meaning of Article 1 of Protocol N.1 cannot amount to the "determination of a criminal charge" within the meaning of Article 6 § 1 of the Convention and should be examined under the "civil" head of that provision' (para. 121).

[64] See Chapter 3.

[65] See, e.g., *Welch v UK* (1995) 20 EHRR 247, App. No. 17440/90 where the Strasbourg Court determined the confiscation order to be a penalty and thus in breach of Article 7.

[66] These issues are explored in more depth in Chapter 6.

Preventive

Such labels and descriptions require elaboration, not least because while civil recovery can be 'preventive' in the sense that the state can *take*[67] potential working capital for further criminal activity, this is not necessarily to say that it does not punish. Just because a measure is preventive does not preclude that it is also punitive. Moreover, even if the courts are satisfied that the property in question constitutes proceeds of crime, there is no basis to the assumption that it necessarily will be used for future criminality. For example, a person in possession of proceeds of crime might instead spend that money lavishly, meaning it would not be working capital for further criminal activity. Another possible dimension of civil recovery's preventive character, then, is how it 'prevent[s] criminals benefiting from the proceeds of crime',[68] reinforcing the policy that *crime should not pay.* While this is, arguably, and as we discuss more expansively in Chapter 6, a more justifiable characterization, the emphasis on 'criminals' betrays the fiction underpinning civil recovery, which is to say, the notion that it does not operate against the person. Its supposed *in rem* nature is relied upon—repeatedly, consistently—to justify the circumvention of criminal procedural safeguards, when it is apparent that the preventive aim concerns the *criminal benefit,* and this without the added protection of those safeguards.[69]

Reparative

By contrast to the preventive label, the reparative nature of civil recovery stands on more solid ground. The rationale here is that the respondent 'has no good title' to the property concerned[70] or 'no right to hold that property'.[71] This is more complex than it initially appears, however. For example, if A steals from B, then it is justifiable to require A to make amends and return the item to B. This would be a private action involving A and B. The reparative characterization thus aligns with the contention that a person has no good title to proceeds of crime and that, in such a situation, the property ought to be returned to the rightful owner. With civil recovery, however, both the reparative

[67] The verb 'take' is deliberately used here, rather than 'recover', as will be explained further below and, in more detail, in Chapter 6.
[68] *Gilligan v Murphy* [2011] IEHC 465, para. 4.8.
[69] See Chapter 5 for consideration of due process arguments.
[70] *Gilligan v. CAB* [1998] 3 IR 185, 237.
[71] *R (Director of the Assets Recovery Agency) v Ashton* [2006] EWHC 1064, para. 43.

and 'no good title' arguments bypass the fact that in these proceedings, it is the *state* who initiates proceedings, not the supposedly rightful owner. It is one thing to say that the rightful owner is entitled to return of the property, but a very different thing to say that the *state* is entitled—in a non-conviction-based proceeding—to all proceeds of crime. The property is neither being 'restored' nor 'recovered', and neither is it being 'given back' or 'taken back'. Instead, it is being *taken* by the state.[72]

Compensatory

Next, the courts have emphasized that civil recovery is not punitive but rather is 'of a preventive and/or compensatory nature'.[73] This compensatory characterization gives rises to further considerations, however. Compensatory to whom? The state? For what harm? Suspected and unproven criminality in general? It is a significant stretch of wording to say that civil recovery proceedings compensate the state on the grounds that property constitutes proceeds of crime. An alternative position might be that it is appropriate to compensate the victim of crime: for example, in *Gogitidze*: 'The compensatory aspect consisted in the obligation to restore the injured party in civil proceedings to the status which had existed prior to the unjust enrichment of the public official in question, by returning wrongfully acquired property either to its previous lawful owner *or, in the absence of such, to the State.*'[74] As this case concerned allegations of corruption in public office, there is a more plausible argument that the proceedings in that instance could be viewed as compensatory, even if the property is confiscated by the state, on the basis that the state itself was a victim of (albeit unproven) wrongdoing. More generally, however, it is both trite and erroneous to say that the state is a victim of all crime and, as such, ought to be compensated using civil recovery.

We reject the judicial characterization of civil recovery as non-punitive simply because it is *something else*, that is, preventive, reparative, compensatory. We take the position that the courts' preference for an either/or approach

[72] Peter Alldridge, 'Civil Recovery in England and Wales: An Appraisal' in Colin King, Clive Walker, and Jimmy Gurulé (eds), *The Palgrave Handbook of Criminal and Terrorism Financing Law* (Palgrave 2018). See also Chapter 6, 'No good title'.

[73] *Gogitidze v Georgia* [2015] ECHR 475, App. No. 36862/05, para. 126. Of course, 'prevention' and 'compensation' are very different, however—by saying that civil recovery is not punitive, but rather is instead *something else*, namely being of a preventive and/or compensatory nature—the court here blurs the conceptual lines between them.

[74] *Gogitidze v Georgia* [2015] ECHR 475, App. No. 36862/05, para. 102. Emphasis added.

has led to repeated mischaracterization of civil recovery as non-punitive. That is not to say that civil recovery cannot be reparative; rather, our argument is that it can be *both* reparative *and* punitive. Or, compensatory *and* punitive, or preventive *and* punitive. The definition need not be exclusionary. Yet given that the punishment/non-punishment classification is so determinative here, and the waters so muddy—with relatively similar actions falling either side of this line, for example financial penalties—it is necessary to scrutinize the meaning of punishment, and specifically whether civil recovery can be said to constitute punishment.

Difficulty immediately arises, however, due to the nebulous approach taken to 'punishment'. As Kelly notes:

> The approaches to punishment in articles 5, 6, and 7 [of the ECHR] are not only internally problematic, but are inconsistent with each other. In other words, there is no consistent Convention-wide approach to assess if a measure is penal. The lack of a universal approach is problematic given the ECtHR's self-proclaimed desire for consistency.[75]

He goes on to say that a measure 'could also, conceivably, be found to be punitive for the purposes of one article, but not another'.[76] Such inconsistency is particularly evident in the context of measures that purport to be preventive. In *M v Italy*, for example, the Commission rejected the argument that 'there is an affinity between criminal proceedings and proceedings on an application for a preventive measure', and went on to say that '[p]reventive measures must, in principle, be regarded as distinct not only from criminal penalties but also from disciplinary penalties ... administrative penalties ... and other forms of penalty ... since they are not designed to punish a specific offence'.[77] Preventive measures and punishment are thus seen in *M* as alternatives, whereas elsewhere the Strasbourg Court viewed them as complementary. In *Welch*, another confiscation case, it was said that 'the aims of prevention and reparation are consistent with a punitive purpose and may be seen as constituent elements of

[75] Rory Kelly, *Behaviour Orders: Preventive and/or Punitive Measures?* (PhD Thesis, University of Oxford, 2019) 71.

[76] Ibid 71. As is evident in the US civil forfeiture context in *US v Ursery* 518 US 267 (1996) (concerning double jeopardy) and *Austin v US* 509 US 602 (1993) (concerning the prohibition against excessive fines).

[77] M *v Italy* App. No. 12386/86, 15 April 1991, 97. In-quotation references omitted. For a critique of this judgment, see Colin King, 'Civil Forfeiture and Article 6 of the ECHR: Due Process Implications for England & Wales and Ireland' (2014) 34(3) *Legal Studies* 371, 379 et seq.

the very notion of punishment'.[78] This incompatibility of approach perpetuates a problematic incoherence, and one whose effects transcend civil recovery alone. What these cases do demonstrate are the difficulties inherent to determining whether a measure involves punishment or not. Such difficulties are particularly evident in the context of so-called preventive measures.

As outlined above, and given the judicial emphasis on civil recovery being such a measure, distinguishing punishment and prevention is a necessary starting point, not least because, as Kelly and Ashworth note, 'it may be harder to distinguish preventive orders from punishment than may be thought'.[79] Prevention and punishment are not mutually exclusive.[80] As Ashworth and Zedner note, 'there are measures (such as the confiscation order) that are preventive in purpose but substantially punitive in nature or effect, which we may term punitive-preventive measures'.[81] They continue here to note that other measures might be preventive in purpose and not significantly punitive in nature and effect, such that they can be classified as preventive measures. The key issue is whether the measure is *punitive*, irrespective as to whether its stated or ancillary purpose is prevention. As we propose below, civil recovery constitutes a punitive sanction imposed as a response to past wrongdoing.[82]

That notwithstanding, and as discussed earlier, the issue of prevention cannot be disregarded. The preventive label has historically performed something of a masking operation, whereby something that is preventive (forward-looking) cannot also be punitive (backward-looking).[83] We have to be careful

[78] *Welch v UK* App. No. 17440/90, 09 February 1995, para. 30. See also *Ezeh and Connors v UK* [2004] 39 EHRR 1, concerning prison disciplinary proceedings, where the Grand Chamber rejected the UK government's contention that the punitive purpose of the offences in question was secondary to the primary preventive purpose.

[79] Rory Kelly and Andrew Ashworth, 'State Responses to Criminal Offences in England and Wales and the Problem of Equality' in Matthew Dyson and Benjamin Vogel (eds), *The Limits of Criminal Law: Anglo-German Concepts and Principles* (Intersentia 2018) 356–7. See also Rory Kelly, 'Reconsidering the Punishment-Prevention Divide' (2019) 135 *Law Quarterly Review* 12.

[80] James R Edwards and AP Simester, 'Prevention with a Moral Voice' in AP Simester, Antje du Bois-Pedain, and Ulfrid Neumann (eds), *Liberal Criminal Theory: Essays for Andreas von Hirsch* (Hart 2014). But contrast Michael Moore, *Placing Blame: A Theory of the Criminal Law* (Oxford University Press 1997).

[81] Andrew Ashworth and Lucia Zedner, *Preventive Justice* (Oxford University Press 2014) 16.

[82] A related issue concerns the justification for punishment. In the context of civil recovery, a central focus is not so much the 'why', but rather the 'how'. The justifications advanced in support of civil recovery have been explained in Chapter 3; for present purposes, the key point is that *crime should not pay*. That objective is uncontroversial, and one that we endorse. Contention arises, however, in *how* that objective is realized: as has been articulated in earlier chapters, post-conviction confiscation follows a criminal conviction, whereas civil recovery does not require a criminal conviction. This non-conviction-based approach is examined further in Chapter 5; for now we are concerned with the emphasis on civil recovery being a punitive measure.

[83] Matthew Dyson and Benjamin Vogel, 'Alternative Enforcement Compared: Between Punishment and Prevention' in Matthew Dyson and Benjamin Vogel (eds), *The Limits of Criminal Law: Anglo-German Concepts and Principles* (Intersentia 2018). The authors note that such a distinction 'might offer a clear demarcation between criminal law and police law in Germany. However, such a distinction

not to overemphasize this characterization, however: as Zedner states, 'the claim that a measure is primarily preventive does not necessarily take it outside the realm of punishment'.[84] It is therefore not an either/or question; a preventive measure can also punish. Indeed, different rationales of punishment, whether deterrence, incapacitation, rehabilitation, or retribution, can all be said to be preventive. These rationales of punishment are each markedly apparent within the civil recovery discourse:

- by targeting the criminal wealth, the individual concerned is discouraged from engaging in crime, as are other individuals (deterrence—both specific and general);
- by removing the proceeds of crime, the individual is deprived of the working capital for future criminal actions (incapacitation);
- by returning it to its rightful owner[85] the property itself is made 'good' again (rehabilitation);[86]
- by depriving them of proceeds of crime, the state is able to hit criminals 'in the pocket' (retribution).[87]

There are clear overlaps between both the justifications and goals of civil recovery and the rationales of punishment. Indeed, and notwithstanding legislative and judicial insistence in focusing on the civil label and non-punitive nature of the process, our contention is that civil recovery *does* result in both censure—that is, the determination that the individual concerned engaged in criminal conduct, even though the proceedings are purportedly against the property[88]—and hard treatment, in this case the deprivation of property.

This position can be explained as follows. A punitive measure will involve, first, the censure of an offender for an offence, and second, the intentional

between the punitive and the prevention is not that clear-cut in English law, not least in view of the broad availability of preventive orders' (400).

[84] Lucia Zedner, 'Penal Subversions: When Is A Punishment Not Punishment, Who Decides and on What Grounds' (2016) 20 *Theoretical Criminology* 3, 7.

[85] The issue of good title is explored in Chapter 6.

[86] Of course, this is a complete fiction: rehabilitation is typically concerned with the offender's behaviour and it is entirely superficial to say that the property, having committed the wrong, is *rehabilitated* by virtue of being subject to civil recovery proceedings. The supposed *in rem* nature of civil recovery is critiqued in Chapter 6.

[87] These justifications are explored in more detail in Chapter 3.

[88] See, e.g., Conor Lally, 'CAB officers carry out raids across eight counties', *The Irish Times* (14 November 2019) which refers to 'a large family-based network of drug dealers'; National Crime Agency, 'Eight-year NCA investigation denies organised crime group £17 million property portfolio' (26 August 2020) where it is stated that 'NCA officers established that the properties were acquired using the proceeds of crime including heroin importation and distribution, fraud and money laundering'.

imposition of hard treatment.[89] The emphasis on censure reinforces the communicative nature of punishment, calling an offender to account,[90] while the hard treatment component involves either the deprivation of liberty or property. In the context of civil recovery, the censorious element is overt in terms of the individual concerned: *you have engaged in criminal conduct, so we are going to take this particular property away from you*. In practice, the preponderance of civil recovery proceedings is taken against those alleged to have themselves perpetrated criminal conduct and who are as a result seen to be deserving of censure and hard treatment – in this instance, the deprivation of *their* property.[91] Such deprivation is regarded as *fair* because the 'perpetrator' does not *deserve* the enjoyment of property obtained as a result of criminal conduct.[92]

Where a measure involves both censure and hard treatment, the question arises as to what procedural safeguards ought to apply in these circumstances. In Chapter 2 we outlined how enhanced procedural protections become operative where a person is charged with a criminal offence, and how a balance has to be struck between maintaining respect for the individual as a citizen and protecting innocent people from wrongful conviction.[93] With civil recovery, like other civil/criminal hybrids, the hybrid process has the effect of circumventing those procedural safeguards inherent to criminal processes, thus generating ambiguity as to whether such hybrid procedures constitute punishment.[94] This then creates uncertainty as to what safeguards *should* apply, and the general adoption of an explicitly pragmatic stance that asserts these to be civil proceedings with the result that civil rules apply.[95] But this stance—focusing solely on the 'civil' classification—is problematic, not least because it seems to overlook both the censure and hard treatment experienced by an individual deprived of property in civil recovery proceedings.

[89] Andrew Ashworth and Lucia Zedner, *Preventive Justice* (Oxford University Press 2014) 14.

[90] Ambrose Lee, 'Defending a Communicative Theory of Punishment: The Relationship Between Hard Treatment and Amends' (2017) 37(1) *Oxford Journal of Legal Studies* 217; Antony Duff, Lindsay Farmer, Sandra Marshall, and Victor Tadros, *The Trial on Trial, Volume 3: Towards a Normative Theory of the Criminal Trial* (Hart Publishing 2007) 119.

[91] See Chapter 6 for consideration of 'no good title' arguments.

[92] This is not to say that all civil recovery proceedings will be so straightforward; complications arise where the alleged offender is not the subject of the civil recovery proceedings, for example where the respondent is an innocent third party (discussed further in Chapter 6), but it suffices as an illustration.

[93] Antony Duff, Lindsay Farmer, Sandra Marshall, and Victor Tadros, *The Trial on Trial, Volume 3: Towards a Normative Theory of the Criminal Trial* (Hart Publishing 2007).

[94] For wider discussion, see Simon Young, 'Enforcing Criminal Law Through Civil Processes: How Does Human Rights Law Treat "Civil for Criminal Processes"?' (2017) 4(2) *Journal of International and Comparative Law* 133; Rory Kelly, *Behaviour Orders: Preventive and/or Punitive Measures?* (PhD Thesis, University of Oxford, 2019).

[95] This pragmatic argument is considered further in Chapter 7.

Our view is that civil recovery *is* punitive, although, and as the next three empirical chapters demonstrate, there is considerable disagreement about this categorization. Moreover, that a measure might be punitive is not determinative,[96] which leads to our next point of dispute with the courts: is civil recovery *de facto* a criminal proceeding under a civil guise?[97]

Civil Classification

As is evident from our empirical data in the following chapters, the civil classification is an issue that sits at the heart of our discussion of civil recovery. While there might be broad consensus on some issues, including the idea that crime should not pay and the importance of due process, it is the *civil* classification that provokes much dispute. At its core, civil recovery is concerned with ensuring that *criminals* do not enjoy proceeds of their criminality. The reality is that 'in a significant percentage of the claims brought by CAB under s. 3 of the Act there are co-existing criminal proceedings'.[98] As a matter of procedural justice, then, would it not be appropriate for deprivation of assets—on the grounds that they constitute proceeds of crime—to be dealt with in criminal

[96] As Packer notes: 'Criminal punishment means simply any particular disposition or the range of permissible dispositions that the law authorizes (or appears to authorize) in cases of persons who have been judged through the distinctive processes of the criminal law to be guilty of crimes. Not all punishment is criminal punishment but all criminal punishment is punishment.' Herbert L Packer, *The Limits of the Criminal Sanction* (Stanford University Press 1968) 35. In *Enright v Ireland* [2003] 2 IR 321, 332 the court said that for a sanction to be considered a penalty in the criminal sense, it must be punitive in nature, but the fact that a sanction is punitive does not *necessarily* mean that it will be a criminal sanction. For consideration of the changing nature of criminal punishment, see Albert W Alschuler, 'The Changing Purposes of Criminal Punishment: A Retrospective on the past century and Some Thoughts about the Next' (2003) 70(1) *University of Chicago Law Review* 1. For Zedner, '[t]he pains and prohibitions imposed by formally non-penal measures may be burdensome or restrictive of liberty but they are not justifiable as punishment'. Lucia Zedner, 'Penal Subversions: When Is A Punishment Not Punishment, Who Decides and on What Grounds' (2016) 20 *Theoretical Criminology* 3, 9.

[97] Note, though, that even if it were accepted that civil recovery is indeed *civil*, as the courts have determined, that does not rule out application of enhanced procedural protections. Civil measures can also attract such additional safeguards—an obvious example is the criminal standard of proof applying in an application for an ASBO (*Clingham v Royal Borough of Kensington and Chelsea; R v Crown Court at Manchester, Ex p McCann* [2002] UKHL 39). Indeed, there is extensive literature arguing for application of criminal procedural safeguards in the context of two-step civil preventive orders, with particular emphasis on the right to liberty (e.g. Mark James and Geoff Pearson, '30 Years of Hurt: The Evolution of Civil Preventive Orders, Hybrid Law, and the Emergence of the Super-Football Banning Order' [2018] *Public Law* 44; Simon Hoffman and Stuart MacDonald, 'Should ASBOs be Civilised?' [2010] *Criminal Law Review* 457). Of course, civil recovery is not concerned with liberty, but rather property—which is considered further in Chapter 6. Our contention is that the downplaying of the deprivation of property—i.e. by casting civil recovery as an action *against that property* (*in rem*, rather than *in personam*)—is instrumental in skewing civil recovery towards a civil classification.

[98] This point was relied upon by counsel for the Criminal Assets Bureau in *CAB v Connors* [2018] IECA 371, para. 14.

proceedings?[99] Even Kennedy, a leading proponent of civil recovery, acknowledges that 'while, as a matter of theory, civil forfeiture proceedings are preventive and reparative, this may be of no comfort to a respondent in a civil recovery action whose property is the subject of a recovery order'.[100]

We have been critical of the adoption of civil recovery, arguing that, 'it is hard not to rue their introduction as a privileging of instrumentality over considerations of due process, not least because there are manifest reasons for the enhanced procedural safeguards inherent in the criminal process'.[101] Our concern is that the courts have too readily accepted the 'civil' label in deference to legislative intention, at the expense of due process. Indeed, we have argued that '[t]he robustness of this judicial position is disconcerting, however, not least because, in spite of civil recovery's adoption of civil processes, it is still evidently concerned with allegations of criminal wrongdoing'.[102] For example, in the High Court hearing in *Gale* Griffith Williams J stated: 'I am in no doubt that DG and TG engaged in unlawful conduct—in DG's case, money laundering and drug trafficking, in TG's case, money laundering. There is also evidence of tax evasion in four jurisdictions.'[103] In giving judicial imprimatur to the use of the civil process, the courts—in Ireland and England & Wales—have ignored that civil recovery is 'a wholly instrumental approach conceived to employ civil law processes in pursuing criminal law objectives, and to circumvent those procedural safeguards that inhere in a criminal trial'.[104] This stance is explored further using our empirical research in the next chapter.

It is worth returning to the *Engel* criteria here. In determining whether a particular matter ought to be deemed a criminal matter, the Strasbourg Court relies upon these three criteria: the domestic classification of the proceedings at issue, the nature of the offence in question, and the nature and severity of the penalty that may be imposed.[105] In relation to the first criterion,

[99] Our interviewees are legal practitioners, enforcement officials, and representatives of non-governmental organizations. This book does not offer insights into the views of those who have been confronted with civil recovery proceedings, which requires future research. For consideration of procedural justice in the context of post-conviction confiscation, see Craig Fletcher, *"Double Punishment"—The Proceeds of Crime Act 2002 (POCA): A Qualitative Examination of the Post-Conviction Confiscation Punishment in England and Wales* (PhD Thesis, Manchester Metropolitan University, 2019).

[100] Anthony Kennedy, 'Justifying the Civil Recovery of Criminal Proceeds' (2005) 12(1) *Journal of Financial Crime* 8, 17.

[101] Jennifer Hendry and Colin King, 'Expediency, Legitimacy, and the Rule of Law: A Systems Perspective on Civil/Criminal Procedural Hybrids' (2017) 11(4) *Criminal Law and Philosophy* 733, 746.

[102] Ibid, 748.

[103] *SOCA v Gale* [2009] EWHC 1015 (QB), para. 140.

[104] Jennifer Hendry and Colin King, 'Expediency, Legitimacy, and the Rule of Law: A Systems Perspective on Civil/ Criminal Procedural Hybrids' (2017) 11(4) *Criminal Law and Philosophy* 733, 748.

[105] *Engel v Netherlands* [1976] 1 EHRR 647. For a critique of these criteria, see the dissenting opinion of Judge de Meyer in *Putz v Austria* [2001] 32 EHRR 13.

the legislative intention certainly appears to have been to create a civil procedure, as evidenced by the civil standard of proof; the hallmarks of criminal proceedings (e.g. arrest, search, detention) are absent; there is no prospect of prosecution with potential for criminal punishment; and the language of the criminal law (e.g. 'offence', 'prosecution', 'conviction') is not used in the legislation. Legislative intent alone is insufficient however;[106] intention does not dictate substance.[107] Indeed, civil recovery is available to the Criminal Assets Bureau (in Ireland) and different 'enforcement authorities'[108] (in England & Wales) that are able to draw upon extensive powers of investigation and/or prosecution. These powers can thus be used in a civil setting to pursue criminal law objectives. While words like 'prosecution' or 'conviction' are not used, and there is no prospect of deprivation of liberty, civil recovery is concerned with 'proceeds of crime' and is widely used against those with criminal convictions and/or those suspected of involvement in criminality, as evident in the findings against David and Teresa Gale in the above quotation.[109] This notwithstanding, it is apparent that the legislative intention, in both jurisdictions, was to create a civil process and so to benefit from all of the procedural advantages generated by such a step.[110]

The first criterion is not determinative, however.[111] The fact that domestic legislation might classify a particular process as 'civil' does not automatically mean that that process is indeed a civil one. If that were the case, then protections of the ECHR, for example, would be undermined—countries could simply label a matter as 'civil' or 'non-criminal' and that would be decisive. Such an outcome would be unconscionable. As Zedner states: 'Where the courts simply defer to the legislature, they tacitly condone state subversion of criminal process protections and the strictures of proportionality that apply to

[106] *Öztürk v Germany* [1984] 6 EHRR 409.

[107] Colin King, 'Using Civil Processes in Pursuit of Criminal Law Objectives: A Case Study of Non-Conviction-Based Asset Forfeiture' (2012) 16(4) *International Journal of Evidence and Proof* 337, 347.

[108] Namely, HM Revenue and Customs, the Financial Conduct Authority, the National Crime Agency, the Director of Public Prosecutions, the Director of the Serious Fraud Office, the Scottish Ministers, or the Director of Public Prosecutions for Northern Ireland. POCA, s. 316(1).

[109] See also *Olupitan v Director of the Assets Recovery Agency* [2008] EWCA Civ 104, para. 24, where the court referred to allegations specified in the claim form: 'The claimant alleges that Olupitan has proven himself to have a propensity to commit crime for financial gain and to lie for person gain. Olupitan has committed immigration offences, acquisitive criminal offences, mortgage fraud and laundered the proceeds of these (and possible other offences) in addition to cheating the public revenue.'

[110] See also political discourse in Chapter 3. On the prosecutorial and evidentiary advantages of civil/criminal hybrid procedures, see Chapter 2.

[111] *Öztürk v Germany* [1984] 6 EHRR 409, para. 52.

punishment.'[112] The courts thus play a key scrutiny role.[113] We turn now to the second and third *Engel* criteria.

The second criterion concerns the nature of the offence in question. Civil recovery proceedings do 'not impute guilt of a specific offence; the proceedings do not seek to impose a penalty other than the recovery of assets acquired through criminal conduct; and they are initiated by the director of an agency, which, although it is a public authority, has no prosecutorial function or competence'.[114] Indeed, proceedings can be initiated against a person in possession of property *even where* that person has not been convicted, under the convenient legal fiction that it is the property that is guilty, not the person in possession.[115] As can be seen from above judicial quotations, however, such proceedings *do* involve general allegations of criminality, such as money laundering and drug trafficking in *Gale*.[116] While it need not be established that specific property is derived from a specific instance of criminal conduct, the courts must be satisfied that the property is derived from criminal conduct. In practice, proceedings have tended to be initiated against those suspected of, and/or convicted of, criminal activity.[117] Moreover, the possibility of civil recovery post-acquittal raises concerns that the acquittal in criminal proceedings is effectively being undermined by subsequent non-conviction-based proceedings based on similar—if not the same—allegations and evidence. As will be shown in the next chapter, in our interviews respondent-focused practitioners expressed concern as to the making of criminal allegations in this purportedly civil process.

Finally, the third *Engel* criterion is concerned with the nature and severity of the penalty that may be imposed. As noted in the previous paragraph, in *Walsh* the court stated that 'the proceedings do not seek to impose a penalty other than the recovery of assets acquired through criminal conduct'.[118] This was similarly the case in *Gilligan*, where the court stressed that:

[112] Lucia Zedner, 'Penal Subversions: When Is A Punishment Not Punishment, Who Decides and on What Grounds' (2016) 20 *Theoretical Criminology* 3, 11.

[113] As Lord Woolf states, 'ultimately there are limits on the supremacy of Parliament which it is the courts' inalienable responsibility to identify and uphold'. Lord Woolf, 'Droit Public—English Style' [1995] *Public Law* 57, 68.

[114] *Walsh v Director of the Assets Recovery Agency* [2005] NICA 6, para. 29

[115] This *in rem* classification is discussed in more detail in Chapter 6.

[116] *SOCA v Gale* [2009] EWHC 1015 (QB), para. 140.

[117] A developing aspect of proceeds of crime jurisprudence concerns third party rights in property, which is explored in Chapter 6.

[118] *Walsh v Director of the Assets Recovery Agency* [2005] NICA 6, para. 29.

> there is no question of the arrest of a Respondent or his remand in custody or on bail and there is no specific penalty of fine or imprisonment. It is true that money or property may be removed from the possession or control of a Respondent, but *if this money or property can be shown to the satisfaction of the Court to be the proceeds of crime, its removal could well be viewed in the light of reparation rather than punishment or penalty.*[119]

We respectfully disagree, and contend that confiscating 'proceeds of crime' is, in essence, a sanction for criminal wrongdoing, particularly when combined with allegations of criminality (as discussed above).[120] It is contrived to say that civil recovery operates merely as a means of recovering such proceeds; an individual subject to such an order will be deprived of property and also be perceived as 'criminal', if not in law, then at least in the eyes of other citizens.[121] It is disingenuous to suggest that an individual is not being punished, that there is no imputation of criminal liability, and that these *in rem* proceedings are concerned solely with the property and not the individual. In our interviews even enforcement officials did acknowledge the reality that the criminal conduct at issue is linked back to a specific individual. Such insights are explored in the following three chapters.

[119] *Gilligan v CAB* [1998] 3 IR 185, para. 86. Emphasis added. See also *M v D* [1998] 3 IR 175, 178.

[120] For wider discussion, see Lucia Zedner, 'Penal Subversions: When Is A Punishment Not Punishment, Who Decides and on What Grounds' (2016) 20 *Theoretical Criminology* 3.

[121] See, e.g., National Crime Agency, Press Release—North-west organised crime suspect loses family home (1 May 2015).

5

Critiquing Civil Recovery

Introduction

Now that we have charted the substantive law establishing and administering civil recovery in both Ireland and England & Wales, and discussed the judicial response, we turn our attention to providing a critique of civil recovery and its operation in both jurisdictions. In doing so, we draw on empirical work undertaken during 2015, 2016, and 2019 (Ireland) and 2018, 2019, and 2021 (England & Wales), when semi-structured 'elite' interviews were conducted with twenty-seven practitioners experienced with active involvement in civil recovery proceedings.[1] In this and subsequent chapters, we provide an empirically informed insight into the practical operation of these controversial powers.

We have previously been critical of the use of the hybrid civil/criminal procedure of civil recovery from both doctrinal and theoretical perspectives,[2] arguing—as earlier chapters will attest—that such non-conviction-based (NCB) confiscation provisions go too far in privileging crime control over due process and individual civil liberties. We are not alone in adopting this condemnatory stance,[3] nor the view that civil recovery comprises a hybrid model, indifferent to either compliance or prosecution,[4] and geared towards the circumvention of procedural standards through the strategic use of civil, administrative, and regulatory mechanisms.[5] Indeed, the adoption of proceeds of

[1] For details, see the 'Methods' section in Chapter 1.

[2] Jennifer Hendry and Colin King, 'Expediency, Legitimacy, and the Rule of Law: A Systems Perspective on Civil/ Criminal Procedural Hybrids' (2017) 11(4) *Criminal Law and Philosophy* 733; Jennifer Hendry and Colin King, 'How Far Is Too Far? Theorising Non-Conviction-Based Asset Forfeiture' (2015) 11(4) *International Journal of Law in Context* 398; Colin King, 'Using Civil Processes in Pursuit of Criminal Law Objectives: A Case Study of Non-Conviction-Based Asset Forfeiture' (2012) 16(4) *International Journal of Evidence and Proof* 337.

[3] Anthony Gray, 'Forfeiture Provisions and the Criminal/Civil Divide' (2012) 15 *New Criminal Law Review* 32; Liz Campbell, 'Theorising Asset Forfeiture in Ireland' (2007) 71(5) *Journal of Criminal Law* 441.

[4] Patrick Ryan, *An Examination of How the Methods Employed by the Criminal Assets Bureau Move Ireland in a New Direction of Crime Control* (PhD Thesis, University of Limerick, 2019) 23.

[5] Michelle Gallant, *Money Laundering and the Proceeds of Crime: Economic Crime and Civil Remedies* (Edward Elgar 2005).

Civil Recovery of Criminal Property. Colin King and Jennifer Hendry, Oxford University Press.
 DOI: 10.1093/oso/9780198824251.003.0005

crime legislation, specifically NCB powers, in Ireland in 1996 and in England & Wales in 2002 has attracted significant criticism and legal challenge over *inter alia* the absence of conviction, the impact upon the presumption of innocence, the use of the civil standard of proof—all of which are analysed in this chapter—and the implications for rights in property, which we discuss in Chapter 6.

In conducting the elite interviews, therefore, we were keen to ascertain the views of practitioners and law enforcement officials, and whether such views aligned with the prevailing, critical academic view of the contentious powers of civil recovery.[6] As this chapter and the next two illustrate, our interviews gave nuanced insights into practitioner understandings and views of this hybrid procedure, particularly in terms of identifying important recurring themes. The most prominent difference of views we identified concerned the dichotomy between due process and individual rights on the one side, and increased effectiveness and pragmatism on the other. Perhaps unsurprisingly, this split mapped generally, although not entirely, onto the respective camps of applicant- (state officials and barristers acting for them) and respondent-focused interviewees. Such apparently entrenched positions only tell part of the story, however. For example, it would be erroneous to suggest that law enforcement officials and enforcement-focused legal practitioners are not concerned with due process and human rights, fundamental legal principles,[7] and—as Mann put it—the 'hierarchy of values',[8] as our interviews highlighted these as recurrent concerns and very real challenges, both practical and existential. By the same token, even practitioners critical of civil recovery—and likewise academics—recognize the importance of an effective confiscation regime. Moreover, our interviews showed no disagreement whatsoever as to the underlying issue, namely, that crime should not pay.

[6] For discussion of civil recovery from an enforcement perspective, see, e.g., Francis Cassidy, 'Targeting the Proceeds of Crime: An Irish Perspective' in Theodore Greenberg, Linda Samuel, Wingate Grant, and Larissa Gray, *Stolen Asset Recovery: A Good Practices Guide for Non-Conviction Based Asset Forfeiture* (World Bank 2009); Jeffrey Simser, 'Perspectives on Civil Forfeiture' in Simon Young (ed.), *Civil Forfeiture of Criminal Property: Legal Measures for Targeting the Proceeds of Crime* (Edward Elgar 2009); Stef Cassella, 'The Case for Civil Forfeiture: Why *in rem* Proceedings are an Essential Tool for Recovering the Proceeds of Crime' (2008) 11(1) *Journal of Money Laundering Control* 8; Anthony Kennedy, 'Justifying the Civil Recovery of Criminal Proceeds' (2005) 12(1) *Journal of Financial Crime* 8.

[7] On principles, see Johan Boucht, 'Asset Confiscation in Europe—Past, Present, and Future Challenges' (2019) 26(2) *Journal of Financial Crime* 526, 538: 'How far can we go in circumventing, or diluting, traditional criminal law standards in the field of asset confiscation, before we leave the domains of a liberal criminal law in the tradition of a democratic *Rechtsstaat* based on the rule of law?'

[8] Kenneth Mann, 'Punitive Civil Sanctions: The Middleground Between Criminal and Civil Law' (1992) 101 *Yale Law Journal* 1795, 1869.

Another clear point that can be drawn from the practitioner interviews is that a great deal turns upon the classification of civil recovery as either a civil or criminal procedure. In their contention that it is a civil procedure, proponents of civil recovery can cite the support of the courts, as discussed in the previous chapter. The use of administrative tools within a 'follow the money' approach, combined with an *in rem* process, provides ground for the argument that civil recovery concerns neither 'the individual *per se* or his or her guilt and potential punishment [but rather . . .] the assets held by that individual', and is as such 'a framework of justice that is apersonal, non-moral, regulatory and administrative in nature'.[9] Critics reject this view as being reliant on a strategic mislabelling, insisting—in spite of its name—that civil recovery is a manifestly criminal procedure and ought to be regarded as such, with all the attendant procedural protections afforded by the criminal law.

For the purposes of this chapter, the three key fault-lines we identified through these elite interviews are (i) the non-conviction-based route, (ii) the presumption of innocence, and (iii) the standard of proof. Our account will consequently centre on each of these issues in turn.

The Non-Conviction-Based Approach

Of all the justifications given for the NCB approach of civil recovery, the most prominent is that of *pragmatism*. The notion that civil recovery is a necessary and proportionate addition to the law enforcement response, particularly to organized crime, considering the ineptness of traditional criminal law mechanisms, saturates the debate to the extent that we have dedicated a full chapter to its discussion.[10] Our focus for the moment is the critical view raised by (mainly respondent-focused) legal practitioners.

First, the context for this position: civil recovery has been heavily criticized as undermining due process. Lea has described this approach to seizing assets as 'a frontal assault on due process',[11] while Gallant has observed that 'the chronic critique of asset recovery is that the takings do not, for the most part, comply with procedural and substantive rights [and that regulation] manages to secure

[9] Patrick Ryan, *An Examination of How the Methods Employed by the Criminal Assets Bureau Move Ireland in a New Direction of Crime Control* (PhD Thesis, University of Limerick, 2019) 24.

[10] See Chapter 7.

[11] John Lea, 'Hitting Criminals Where It Hurts: Organised Crime and the Erosion of Due Process' (2004) 35 *Cambria Law Review* 81, 83.

title to tainted assets at the expense of the rule of law'.[12] We have also previously questioned the legitimacy of the NCB approach, alleging a privileging of instrumental considerations over those of due process, and querying its compliance with the rule of law,[13] while Campbell goes even further, arguing that civil recovery represents 'a fundamental alteration of the traditional norms of the criminal justice system'.[14]

Arguments that civil recovery undermines due process were therefore explored during our interviews.[15] Respondent-focused practitioners by and large rejected contentions that the NCB approach was necessary given the nature of crime that it was intended to target. One defence solicitor refuted the proposition that there are numerous so-called Mr Bigs beyond the reach of criminal law, stating instead that '[m]ost people's clients are in fact very stupid criminals'.[16] They continued:

> The people who I think are very clever criminals are people who first of all never reside long enough in the jurisdiction to be tax resident. Secondly, apparently have no assets whatsoever. Thirdly, apparently have no bank accounts whatsoever. Fourthly, always travel in their own identity. Fifthly, always have access to funding somehow or another. Sixthly, always have access to motor vehicles. Very, very few of them around.[17]

In light of these low numbers of potential targets, this interviewee rejected the adoption of NCB processes for this explicit purpose. In sharp contrast to the pragmatic argument put forward by supporters of civil recovery, who contend that criminal procedural protections are not applicable due to the civil nature of this process,[18] this interviewee took the position that criminal procedural protections were vitally important in this context and should not be

[12] Michelle Gallant, 'Money Laundering Consequences: Recovering Wealth, Piercing Secrecy, Disrupting Tax Havens and Distorting International Law' (2014) 17(3) *Journal of Money Laundering Control* 296, 299.

[13] Jennifer Hendry and Colin King, 'Expediency, Legitimacy, and the Rule of Law: A Systems Perspective on Civil/ Criminal Procedural Hybrids' (2017) 11(4) *Criminal Law and Philosophy* 733.

[14] Liz Campbell, 'Theorising Asset Forfeiture in Ireland' (2007) 71 *Journal of Criminal Law* 441, 456. She continues: 'no longer is the State the entity from which individuals must be protected, rather it is the State that protects us from each other. While due process safeguards sought to defend the individual from the might of the State, civil forfeiture circumvents these protections, implying a more benign view of State power.'

[15] By 'talking back' to interviewees, we were able to put different perspectives to interviewees so as to allow them to engage with opposing views and to offer their own rebuttal or agreement. See the 'Method' section in Chapter 1.

[16] IRE08.

[17] IRE08.

[18] See Chapters 3 and 7.

jettisoned: 'If some people get away with it, it's just too bad. The problem is that you're turning the whole legal system up to try and get after people like that.'[19] Indeed, the importance of procedural rights was emphasized repeatedly, as was the categorization of proceedings as civil, as shown here: 'You can bring a civil case, it looks like a civil case, it smells like a civil case—but it really is a criminal case, and if that's the case then the protections under Article 6 really should apply.'[20] A defence solicitor further stressed that 'even people suspected of heinous criminal offences have a full panoply of rights', continuing with '[i]t's an unfortunate part of living in a constitutional democracy and if those rights are ridden roughshod over in the name of the war against crime, I think it's a wrong thing'.[21] The brunt of the criticisms levied against civil recovery in the interviews were in fact borne by this civil/criminal procedural line-blurring:

> [T]he reality is that most of the cases that I've done have not been third party cases at all, they have been cases where an individual is holding the property and is actually, in reality, accused of taking it criminally. So, I think to that extent that when people have said, particularly in the academic context, this is a cop-out, doing criminal justice by the back door, I think there's some truth in that.[22]

The same interviewee continued in this vein:

> When you've got a person who is alleged to have obtained property through criminal conduct, and you've got a civil recovery action, it's completely artificial to say that the action is against the property, rather than an action against the individual. The reality is that you're not going to get the case home unless you prove that it is the individual who has committed crime. Only difference is you are proving it on the balance of probabilities, and not beyond reasonable doubt.[23]

To be clear: the use of a 'civil' process to confiscate 'criminal' assets has the result that the rules of criminal evidence do not apply. This paves the way for the admission of evidence that would not otherwise be admissible at a criminal trial,

[19] IRE08. That interviewee was in favour of targeting criminal proceeds by other avenues: 'Do it with the tax system. The tax system's cheap. It's dirt cheap. Just whack them with notices of assessment.'
[20] EW04.
[21] IRE08.
[22] EW07.
[23] EW07.

such as inferences from silence, previous behaviour, illegally obtained evidence and abuse of process, and hearsay evidence.[24] Not only does this amount to an attrition of formerly robust and entrenched procedural protections, but it also introduces the problematic idea that certain individuals suspected of criminal activity might not deserve the full protection of the criminal justice process.

Although the hybrid nature of civil recovery[25] has rendered it a prominent example of this erosion of criminal procedural safeguards, recent decades have witnessed other, previously unthinkable, intrusions upon these protections, including: curtailments of the right to silence, the increased admissibility of hearsay evidence in criminal proceedings, changes to the admissibility of character evidence, and restrictions on the right to jury trial, to name but a few examples.[26] Moreover, when seen as one aspect of a more widespread change, it is evident that such developments have radically altered not just the criminal justice system but also the relationship between the state and the individual.[27] As Duff et al. point out:

> [N]otwithstanding the continuing adherence to the principle of the presumption of innocence, it seems clear that the standing of the accused person has shifted. As a consequence of changes in policing and prosecution they are no longer seen as an innocent, an equal who happens to have been charged with a crime, but are instead frequently viewed as suspects, required to answer the charges, and whose silence is seen as an obstacle to criminal justice.[28]

Neither is this situation confined to high-level criminality and concerns about organized crime, corruption, and terrorism, for there has been a similar shift in terms of 'low level' criminality, such as anti-social behaviour and public order

[24] Peter Alldridge, 'Proceeds of Crime Law since 2003—Two Key Areas' [2014] *Criminal Law Review* 171, 185–7. There are, of course, statutory provisions whereby such types of evidence might be admitted in a criminal case.

[25] See Chapter 2 on civil recovery's procedural hybridity. For discussion of hybridity in other contexts see, e.g., Simon Bronitt and Susan Donkin, 'Australian Responses to 9/11: New World Legal Hybrids?' in Aniceto Masferrer (ed.), *Post 9/11 and the State of Permanent Legal Emergency Security and Human Rights in Countering Terrorism* (Springer 2012); Stuart MacDonald, 'ASBOs and Control Orders: Two Recurring Themes, Two Apparent Contradictions' (2007) 60(4) *Parliamentary Affairs* 601; Jennifer Hendry, 'The Hostile Environment and Crimmigration: Blurring the Lines between Civil and Criminal Law' (2020) 76 *Soundings* 26.

[26] See, generally, Liz Campbell, Andrew Ashworth, and Mike Redmayne, *The Criminal Process* (5th edn, Oxford University Press 2019); Dermot Walsh, *Walsh on Criminal Procedure* (Round Hall 2016).

[27] For wider discussion see, generally, Antony Duff, Lindsay Farmer, Sandra Marshall, and Victor Tadros, *The Trial on Trial, Volume 3: Towards a Normative Theory of the Criminal Trial* (Hart 2007); Shane Kilcommins and Barry Vaughan, 'Reconfiguring State-Accused Relations in Ireland' (2006) 41 *Irish Jurist* 90.

[28] Antony Duff, Lindsay Farmer, Sandra Marshall, and Victor Tadros, *The Trial on Trial, Volume 3: Towards a Normative Theory of the Criminal Trial* (Hart 2007) 52–3.

offences.[29] Contrary to perceptions that the criminal law/process is 'soft' or that due process safeguards overly favour suspects or accused persons, there is instead a noticeable shift towards a crime control model of criminal justice, as well as a sense of populist punitiveness.[30]

Zedner has referred to this shift as 'politicians and policymakers ... press[ing] the fast-forward button on criminal justice',[31] while our view is that this attrition of formerly robust and entrenched procedural protections, whether undertaken by means of procedural hybridization or otherwise, is problematic.[32] In our interviews, the representative from the Irish Council for Civil Liberties raised similar concerns about the erosion of procedural safeguards in civil recovery proceedings:

> It's the slippery slope argument for sure with this, but I think it's even more dangerous ... once you put in the minds of decision-makers and power-holders that this process will work and that the legal community will accept it, that the public will accept it, that it will actually be supported and their positive vibes given about it, well then it will bring about a shift in how they approach things, and a shift in the dynamics, the paradigm that they are looking at. So, in many ways I think it is more dangerous than just itself on the face of it.[33]

Critical views along these lines go to the heart of debates on civil recovery. There is little dispute over the general principle that crime should not pay, yet significant disagreement concerning *how* it is that 'criminals' should be deprived of the proceeds of illegal activities. A core concern for this same interviewee was that the non-conviction-based approach, introduced to deal with the kingpins and Mr Bigs of organized crime, could potentially be used for much lower level criminality.[34] This has already proven to be the case in the Irish context, where the Criminal Assets Bureau (CAB) is now actively targeting civil

[29] For wider discussion, see Eamonn Carrabine, 'Youth Justice in the United Kingdom' (2010) 7(1) *Essex Human Rights Review* 12; Ursula Kilkelly, 'Diverging or Emerging from Law? The Practice of Youth Justice in Ireland' (2014) 14(3) *Youth Justice* 212.

[30] Liz Campbell, 'Criminal Justice and Penal Populism in Ireland' (2008) 28(4) *Legal Studies* 559. See also Ian Loader, 'Fall of the Platonic Guardians: Liberalism, Criminology and Political Responses to Crime in England and Wales' (2006) 46 *British Journal of Criminology* 561.

[31] Lucia Zedner, 'Dangers of Dystopias in Penal Theory' (2002) 22(2) *Oxford Journal of Legal Studies* 341, 341.

[32] Jennifer Hendry and Colin King, 'How Far Is Too Far? Theorising Non-Conviction-Based Asset Forfeiture' (2015) 11(4) *International Journal of Law in Context* 398, 406.

[33] IRE10.

[34] IRE10. The 'massive danger with this type of approach is that it's going to just trickle down, that it's going to become normal, and it's going to become standard'. IRE10.

recovery powers at lower-level targets and the monetary threshold for an action has been reduced to a mere €5,000.[35] This expansion of the scope of civil recovery should be taken seriously, not least because advantages in efficiency and expediency over criminal process alternatives are already making the non-conviction-based route more attractive to law enforcement agencies, and this is a worrisome combination from a procedural rights perspective.

By avoiding the enhanced procedural protections of the criminal process, civil recovery has obvious advantages: it is quicker, cheaper, more certain of 'success', and—whether or not one concedes the punitive point—in the seizure of alleged criminal assets provides an outcome that is undeniably a financial consequence and thus, at the very least, *punishment-adjacent*. The functional equivalence of civil recovery to a post-*conviction* confiscation of property following a deprivation order under the Sentencing Act 2020 is striking—they are identical in substance, if not in either derivation or classification. If the outcome is effectively the same and the process is more straightforward, why then not make liberal use of the easier 'civil' approach in lieu of the more burdensome criminal prosecution? There are several interrelated issues here that need to be disentangled.

The first thing that begs consideration is the particular role of the criminal law[36] and its unique functions, of which there are three: criminalization, conviction, and punishment.[37] Condemnatory in nature, criminal law controls the behaviour of those subject to it by means of rules, backed up by threats, and by holding wrongdoers publicly to account.[38] Again here, the civil/criminal distinction arises. The use or otherwise of the non-conviction-based approach must therefore be considered in this specific context. Do the purported benefits of civil recovery—that it is more efficient, more affordable, more likely to achieve a result—suffice, cumulatively, in justifying the loss of criminal procedural protections, not least given than civil recovery proceedings are initiated by the state and often involve censure? Our position is that they do not, a viewpoint reinforced by some respondent-focused interviewees: 'it's actually very short-sighted in my view. We should be prosecuting these people.'[39]

[35] Proceeds of Crime (Amendment) Act, 2016. See also Luke Byrne, 'Targeting the "Godfathers of Tomorrow"—Why the Criminal Assets Bureau is Seeking Out "Man Caves" in the Fight Against Crime', *The Irish Independent* (18 October 2019).

[36] See Chapter 2.

[37] AP Simester, et al., *Simester and Sullivan's Criminal Law: Theory and Doctrine* (7th edn, Hart 2019) 5.

[38] Anthony Duff, Lindsay Farmer, Sandra Marshall, and Victor Tadros, *The Trial on Trial, Volume 3: Towards a Normative Theory of the Criminal Trial* (Hart 2007) 137 et seq.

[39] EW02. Some respondent-focused interviewees, however, expressed a different view, which is explored in Chapter 7 in the context of pragmatism.

The second issue here is the more practical one of resources. Indeed, from the perspective of respondent-focused practitioners, criminal prosecution is arguably the preferred avenue, although they acknowledged that resourcing considerations were a significant influence in law enforcement going down the civil recovery route.[40] One defence solicitor described this approach as 'a much easier regime',[41] continuing with this rhetorical question: 'Why would the state want to prosecute people and lock them up, when actually it's much easier to just nick all the money? That's the reality, isn't it.'[42] Another emphasized the strategic aspect of civil recovery in this regard, citing it not only as 'a disruptive tactic' but also as a cheaper and more certain alternative to prosecution.[43] The disruption of serious and organized criminal activity and the undermining of the profit incentive is, of course, a central feature of 'follow the money' approaches, but there is a fundamental question to be posed about what is, in essence, a compromise. This compromise is basically the choice not to prosecute the criminal activity and instead to follow the money, which is more likely to be successful even if it is less satisfactory. Classic crime control model reasoning tells us that, while efficient and expeditious options are often preferred, they invariably lead to errors[44]—in civil recovery cases errors constitute miscarriages of justice in the form of harmful, wrongful deprivations.[45]

This takes us to our third consideration here, which is the public interest, and which arguably overlaps with both of the foregoing matters—punishment and public resource management. To these we can add this notion of compromise, that is, the alternative 'successes' of disruption and disincentivization, and the related goal of improved public security. The non-conviction-based approach of civil recovery has a very different quality of justice to a conviction-based, overtly criminal law approach, and all of these countervailing issues make it challenging to ascertain what, in fact, is in the best interests of the public when it comes to civil recovery; indeed, our respondent-focused interviewees found this no more straightforward. One criminal defence solicitor seemed to think that money provided the central motivation: 'There is a general attraction in simply just getting the funds. Maybe I'm just cynical though, but that is my experience of it.'[46] Another defence solicitor noted that, while the decision

[40] EW01; EW02; EW04. Similar points about resourcing of the criminal justice system were aired in Ireland, e.g. IRE10.
[41] EW01.
[42] EW01.
[43] EW02.
[44] Herbert L Packer, *The Limits of the Criminal Sanction* (Stanford University Press 1968).
[45] For consideration of property, see Chapter 6 and for pragmatic arguments, see Chapter 7.
[46] EW06.

'to pursue civil recovery or to stick with a criminal investigation' is likely to be decided on a case-by-case basis, 'eventually, what we kind of feel is that, there will be a sea change where it will start becoming the converse: is it actually in the public interest to prosecute this when we could do this anyway?'[47] Similar concerns have been expressed in academic literature, that is, the non-conviction-based approach 'holds the potential to usurp ordinary police work, as a softer option to the normal and more onerous investigative and prosecution process.'[48]

Worries that civil recovery is increasingly being used as a substitute for criminal prosecution have been aired in England & Wales, while similar disquiet was raised amongst practitioners as early as 2010: 'one must be mindful of the danger that the Crown, lured by the relative simplicity of the civil courts, will opt for civil recovery at the expense of the criminal trial and its attendant range of protections.'[49] It is unclear as to whether this is an entirely unintended consequence of adopting this hybrid procedure,[50] whose innately malleable design always had the potential to expand into any available space that might arise. Indeed, Home Office Guidance now recognizes:

> Whilst in general the reduction of crime is best secured through criminal investigations and proceedings, civil powers under Parts 5 and 6 of POCA (also referred to in this Guidance as 'non-conviction based asset recovery powers') also make an important contribution to the reduction of crime... There is no strict hierarchy to denote the use of the powers. Nothing in this guidance should prohibit the use of non-conviction based asset recovery powers in an individual case.[51]

[47] EW01.

[48] Liz Campbell, 'The Recovery of "Criminal" Assets in New Zealand, Ireland and England: Fighting Organised and Serious Crime in the Civil Realm' (2010) 41 *Victoria University Wellington Law Review* 15, 35.

[49] Mark Sutherland Williams and Thomas Jaggar, 'Civil Recovery: Then and Now' [2010] *Criminal Bar Quarterly* 5, 6.

[50] For wider discussion of unintended regulatory consequences, see Peter Grabosky, 'Counterproductive Regulation' (1995) 23 *International Journal of the Sociology of Law* 347; Gunther Teubner, 'Legal Irritants: Good Faith in British Law or How Unifying Law Ends Up in New Divergencies' (1998) 61(1) *Modern Law Review* 11.

[51] Home Office, *The Proceeds of Crime Act 2002 (POCA) Guidance Under Section 2A for Relevant Authorities* (28 June 2021), para. 5. Relevant principles for application of criminal and civil powers under POCA are set out at para. 8 of this Guidance. An enforcement official noted: 'In essence the guidance acknowledges that there are many ways to skin a cat if you will pardon the expression. LEAs are encouraged to consider NCB interventions alongside criminal interventions at the outset. Significantly the guidance recognises that NCB may be a better deployment of resources in order to achieve a manageable and proportionate outcome.' EW14.

What is clear, however, is that there is no appetite among respondent-focused interviewees for criminal recovery to replace criminal proceedings: one barrister, who took pains to emphasize that they thought such a development unlikely, told us that for 'there to be no change but that civil recovery were to effectively replace criminal prosecution' would be 'very dangerous'.[52]

The general mood in this regard is one of caution, not least because there is 'no collateral relationship with criminal proceedings at all, and currently there is little to prevent the [enforcement authority] opting for civil recovery as by far the easiest option'.[53] This 'easiest option' emphasis is both notable and pervasive: civil recovery is presented as a more expedient method of targeting criminal assets outside 'the clumsy and expensive unpredictability of the full criminal trial'.[54] As Sittlington and Harvey observe:

> [R]ather than prosecute for the predicate offence, asset recovery and gathering in of criminal funds provides a "route of least resistance". As a consequence, and somewhat rationally, a civil recovery appears to be preferred to a costly time and resource intensive investigation even though a prima facia [*sic*] case is presented.[55]

Resourcing considerations were starkly evidenced by an enforcement official, as follows:

> There are arguments that certain investigations, in terms of value for money, might be better pursued via NCB as opposed to the criminal route... an NCB case we brought saw the recovery of in excess of £10m of assets, a parallel criminal investigation had also resulted in the convictions of a number of targets involved in the supply of drugs. Both investigations took roughly the same amount of time but whereas the criminal investigation was resourced by a whole Branch, the NCB investigation involved only half a dozen members of staff. In terms of resourcing we were able to deliver an outcome that was as impactful in many ways as the criminal outcome, but with a fraction of the resource.[56]

[52] EW07.
[53] Edward Rees, Richard Fisher, and Richard Thomas, *Blackstone's Guide to The Proceeds of Crime Act 2002* (5th edn, Oxford University Press 2015) 171.
[54] Mark Sutherland Williams and Thomas Jaggar, 'Civil Recovery: Then and Now' [2010] *Criminal Bar Quarterly* 5, 6.
[55] Samuel Sittlington and Jackie Harvey, 'Prevention of money laundering and the role of asset recovery' (2018) 70 *Crime, Law and Social Change* 421, 433. There are inherent difficulties with such a pragmatic argument, however; as already mentioned, we will cover these in more detail in Chapter 7.
[56] EW14.

In this example, civil recovery proceedings ran parallel to a criminal investigation and prosecution. It is possible, though, to envisage situations where cost considerations might influence decisions to pursue a civil recovery case *instead of* a criminal prosecution.[57] And there is evidently significant trepidation amongst practitioners representing respondents in civil recovery proceedings concerning the lack of criminal conviction and the sidestepping of criminal procedural safeguards. Such concerns are particularly apparent in relation to the presumption of innocence and the standard of proof, to which we now turn our attention.

Presumption of Innocence

It is axiomatic that a person ought to be regarded as innocent until such time as a guilty verdict is rendered following criminal trial.[58] In a criminal trial, in both Ireland and England & Wales, the burden of proof is on the prosecution to establish the defendant's guilt beyond reasonable doubt. Although the presumption of innocence does not strictly require such a standard, the beyond reasonable doubt standard of proof is a product of the values that underlie the presumption.[59] The presumption is further enshrined in international instruments, notably Article 6(2) of the European Convention on Human Rights (ECHR), which states: 'Everyone charged with a criminal offence shall be presumed innocent until proved guilty according to law.'

The use of purportedly civil or hybrid processes bypasses this important safeguard.[60] Moreover, the underpinning crime control rationale is clear: the operation of the higher standard can make it impossible to prosecute and/or convict in criminal proceedings—for example, there may be no or insufficient evidence linking an individual to a particular offence—and the NCB approach

[57] A possibility reflected in the Guidance: 'Where there is a criminal investigation or prosecution, a relevant authority may decide that non-conviction based asset recovery, in whole or in part, is a better deployment of resources to the asset recovery aspects of the case, in order to achieve a manageable and proportionate outcome.' Home Office, *The Proceeds of Crime Act 2002 (POCA) Guidance Under Section 2A for Relevant Authorities* (28 June 2021) para. 8.

[58] *Woolmington v DPP* [1935] AC 462; *O'Leary v AG* [1993] 1 IR 102.

[59] Antony Duff, Lindsay Farmer, Sandra Marshall, and Victor Tadros, *The Trial on Trial, Volume 3: Towards a Normative Theory of the Criminal Trial* (Hart 2007) 89. The standard of proof is considered further later in this chapter.

[60] See, e.g., Simon Young, 'Enforcing Criminal Law Through Civil Processes: How Does Human Rights Law Treat "Civil for Criminal Processes"?' (2017) 4(2) *Journal of International and Comparative Law* 133; Jennifer Hendry and Colin King, 'Expediency, Legitimacy, and the Rule of Law: A Systems Perspective on Civil/ Criminal Procedural Hybrids' (2017) 11(4) *Criminal Law and Philosophy* 733.

offers a viable, if admittedly lesser, alternative.[61] 'What could be simpler,' asks Ashworth in the context of the presumption of innocence, 'than for a government to circumvent the presumption by promoting legislation that provides for the imposition of civil orders on citizens?'[62]

Given that civil recovery proceedings will often include an allegation that the respondent has engaged in, or benefitted from, criminal conduct, there is an intuitive appeal in the argument that the presumption of innocence ought to apply. Such an argument is strengthened by the fact that a successful civil recovery application will almost inevitably expose the respondent to stigma and/or community condemnation; as Campbell states, asset recovery 'incorporates a substantial stigma and incorporates the blame that distinguishes criminal from civil measures'.[63] According to Boucht, 'the holder of the property is in effect singled out as having been associated with criminal activity. Conceptual re-labelling from criminal to civil does not necessarily affect the factual perception of the measure.'[64] Moreover, the terminology of the legislation in both England & Wales and Ireland reinforces this concern—'proceeds of crime', 'unlawful conduct' (England & Wales), and 'criminal conduct' (Ireland) inevitably lead the general public to believe that a person subject to a civil recovery order is, or has previously been, involved in criminality.[65] The contention that the civil recovery action is directed against the property itself (actions *in rem*)[66] rather than against the individual (actions *in personam*) is similarly difficult to defend.[67] This *in rem* justification is based on the premise that it is not the individual in possession of the property who is punished but rather *the property itself*. As Gallant points out, '[i]t is of course entirely artificial to say that the property is "at fault". Property has no ability to act on its own; it is controlled or used by an individual'.[68] The confiscation of property in civil recovery

[61] Anthony Kennedy, 'Designing a Civil Forfeiture System: An Issues List for Policymakers and Legislators' (2006) 13(2) *Journal of Financial Crime* 132.

[62] Andrew Ashworth, 'Four Threats to the Presumption of Innocence' (2006) 10(4) *International Journal of Evidence and Proof* 241, 270.

[63] Liz Campbell, 'Criminal Labels, the European Convention on Human Rights and the Presumption of Innocence' (2013) 76(4) *Modern Law Review* 681, 705.

[64] Johan Boucht, 'Asset Confiscation in Europe—Past, Present, and Future Challenges' (2019) 26(2) *Journal of Financial Crime* 526, 541.

[65] See, e.g., Conor Lally, 'CAB officers carry out raids across eight counties', *The Irish Times* (14 November 2019) which refers to 'a large family-based network of drug dealers'; National Crime Agency, 'Eight-year NCA investigation denies organised crime group £17 million property portfolio' (26 August 2020) where it is stated that 'NCA officers established that the properties were acquired using the proceeds of crime including heroin importation and distribution, fraud and money laundering'.

[66] For wider discussion, see George Fraser Jr, 'Actions in Rem' (1948) 34(1) *Cornell Law Review* 29.

[67] See Chapter 6 for a discussion of property rights and the designation of civil recovery as an action *in rem*.

[68] Michelle Gallant, *Money Laundering and the Proceeds of Crime: Economic Crime and Civil Remedies* (Edward Elgar 2005) 57.

proceedings might present as an action taken against the property itself, but it is frankly impossible 'to declare a car or house or bank account to be the proceeds of cocaine sales, for example, without simultaneously smearing its owner with the accusation of drug trafficking'.[69] Thus, deprivation of property is *de facto* accompanied by allegations of criminality and associated criminal labelling and stigma, which inevitably go to the heart of the presumption of innocence.[70]

A further concern is that the non-conviction-based route can give the state another bite at the cherry: where a criminal prosecution has been unsuccessful, for whatever reason, the acquitted defendant can nonetheless still be pursued in civil recovery proceedings based on *the very same allegations and evidence*.[71] In *SOCA v Olden*, Holroyde J opined that an enforcement agency:

> may seek, and the court grant, a recovery order *even though* the respondent has either not been prosecuted or has been prosecuted and acquitted; *even though* the criminal and civil proceedings raise similar issues; and *even though* the evidence relied upon in the civil proceedings is the same as, or includes, the evidence used in the unsuccessful prosecution. There is therefore built into the statute the prospect that there may be different outcomes to criminal and civil proceedings founded on the same evidence and allegations.[72]

While an acquittal does not, of course, establish factual innocence,[73] the subsequent use of civil recovery in such circumstances effectively runs roughshod over that acquittal. At a minimum it undermines the certainty of the acquittal—a point acknowledged by Collins J in *T*:

> I appreciate the argument that there is considerable oppression as the matter is viewed from the point of view of the defendants. They were acquitted, they believed that was the end of the matter, they heard a judge state that in his view the system had gone wrong and the prosecution should not proceed. Unfortunately, the law is now such that these Part V proceedings can be

[69] RT Naylor 'Wash-out: A Critique of Follow-the-Money Methods in Crime Control Policy' (1999) *Crime, Law and Social Change* 1, 41.

[70] Such issues are explored further in relation to the standard of proof in the next section.

[71] *Director of the Assets Recovery Agency v Taher* [2006] EWHC 3406 (Admin); *Director of the Assets Recovery Agency v Kean* [2007] EWHC 112 (Admin).

[72] [2009] EWHC 610 (QB), para. 30, emphasis added. In *Gale v SOCA* [2011] UKSC 49, para. 44 Lord Phillips stated: 'If confiscation proceedings do not involve a criminal charge, but are subject to the civil standard of proof, I see no reason in principle why confiscation should not be based on evidence that satisfies the civil standard, notwithstanding that it has proved insufficiently compelling to found a conviction on application of the criminal standard.'

[73] An acquittal establishes that guilt has not been established to the criminal standard of proof.

> brought. Even an acquittal is not necessarily nowadays the end of the matter. If the Director feels that she is able to establish that particular property has been obtained through unlawful means, then she can take these proceedings. It is in the public interest, so Parliament has decided, that no-one shall profit from ill-gotten gains, if they can be identified.[74]

Of course, an acquittal in criminal proceedings does not preclude subsequent action from being taken against the now-acquitted defendant: for example, even though a defendant might be acquitted of assault charges, civil proceedings might be initiated by the victim against that same person for the same actions.[75] That notwithstanding, 'the voicing of suspicions regarding an accused's innocence is no longer admissible' post-acquittal.[76] Of central importance in this regard is whether the relevant issues are a consequence of the criminal proceedings that resulted in the acquittal,[77] which is to say: is there a link between the question of criminal responsibility and the subsequent legal proceedings?[78] The acquittal must also be respected by any authority's reference—whether directly or indirectly—to the criminal liability of the individual concerned.[79] In *Allen*, the Grand Chamber reinforced the effect of the presumption of innocence:

> Article 6(2) safeguards the right to be 'presumed innocent until proved guilty according to law'. Viewed as a procedural guarantee in the context of a criminal trial itself, the presumption of innocence imposes requirements in respect of, *inter alia*, the burden of proof ...; legal presumptions of fact and law ...; the privilege against self-incrimination ...; pre-trial publicity ...; and premature expressions, by the trial court or by other public officials, of a defendant's guilt ....
>
> However, in keeping with the need to ensure that the right guaranteed by Article 6(2) is practical and effective, the presumption of innocence also has another aspect. Its general aim, in this second aspect, is to protect individuals who have been acquitted of a criminal charge, or in respect of whom criminal proceedings have been discontinued, from being treated by public officials

[74] *Director of the Assets Recovery Agency v T* [2004] EWHC 3340 (Admin), para. 21.
[75] *Y v Norway* [2005] 41 EHRR 7, para. 41.
[76] *Rushiti v Austria* [2001] 33 EHRR 56, para. 31.
[77] *Moullet v France* App. No. 27521/04, 13 September 2007; *Sekanina v Austria* [1994] 17 EHRR 221.
[78] *Allen v UK* App. No. 25424/09, 12 July 2013.
[79] *Vassilios Stavropoulos v Greece* App. No. 35522/04, 27 September 2007; *Tendam v Spain* App. No. 25720/05, 13 July 2010.

> and authorities as though they are in fact guilty of the offence charged. In these cases, the presumption of innocence has already operated, through the application at trial of the various requirements inherent in the procedural guarantee it affords, to prevent an unfair criminal conviction being imposed. Without protection to ensure respect for the acquittal or the discontinuation decision in any other proceedings, the fair-trial guarantees of Article 6(2) could risk becoming theoretical and illusory. What is also at stake once the criminal proceedings have concluded is the person's reputation and the way in which that person is perceived by the public. To a certain extent, the protection afforded under Article 6(2) in this respect may overlap with the protection afforded by Article 8 . . . .[80]

In the context of compensation following miscarriages of justice, specifically following the quashing of a conviction, the Grand Chamber stated the following:

> [T]he presumption of innocence means that where there has been a criminal charge and criminal proceedings have ended in an acquittal, the person who was the subject of the criminal proceedings is innocent in the eyes of the law and *must be treated in a manner consistent with that innocence.* To this extent, therefore, the presumption of innocence will remain after the conclusion of criminal proceedings in order to ensure that, as regards any charge which was not proven, the innocence of the person in question is respected.[81]

Post-acquittal, therefore, an individual is *entitled* to be presumed innocent. Difficulty arises, however, where—based on the same allegations and often on the same evidence—that acquitted individual is alleged to have benefitted from their own criminal conduct and is subsequently confronted with civil recovery proceedings. In *Olden*, for example, the application was for 'a Recovery Order in relation to property which is alleged to be, or to represent, the proceeds of the unlawful conduct of the Respondent ("Mr Olden")'.[82] The effect in such

[80] *Allen v UK* App. No. 25424/09, 12 July 2013, paras 93–94 (references omitted). See also *Balsamo v San Marino* App. Nos 20319/17 and 21414/17, 10 September 2019 and 8 October 2019, paras 71–72 in the context of asset confiscation.

[81] *Allen v UK* App. No. 25424/09, 12 July 2013, para. 103, emphasis added. In that instance, the Strasbourg Court determined that the application was admissible but that, on the facts, there was no violation of Art. 6(2).

[82] *SOCA v Olden* [2009] EWHC 610 (QB), para. 1. The false statements underpinning the unlawful conduct of Mr Olden are set out in detail at para. 47 et seq. The court went on to state, *inter alia*: 'it is perfectly clear from the evidence adduced by SOCA that Mr Olden was acting dishonestly in each and every one of the mortgage transactions to which SOCA point' (para. 57). Similarly, in *Taher* [2006] EWHC 3406 (Admin) the allegations were that the respondent engaged in advance fee fraud.

situations, as Gallant and King argue, is that '[i]n essence, a person is being "punished" for his wrongdoing, albeit in civil proceedings, having been found "guilty", in the eyes of both the State and his fellow citizens, of the offence for which he had been previously acquitted'.[83] For Campbell, what is most problematic in this context is a declaration of guilt *in the guise* of asset seizure described as 'proceeds of crime', without proof beyond reasonable doubt.[84]

Criticisms of the NCB approach, and its impact on the presumption of innocence, were explored in our interviews. Unsurprisingly, any levelling of criminal allegations without respect for the criminal process' enhanced procedural protections attracted serious consternation. One criminal defence solicitor conveyed this in the following colourful example:

> I had a client a couple of years ago who I suspect was a serious player in the drug business; although in fact he was never accused of drugs offence .... But in the affidavit, in the Grounding Affidavit, he was nominated for at least six murders, at least six murders. Named as the person being responsible. The person responsible can be a remote person so you can just give an order that someone be shot and that's fine but one would have thought that, if you were going to nominate somebody for six murders, you would at least carry out a rudimentary criminal investigation to the extent that the person should be arrested and questioned. But that man was never questioned for murder. In fact he was never questioned about a drugs offence, so he was a very slippery character in Teflon terms if he was the big criminal that CAB had him fingered as being. Now I don't have a problem with CAB going after people who are such successful criminals that they have no obvious assets to get hold of and I've no particular problem with CAB using the tax system to get after people like that but I do have a problem with them putting up affidavits to say that they are responsible for murders because it has no relevance to the proceeds of crime application.[85]

In this regard, the principle of legality is undermined. Referring to the well-known example of Al Capone being convicted of tax evasion,[86] Alldridge explains: 'The principle of legality requires that if the authorities want to claim

[83] Michelle Gallant and Colin King, 'The Seizure of Illicit Assets: Patterns of Civil Forfeiture in Canada and Ireland' (2013) 42 *Common Law World Review* 91, 97.
[84] Liz Campbell, 'Criminal Labels, the European Convention on Human Rights and the Presumption of Innocence' (2013) 76(4) *Modern Law Review* 681, 706.
[85] IRE08.
[86] See, e.g., *Capone v US*, 56 F.2d 927 (7th Cir. 1932).

that Capone is a murdering racketeer they should be compelled to make that allegation in court, and produce evidence of those offences.'[87] Another defence solicitor adopted a broad approach to the presumption of innocence,[88] stating that unless the authorities prove that an individual has committed a crime 'then everyone is innocent. There are no two ways about it, you are innocent until proven guilty'. They contended that, absent conviction, all civil recovery proceedings 'are against innocent people'.[89]

Notwithstanding the view that civil recovery might be against *innocent* people, it is evident that such proceedings are often taken against suspected criminals where criminal prosecution is, for whatever reason, not possible. In such circumstances, suspicion comes very much to the fore. One defence solicitor referred to an instance where civil recovery proceedings were initiated even though there was nothing unlawful in what the individual was doing; they noted that the authorities 'don't believe that he's telling the truth, because it's highly suspicious'.[90] That interviewee expressed the view that the circumstances may have appeared suspicious to the police, but that it was not out of the ordinary for the individual involved to be dealing with large sums of cash.[91] Suspicion is thus the central focus: as the example above shows, it is seen as fair game to include within civil recovery proceedings any other suspicions, no matter whether there is evidence to support it. This is deeply concerning: in criminal proceedings there are detailed rules as to when, for example, evidence of bad character might be admitted,[92] but civil proceedings are subject to no comparable restriction. Such opening up of the process to influences such as suspicion is hugely problematic,[93] not least in terms of the ease with which suspicion pivots into prejudice.[94]

In the interviews, we asked whether the *in rem* nature of civil recovery was a safeguard for the respondent, in that the action is against the property and there are no allegations against that person. Even some enforcement-focused barristers acknowledged:

[87] Peter Alldridge, *Money Laundering Law: Forfeiture, Confiscation, Civil Recovery, Criminal Laundering and Taxation of the Proceeds of Crime* (Hart 2003) 248.

[88] For consideration of broad and narrow approaches, see Pamela Ferguson, 'The Presumption of Innocence and its Role in the Criminal Process' (2016) 27 *Criminal Law Forum* 131.

[89] EW08.

[90] EW01.

[91] EW01.

[92] Mike Redmayne, *Character in the Criminal Trial* (Oxford University Press 2015).

[93] For further consideration of suspicion, see Chapter 7.

[94] For more on prejudice relative to the use of hybrid procedures, see Jennifer Hendry, '"The Usual Suspects": Knife Crime Prevention Orders and the "Difficult" Regulatory Subject' (2022) 62(2) *British Journal of Criminology* 378.

> It's a complete fiction obviously, that you sue the piece of property or you apply in relation to the property... ultimately you do have to have an identifiable party who you say is responsible for the wrongdoing or for the shielding of the profits of the wrongdoing.[95]

There was also considerable scepticism amongst respondent-focused practitioners concerning the *in rem* argument,[96] with interviewees pointing out that, in reality, more often than not it is the respondent who is accused of criminality.[97] Such contentions echo academic criticism of the *in rem/in personam* distinction in civil recovery proceedings.[98] One interviewee emphatically rejected the contention of proponents that civil recovery proceedings only target property and do not involve criminal allegations: 'It doesn't work like that in practice. I'm fed up with [this argument]. They know it's artificial. They can't get their case proven, even on the balance of probabilities, without showing that the person who is the respondent has committed the crime.'[99] While opinions from respondent-focused interviewees on this point were broadly consistent across both jurisdictions, one clear difference identified across the practitioner interviews was the issue of civil recovery proceedings post-acquittal, which has tended to arise in England & Wales more so than in Ireland. In interviews, post-acquittal civil recovery did not arise in discussion with Irish participants,[100] whereas it generated significant debate in the England & Wales interviews. Moreover, the possibility of post-acquittal civil recovery was explicitly acknowledged in Parliamentary debates prior to the enactment of the Proceeds of Crime Act (POCA) (England & Wales) in 2002: 'It is clearly conceivable, therefore, that there could be circumstances in which a person's assets could be recovered even though his conviction on a specific offence had failed.'[101] Proponent interviewees echoed this stance: 'Acquittal at a criminal trial merely means that the evidence wasn't sufficient, it doesn't mean to say that you definitely did not do something. Because of the *in rem* nature of what

[95] IRE09.

[96] We consider the *in rem* nature of civil recovery in more detail in Chapter 6.

[97] EW07.

[98] Colin King, 'Civil Forfeiture and Article 6 of the ECHR: Due Process Implications for England & Wales and Ireland' (2014) 34(3) *Legal Studies* 371, 378–9; Liz Campbell, 'The Recovery of "Criminal" Assets in New Zealand, Ireland and England: Fighting Organised and Serious Crime in the Civil Realm' (2010) 41 *Victoria University Wellington Law Review* 15, 25–6; RT Naylor, 'Wash-out: A Critique of Follow-the-Money Methods in Crime Control' (1999) 32 *Crime, Law & Social Change* 1, 41.

[99] EW07.

[100] Only one practitioner (IRE05) in Ireland addressed this issue and that was to defend post-acquittal civil recovery.

[101] HC Deb 30 October 2001, vol. 373, col. 761, per Mr Denham (Minister for Police, Courts and Drugs).

we do, it's not as if we are having another bite of the cherry at the defendant, what we are doing is targeting the property.'[102] In contrast, respondent-focused interviewees expressed criticism: a barrister described a situation where their client had been acquitted at trial but the National Crime Agency (NCA) subsequently relied upon some of the evidence from the criminal case for civil recovery proceedings. This interviewee objected to this, declaring:

> There is case law on this—basically what the NCA can't do is question an acquittal. However, in the cases I have come across the NCA have appeared to do just that or come very very close to it. Two bites at the cherry in my view should never be permitted. Civil jurisdiction should be used instead of a prosecution not in addition to a prosecution. It smacks of State persecution and relentless pursuit and disregard of a not guilty verdict.[103]

A defence solicitor opined: 'It's absolutely ridiculous. It is a second bite of the cherry, and of course it's exactly the same issues, it's the same case.'[104] They continued: 'You now have to prove on the balance of probabilities that it isn't bent; the prosecution not having been able to prove at criminal trial that it is bent; you now have to prove on the balance of probabilities that it isn't bent. Just to get your money back.'[105] Another interviewee stated, 'It doesn't feel right. But it's not *in personam*, and that is exactly why the legislation is put there. It's very unhappy.'[106]

Furthermore, where acquittal stems from exclusion of evidence,[107] it could be expected that that evidence would also be excluded in any subsequent NCB proceedings:

> If evidence has been excluded from the criminal case because a suspect's Article 6 or 8 rights have been infringed ... and if that's true of the Crown Court, the evidence being excluded, then I can't understand why it's not the same in a civil recovery case, why it's not also excluded.[108]

[102] EW14. This view was echoed by an enforcement barrister: 'I don't see anything really wrong with it. It is what it is, it's a different area of law and it is against the asset.' EW09. Similarly, an Irish enforcement official stated that, post-acquittal, 'We could still bring our proceeds of crime case. There's nothing wrong with that.' IRE05.

[103] EW04.

[104] EW01.

[105] EW01.

[106] EW07.

[107] As was the case in *Olden v SOCA* [2010] EWCA Civ 143. Different considerations impact the weight to be attached to an acquittal: *SOCA v Namli and Topinvest Holding International Ltd* [2013] EWHC 1200 (QBD).

[108] EW04.

To give an example: if evidence obtained during an unlawful arrest, search and interview were excluded from the criminal trial,[109] it might be expected that the same evidence would also be inadmissible in civil recovery proceedings. That has not proven to be the case, however. Indeed, in *Olden* the following was stated: 'It seems to me that there is a clear distinction between the admission of evidence in criminal proceedings leading to imprisonment, and the admission of evidence in civil proceedings aimed at recovering property to which (if the application be made out) the respondent has never had any legitimate entitlement.'[110] In practice, it appears that enforcement officials tread carefully in this regard:

> As an enforcement authority we would certainly want to know exactly what has happened, and if there is any misfeasance around that particular evidence we would not be touching that evidence with a barge pole. We would not be proceeding on the basis of evidence that had been excluded at a previous trial.[111]

In this regard the enforcement officials can be said to act as gatekeepers—a role that is discussed further in Chapter 7. This notwithstanding, the courts are receptive to the use of such evidence, and the absence of specific safeguards in this respect (described as 'fairness provisions') was acknowledged by an enforcement barrister to be 'a serious deficiency'.[112]

In civil proceedings, the courts do, of course, have power to exclude evidence that would otherwise be admissible.[113] In exercising this discretion the courts will seek to give effect to the 'overriding objective' of the Civil Procedure Rules, namely 'enabling the court to deal with cases justly and at proportionate cost'.[114] While there will inevitably be tensions between the administration of justice and the exclusion of material obtained unlawfully,[115] in the context of civil recovery this tension is embodied in the admission of evidence *previously excluded* in the separate criminal proceedings. The effect of this approach is that evidence excluded from a criminal trial in the Crown Court is admissible in civil proceedings in the High Court concerned with, in essence, the very same allegations. As one interviewee put it: there is thus 'a difference

109 This example is based on the facts of *Olden* [2009] EWHC 610 (QB), paras 13–14.
110 *Olden* [2009] EWHC 610 (QB), para. 44.
111 EW14.
112 EW09.
113 CPR 32.1.
114 CPR 1.1.
115 *Jones v University of Warwick* [2003] EWCA Civ 151.

of application between the Crown Court and the High Court of fundamental principles, and that can't be the way forward'.[116]

Standard of Proof

In criminal proceedings, the standard of proof is beyond reasonable doubt,[117] a high standard justified on several grounds.[118] One of these grounds is the minimization of the risk of error, as encapsulated in the maxim that it is better ten guilty people go free than for one innocent person to be punished wrongly.[119] Another justification is that individuals have a right to a fair trial involving a rigorous independent evaluation of the evidence against them. An accused person should not be convicted on the basis of suspicion—even where that suspicion is accompanied by evidence—until the state has established guilt to a high standard. Given the potential consequences of conviction, moreover—not only the deprivation of liberty but also the labelling as 'criminal' and its associated stigma—securing conviction should not be straightforward for the state. As Lippke notes, we 'permit individuals accused of crimes to insist that the evidence developed by state officials against them be put to a rigorous and dispositive test. We make the test a stern one because so much is at stake for those accused of crimes'.[120]

Criminal conviction can thus be distinguished from an adverse civil judgment, where the civil standard of proof—the balance of probabilities—may be more appropriate. The issue of appropriateness is significant here, as this is the standard of proof employed in civil recovery proceedings, notwithstanding the criminal allegations that usually underpin such proceedings. This is the case in both Ireland and England & Wales: although the Irish POCA legislation simply provides that the standard of proof is 'that applicable to civil proceedings',[121]

[116] EW04. A defence solicitor stated that, in civil recovery proceedings, 'Judges will be able to make an assessment about the veracity of the evidence rather than the issue of fairness.' EW08.

[117] Though it is acknowledged that it is possible to conceive of a presumption that requires the prosecution to establish guilt on the balance of probabilities: Andrew Ashworth, 'Four Threats to the Presumption of Innocence' (2006) 10 *International Journal of Evidence and Proof* 241, 250.

[118] For detailed consideration of justifications, see Richard Lippke, 'Justifying the Proof Structure of Criminal Trials' (2013) 17(4) *International Journal of Evidence and Proof* 323.

[119] Different numbers are suggested, such as a 10:1 or a 100:1 ratio. For wider discussion, see Vidar Halvorsen, 'Is it Better that Ten Guilty Persons Go Free Than that One Innocent Person be Convicted?' (2004) 23(2) *Criminal Justice Ethics* 3.

[120] Richard Lippke, 'Justifying the Proof Structure of Criminal Trials' (2013) 17(4) *International Journal of Evidence and Proof* 323, 345–6.

[121] POCA 1996 (Ire), s. 8(2).

this has been interpreted as the balance of probabilities,[122] whereas section 241(3) POCA England & Wales explicitly specifies the balance of probabilities as the requisite standard.[123] The latter approach thus explicitly avoids the possibility of the courts applying fluctuating or variable civil standards of proof.[124] The balance of probabilities has in fact been described as 'the hallmark of civil recovery', to the extent that if it 'were to be replaced with the criminal one (beyond reasonable doubt), then the whole civil recovery regime would almost certainly be fatally damaged'.[125]

Much of this foundational quality within civil recovery stems from how the balance of probabilities standard has been justified relative to difficulties in prosecuting those at the upper echelons of organized criminal activities.[126] In other words, so the argument goes, the balance of probabilities is warranted where 'it is as plain as a pikestaff'[127] that particular property represents the proceeds of crime, but where criminal prosecution is not possible. Its effect, however, is quite clearly to allow for criminal allegations to be tested against the civil standard of proof. This has proven controversial, not least because it is 'significantly easier to prove matters of fact and law to the civil standard of a balance of probabilities than it is to prove the same beyond a reasonable doubt'.[128] Efficiency and instrumentality are thus prioritized over certainty, and due process safeguards are diluted.

Criminal allegations being made on the civil standard did attract criticism from respondent-focused interviewees, although it was acknowledged that this was where the value in civil recovery lay: 'that's what makes it an effective

[122] *Banco Ambrosiano SPA v Ansbacher and Co Ltd* [1987] ILRM 669; *Masterfoods Ltd v HB Ice Cream Ltd* [1993] ILRM 145. In the context of POCA, see *Murphy v GM, PB, PC Ltd, GH; Gilligan v CAB* [2001] 4 IR 113; *FJM v TH and JH*, unreported, High Court, O'Sullivan J, 29 June 2001.

[123] In earlier proceeds of crime legislation, the legislative wording tended to specify 'the standard applicable in civil proceedings' as the relevant standard.

[124] In *Bater v Bater* [1951–52] P 35, 36–37 Denning LG stated: 'in civil cases, the case may be proved by a preponderance of probability, but there may be degrees of probability within that standard. The degree depends on the subject-matter.' See also *Hornal v Neuberger Products Ltd* [1957] 1 QB 247. The authorities are reviewed in *R (On the application of AN) v Secretary of State for the Home Department* [2005] EWCA Civ 1605. For consideration in different contexts, see: *Clingham v Royal Borough of Kensington and Chelsea; R v Crown Court at Manchester, Ex p McCann* [2002] UKHL 39 (anti-social behaviour orders); *Re H (Minors)* [1995] UKHL 16; *Re LU (A Child); Re LB (A Child)* [2004] EWCA Civ 567; *Re B (Children)* [2008] UKHL 35 (child protection cases); *B v Chief Constable of Avon and Somerset Constabulary* [2000] EWHC 559 (sex offender order); and *Gough v Chief Constable of the Derbyshire Constabulary* [2002] EWCA Civ 351 (football banning order). For a critique, see Mike Redmayne, 'Standards of Proof in Civil Litigation' (1999) 62 *Modern Law Review* 167.

[125] Ian Smith, 'Civil Asset Recovery: The English Experience' in Jon Petter Rui and Ulrich Sieber (eds), *Non-Conviction-Based Confiscation in Europe* (Duncker & Humblot 2015) 33.

[126] Dáil Éireann, Private Members' Business—Organised Crime (Restraint and Disposal of Illicit Assets) Bill, 1996, Second Stage, 2 July 1996 vol. 467; HC Deb 30 October 2001, vol. 373, cols 757–760.

[127] HL Deb, Proceeds of Crime Bill, 25 June 2002, vol. 636, col. 1271.

[128] Michelle Gallant, *Money Laundering and the Proceeds of Crime: Economic Crime and Civil Remedies* (Edward Elgar 2005) 19.

piece of legislation from [the enforcement agencies] point of view.'[129] One participant's rejection of the justificatory classification of civil recovery as a civil process was particularly emphatic:

> And they come into court and say it's really a civil action. Fuck off. Sorry. As far as I am concerned, most times, in a civil case, if the proper civil standard was being applied, they wouldn't get their noses across the line. They get their noses across the line because the High Court has made a clear policy decision, and the Supreme Court as well, a clear policy decision, that CAB is to be supported.[130]

Once again, the centrality of the civil/criminal distinction within civil recovery comes to the fore.

In spite of the definitive position adopted by the courts,[131] among respondent-focused interviewees there is still considerable consternation as regards the purposeful undermining of procedural protections. As one barrister stated: 'it's still a lower standard of proof; it shouldn't be',[132] a concern echoed by the Irish Council for Civil Liberties representative: 'I think that that's why I am uneasy about [non-conviction based confiscation].'[133] In the context of levelling criminal allegations within civil proceedings—something that is, of course, not prohibited[134]—it is important here to distinguish between situations whereby one private party sues another, compared to the state taking action against an individual in order to confiscate proceeds of crime. The power asymmetry alone in the latter case should warrant the use of the higher standard of proof.

Respondent-focused interviewees acknowledged that there have been some prominent cases where the civil standard was applied without issue.[135] However, 'once the precedent is established', the more complex cases end up

[129] IRE01. The combination of the civil standard of proof and provision for belief evidence has attracted particular criticism: for further discussion, see Colin King, 'The Difficulties of Belief Evidence and Anonymity in Practice—Challenges for Asset Recovery' in Colin King, Clive Walker, and Jimmy Gurulé (eds), *The Palgrave Handbook of Criminal and Terrorism Financing Law* (Palgrave 2018).

[130] IRE08.

[131] *Murphy v GM, PB, PC Ltd, GH; Gilligan v CAB* [2001] 4 IR 113; *Gale v SOCA* [2011] UKSC 49. For discussion, see Chapter 4.

[132] EW04.

[133] IRE10. This feeling of unease concerning the standard of proof was echoed by a defence solicitor as follows: 'the civil standard makes it easier to keep the assets without even proving that someone has committed a crime, and that is my biggest issue with NCB'. EW08.

[134] For detailed consideration in different contexts, see Simon Young, 'Enforcing Criminal Law Through Civil Processes: How Does Human Rights Law Treat "Civil for Criminal Processes"?' (2017) 4(2) *Journal of International and Comparative Law* 133.

[135] EW01.

falling within that same approach: the authorities bring 'the best [case] that they've got at the start, because then you've got the principles, and judiciary on the principles, and then off you go'.[136] This kind of slippery slope argument was prevalent: that same interviewee expressed the view that it is going 'against all of the principles that we've all grown up with, the criminal standard; it's opening the door a little', continuing to explain that the application of the balance of probabilities standard in more difficult situations would be 'bloody unfair'.[137] There was concern among respondent-focused interviewees about what was perceived as the erosion of procedural protections, even to the extent that, in some instances, they have advised clients to agree a settlement given the practical difficulties that they would face given the lower standard of proof.[138]

In light of criticism as to the standard of proof, the academic literature has considered the option of applying, in civil recovery cases, a higher standard than the balance of probabilities.[139] Such proposals for a third way, middleground, or elevated civil standard are unsurprising given developments in other contexts,[140] not to mention the explicit rejection in Parliamentary debates of the prospect of applying within civil recovery actions the criminal standard of proof beyond reasonable doubt. This rejection was given on the grounds that '[i]t is not practical for the burden of proof in civil recovery ever to be as high as that in criminal proceedings, or one would not be able to succeed where one had already failed',[141] and reinforces our earlier disquiet that the non-conviction-based approach is specifically intended to be used in circumstances where an individual has already been acquitted in criminal proceedings.

Scholars exhibit a range of viewpoints in this regard. For example, Boucht acknowledges that '[t]o assert the criminal standard in NCB confiscation would have practical consequences, and could seriously impede the efficiency of the system'[142] but suggests a compromise. 'Considering the nature of NCB confiscation proceedings,' he notes, 'a plausible standard of proof for civil asset confiscation, particularly where there has been a prior acquittal, would seem to

[136] EW01.
[137] EW01.
[138] EW04.
[139] Calls for a 'clear and convincing' standard of proof have been aired in the United States: see, e.g., Eric Moores, 'Reforming the Civil Asset Forfeiture Reform Act' [2009] 51 *Arizona Law Review* 777, 799–801.
[140] See the caselaw cited in n.124.
[141] HC Deb 26 February 2002, vol. 380, col. 658, per Vera Baird. For consideration in the Irish context, see Dáil Éireann, Proceeds of Crime Bill, 1996: Report and Final Stages, 25 July 1996, vol. 468.
[142] Johan Boucht, *The Limits of Asset Confiscation: On the Legitimacy of Extended Appropriation of Criminal Proceeds* (Hart 2017) 225.

be an *enhanced (or qualified) balance of probability*'.[143] As he explains: 'A higher standard of proof than the balance of probabilities would serve at least two important aims: it would ensure that the property in question truly is liable to confiscation, and it would improve consistency in that NCB confiscation proceedings would resemble criminal proceedings due to their quasi-criminal nature.'[144] In the context of quasi-criminal proceedings, Campbell similarly argues in favour of an elevated civil standard of proof:

> If the state seems to be using the civil process to circumvent the criminal trial, this may suggest that the requisite standard of proof may need to be re-examined. The relevance of the presumption [of innocence] here affects the standard of proof required for establishing liability and implies that the balance of probabilities should be reconsidered in relation to certain official labels. Though the absence of 'hard treatment' implies that proof beyond reasonable doubt is too onerous a standard, I suggest that at least 'clear and convincing evidence' ought be [*sic*] required when the presumption is affected in these contexts.[145]

Campbell explicitly envisages such a standard of proof not only for civil recovery orders but also in proceedings concerned with Anti-Social Behaviour Orders (ASBOs) and control orders[146] where such orders are publicized. She continues:

> In this context not only can stigma accrue, but there is also an intention to label, to deter others from the particular behaviour through expression of suspicion regarding culpability, and to condemn the person's pattern of behaviour or lifestyle. This constitutes a declaration of guilt, albeit in relation to criminality in general rather than one specific crime, based on the civil standard of proof. Nonetheless, I argue that these issues are not irremediable, given that altering of the standard of proof and requiring anonymity would provide sufficient protection for the individual involved.[147]

[143] Johan Boucht, *The Limits of Asset Confiscation: On the Legitimacy of Extended Appropriation of Criminal Proceeds* (Hart 2017) 226–7. Emphasis added.

[144] Johan Boucht, *The Limits of Asset Confiscation: On the Legitimacy of Extended Appropriation of Criminal Proceeds* (Hart 2017) 225. See also Eric L Jensen and Jurg Gerber, 'The Civil Forfeiture of Assets and the War on Drugs: Expanding Criminal Sanctions While Reducing Due Process Protections' (1996) 42 *Crime & Delinquency* 421, 426 et seq.

[145] Liz Campbell, 'Criminal Labels, the European Convention on Human Rights and the Presumption of Innocence' (2013) 76(4) *Modern Law Review* 681, 694.

[146] For more on civil preventive orders, see Chapter 2.

[147] Liz Campbell, 'Criminal Labels, the European Convention on Human Rights and the Presumption of Innocence' (2013) 76(4) *Modern Law Review* 681, 701.

Redmayne is also in favour of this intermediate standard of 'clear and convincing evidence', although his focus was on 'regular' civil cases: for him, the differences between civil and criminal litigation were salient.[148] Our position, however, is that even an elevated civil standard along the lines of those proposed above is insufficient. In spite of the fact that civil recovery cases involve no deprivation of liberty, we contend that the potential for harm[149] means that the criminal standard of proof beyond reasonable doubt ought to be applied.[150] We are not alone in this regard: the criminal standard is also advocated in the civil recovery context by Virdi, primarily on the grounds of protecting the presumption of innocence,[151] while Lord Steyn took a similar position in terms of another procedural hybrid, the ASBO.[152] In his view: 'pragmatism dictates that the task of magistrates should be made more straightforward by ruling that they must in all cases under section 1 apply the criminal standard... This approach should facilitate correct decision-making and should ensure consistency and predictability in this corner of the law.'[153] Our stance is founded on arguments similar to those advanced by Campbell, specifically the goal of deterrence, the levelling of criminal allegations, the potential for stigma, and – fundamentally—the declaration of 'guilt'. This position is largely based on our contention that civil recovery ought to be regarded as a criminal, not civil, measure,[154] although this is not a view shared by the courts, who have on this basis rejected arguments in favour of a heightened standard of proof. In *He and Chen*, for example, the court stated:

[148] Mike Redmayne, 'Standards of Proof in Civil Litigation' (1999) 62 *Modern Law Review* 167, 188. For example, he emphasizes that in a criminal case, the defendant is faced with the might of the State, with its superior resources and coercive powers (e.g. powers to arrest and question); the outcome in criminal cases is more serious than in civil cases (whether in terms of loss of liberty or a monetary fine) and is accompanied by non-material considerations (such as censure and stigma). Such considerations are equally relevant in civil recovery proceedings.

[149] On the issue of harm, specifically bare and moral harm, see Chapter 7.

[150] Jennifer Hendry and Colin King, 'Expediency, Legitimacy, and the Rule of Law: A Systems Perspective on Civil/ Criminal Procedural Hybrids' (2017) 11(4) *Criminal Law and Philosophy* 733; Colin King, 'Using Civil Processes in Pursuit of Criminal Law Objectives: A Case Study of Non-Conviction-Based Asset Forfeiture' (2012) 16(4) *International Journal of Evidence and Proof* 337.

[151] Alexa Virdi, *Legal and Other Fictions of Civil Recovery: Is it Possible to Reconcile the Civil Recovery of the Proceeds of Grand Corruption with Criminal Justice and Human Rights* (PhD thesis, University of Oxford, 2020).

[152] Crime and Disorder Act 1998, s. 1. ASBOs are defunct in England & Wales, but not Scotland. The English & Welsh ASBO legislation influenced Ireland's Criminal Justice Act 2006; for consideration of similarities and differences, see Kevin Brown, 'Examining the Introduction of Legislation in Ireland to Tackle Juvenile Anti-Social Behaviour' (2007) 54(3) *Journal of Community and Criminal Justice* 239. For consideration of preventive and punitive purposes, see Chapter 2.

[153] *Clingham v Royal Borough of Kensington and Chelsea; R v Crown Court at Manchester, Ex p McCann* [2002] UKHL 39, para. 37.

[154] See Chapter 4.

> I recognise, and it is no doubt right, that since it is necessary to establish that there has been criminal conduct in the obtaining of the property, the court should look for cogent evidence before deciding that the balance of probabilities has been met. But I have no doubt that Parliament deliberately referred to the balance of probabilities, and that the court should not place a gloss upon it, so as to require that the standard approaches that appropriate in a criminal case.[155]

This judicial position was emphasized yet further by Kerr LCJ in *Walsh*: 'If recovery proceedings could only be taken on proof beyond reasonable doubt that the person from whom recovery was sought had benefited from crime, the efficacy of the system would be substantially compromised.'[156]

Again, this conspicuously pragmatic attitude is similarly evident even amongst some England & Wales interviewees who represent respondents in civil recovery proceedings: 'There wouldn't be any point in High Court civil recovery proceedings if it was *carte blanche* criminal standard'.[157] Some respondent-focused interviewees noted that, for authorities, 'the civil standard is much more attractive',[158] and that insisting upon a higher (criminal) standard on the basis of allegations of criminality 'would lead to a tiring and long proceedings.'[159] Such views were explicitly described, in a by now familiar manner, as being 'very pragmatic',[160] and echoed enforcement-focused practitioner views that '[i]t needs to be the civil standard because it's civil based. And it's also about the property. It never would work otherwise'.[161]

It has long been established that the civil standard of proof can apply even with allegations of criminality, for example in professional misconduct and family law cases,[162] so the use of the civil standard in civil recovery cases 'is not out of line'.[163] That said, respondent-focused interviewees nonetheless argued for appropriate protections to be put in place where, for example, civil recovery follows post-acquittal:

155 *Jia Jin He and Dan Dan Chen* [2004] EWHC 3021 (Admin), para. 66.

156 *Walsh v Director of the Assets Recovery Agency* [2005] NICA 6, para. 33.

157 EW04.

158 EW06.

159 EW08.

160 EW08. But contrast that solicitor's views at n.133.

161 EW09. As mentioned earlier, the pragmatic dimension of civil recovery will be the focus of Chapter 7.

162 For example, in *F v Cumbria Co Co and M* [2016] EWHC 14 (Fam) the court rejected the argument that a higher standard of proof should be applied (para. 43) and determined that a father had sexually assaulted his daughter (para. 107), a judgment that was subsequently permitted to be published (para. 126).

163 EW07.

> I don't think anybody should be put through the mill a second time at all—but if a civil recovery action is brought based on matters that have already been tried, unless there is new evidence for example, the very least the courts should expect from the state is that the criminal standard would still apply, as this person has faced these allegations before. The notion of non-conviction-based penalties, I haven't got a problem with that—as long as the protections are there.[164]

This holistic view in terms of the overall legitimacy of civil recovery proceedings was fairly common across the respondent-focused interviewees, several of whom were of the view that pragmatic considerations should be mitigated through protections: 'Just because they are civil does not mean that anything goes ... I would expect certain standards of fairness to come with the lowering of the standard of proof.'[165] Indeed even some enforcement-focused interviewees expressed similar views: one barrister with extensive experience representing enforcement authorities stated that were they to deal with a civil recovery case as a judge, their approach would be to require a heightened standard.[166] By contrast, a respondent-focused barrister reiterated the importance of striking a balance between considerations of practicality on the one hand and procedural protections on the other, but ultimately rejected the argument that, due to the state initiating civil recovery proceedings, a higher standard ought to apply: 'All that that does is recognise that there is an imbalance between the parties, which goes back to my earlier point about releasing funds for legal aid, something should be done to put the parties on an equal footing. So the premise is flawed. There should be equality of arms.'[167]

Clearly then, there is no common consensus on the standard of proof, with interviewees demonstrating the vexed nature of the matter. Indeed, some

164 EW04.
165 EW04.
166 EW03.
167 EW07. This opens up the question as to what procedural protections ought to apply in such proceedings. In arguing in favour of a middleground system of justice, Mann recognizes the important role of stringent procedural rules (although not quite as stringent as those in criminal proceedings), but fails to develop this point. He remains content simply to state that a middleground paradigm requires special procedural rules over-and-above the norms in the civil process yet not quite as demanding as the enhanced procedural protections in criminal proceedings. He does not identify those procedural rules that ought to be insisted upon before punitive civil sanctions can be pursued. Kenneth Mann, 'Punitive Civil Sanctions: The Middleground Between Criminal and Civil Law' (1992) 101 *Yale Law Journal* 1795. For critique of Mann's argument on this basis, see Carol S Steiker, 'Punishment and Procedure: Punishment Theory and the Criminal-Civil Procedural Divide' (1996–1997) 85 *Georgetown Law Journal* 775, 814; Aaron Xavier Fellmeth, 'Challenges and Implications of a Systemic Social Effect Theory' (2006) 4 *University of Illinois Law Review* 691, 727.

respondent-focused interviewees expressed views that one might expect from enforcement officials, and vice versa.

Notwithstanding evidently differing views as to the standard of proof, there is no ambiguity in the position taken by the courts in England & Wales on whether an intermediate or floating standard should be applied in civil recovery proceedings. Their position is clear: they 'should not place a gloss upon [the balance of probabilities standard]',[168] and remains clear in spite of the serious connotations and severe consequences of an adverse judgment, as were comprehensively spelled out in *Virtosu*:

> Although civil recovery proceedings under Part V of the 2002 Act are civil, not criminal, the gravity of them is very great indeed. The alleged crime is extremely serious: international trafficking of women to become prostitutes in circumstances where they have no real choice whether to consent or not to consent to engaging in the sexual acts involved. The consequences of a finding in favour of the Director are also very serious indeed. In the present case, which is probably not untypical in this respect, the Order that the Director seeks would have the effect of depriving the Respondents of property which is not only very valuable in money terms (in excess of £1m), but which also, and much more importantly, includes the family home, and effectively all that they possess, other than the flat in South Africa. They will be left penniless in this country. These consequence [*sic*] do not include deprivation of liberty, but they are (and were intended by the legislature to be) more serious than the consequences of the severe prison sentences which were imposed on Mr Virtosu in France and on the Dulghierus in England.[169]

It is therefore interesting to see that, in direct contrast to the approach in England & Wales, an intermediate approach appears to be at play in the Irish context. This state of affairs was acknowledged by an enforcement official: 'That doesn't exist in a structured way, but in reality it does.'[170] It was also suggested by interviewees that 'the court kind of forces itself into a guilty or not guilty approach',[171] and that the CAB *does* apply the criminal standard in its internal decision-making over whether or not to initiate proceedings.[172] Another enforcement official stated, 'while we would acknowledge the civil standard, in

[168] *Jia Jin He and Dan Dan Chen* [2004] EWHC 3021 (Admin), para. 66.
[169] *Assets Recovery Agency v Virtosu* [2008] EWHC 149 (QB), para. 18.
[170] IRE05.
[171] IRE05.
[172] IRE11; IRE13.

reality, we would apply the same level of scrutiny and test to our evidence as you would in a criminal case'.[173] The same interviewee continued: 'we're crime investigators, we're saying it's the proceeds of crime, so in reality the standard of evidence will equate to the criminal standard'.[174] This notion was rejected by criminal defence practitioners, whose scorn in this regard was apparent: 'That's absolute baloney. They know perfectly well that most of their cases would never get into court on a criminal standard. A huge amount of the evidence that they try to lead in POCA cases is simply inadmissible, it's hearsay on hearsay on hearsay. It's absolute baloney'.[175]

While our position is that civil recovery ought to be regarded as a criminal proceeding[176] and as such ought to attract the standard of beyond reasonable doubt, it is worth reiterating our antagonism to the idea of a flexible standard alternative. Beyond a straightforward intermediate standard—such as 'clear and convincing evidence'—there are further practical difficulties with applying a flexible or floating civil standard of proof. For example, when should it apply, in what type of cases, and in what degree?[177] These difficulties make the idea of a flexible standard a generally unpopular one in the academy, even where there is support for an intermediate approach. Some scholars go as far as to suggest that discussion of flexible standards is too much of a distraction, a sideshow: as Mirfield notes, were we to 'hear no more about flexible standards of proof' then there would 'at least, be a better prospect of courts attending to the much more important policy issue of which of our two standards of proof is appropriate to the issue at hand'.[178]

Apropos this 'policy issue', we acknowledge that the courts have already selected the 'appropriate' standard, and have, regrettably, came down in favour of the balance of probabilities. Indeed, there is little prospect of successful legal challenge to this civil standard. What we end up with, then, is an evident preference for downward pressure on the standard of proof, which has been described as 'indicative of increased support for a risk management standard, premised on efficiency rather than certainty, as opposed to a more traditional criminal standard that placed a premium on accuracy and was designed to afford individuals every possible benefit of law'.[179] In contrast to this downward

[173] IRE03.
[174] IRE03.
[175] IRE08.
[176] See Chapter 4.
[177] See Rosemary Pattenden, 'The Risk of Non-Persuasion in Civil Trials: The Case Against a Floating Standard of Proof' (1988) 4 *Civil Justice Quarterly* 220.
[178] Peter Mirfield, 'How Many Standards Of Proof Are There?' (2009) *Law Quarterly Review* 31, 38.
[179] Shane Kilcommins and Barry Vaughan, 'Reconfiguring State-Accused Relations in Ireland' (2006) 41 *Irish Jurist* 90, 109.

pressure, our argument is that the criminal standard ought to be preferred; if that were the case, recourse to a flexible standard of proof as a safeguard would not be necessary. Moreover, the criminal standard would offer a much more 'coherent' approach.[180]

[180] See Ennis McBride, 'Is the Civil "Higher Standard of Proof" a Coherent Concept?' (2009) 8 *Law, Probability and Risk* 323.

6

Civil Recovery and Property

Introduction

While our analysis has to this point focused on the contextualized introduction, judicial reception, and development of civil recovery mechanisms in Ireland and in England & Wales, we now consider the target of this 'follow the money' approach, that is, the property subject to confiscation. As mentioned in the previous chapter, a central issue raised by the adoption of proceeds of crime legislation, specifically non-conviction-based powers, is the implications it has not only for due process but also for rights in property. Property rights considerations are key in analysing the civil recovery of criminal assets due to its operation as an action against the property (*in rem*), as opposed to an action against the person or the individual (*in personam*).

The chapter proceeds in three sections. First, charting the historical development of actions *in rem*, we advance the argument that civil recovery—like many *in rem* actions before it—constitutes a legal fiction, one conceived and employed to attenuate the owner-owned relationship. In this opening section we further contend that this legal fiction has been relied upon at the expense of individual rights in property so that criminal justice agencies can more efficiently target 'dirty assets'; that is, property deemed to have been obtained through unlawful conduct. The *in rem*/*in personam* distinction is integral to understanding the structure and categorization of civil recovery, and we elucidate this throughout the rest of the chapter, drawing upon data from our interviews with practitioners in Ireland and England & Wales.[1] In the second section, we highlight the salient features of civil recovery that render it unusual in terms of property and property rights, and juxtapose these features against considerations of good title and restitution. In the third and final section, taking a position grounded in liberal legal theory, we evidence in our data notably *illiberal* attitudes towards property rights, particularly how this *in rem* 'exercise-in-pretend'[2] is relied upon to downplay the punitive aspect of civil

[1] For the methodology of this data collection, see both Chapters 1 and 5.

[2] On 'exercises in pretend', 'make-believe notions', and legal fictions generally, see Maksymilian del Mar and William Twining (eds), *Legal Fictions in Theory and Practice* (Springer 2015).

Civil Recovery of Criminal Property. Colin King and Jennifer Hendry, Oxford University Press.
 DOI: 10.1093/oso/9780198824251.003.0006

recovery. We argue that this 'make-believe' notion of liability resting with the property itself leads, in the context of civil recovery, to the untenable justification of confiscation on the grounds of suspicion, the unjustifiable dissolution of the legal relationship between owner and owned, and the worrisome disregard of liberal tenets concerning those requirements on the part of the state to respect and protect individual 'life, liberty, and estate'.[3]

The Legal Fiction of Actions *in rem*

Much of the procedural innovation of civil recovery turns on it being an action *in rem* and thus operating against the property itself. The characterization of these non-conviction-based proceedings as against the property instead of against the person is central to many of the problems we identify with civil recovery. Being cast as an action *in rem* influences civil recovery's categorization as a civil process, and supports the resultant inference that being deprived of property is not punitive—at least, not in the way that being deprived of liberty is punitive.[4] These issues are interconnected: by bringing the action against the property the procedural safeguards that inhere in a criminal trial are effectively bypassed, while those legal protections that would, under usual circumstances, arise in an action against an owner (*in personam*) are denied. Far from being convenient accidents, the focus on targeting *criminal* property through a purportedly civil process indicates that these advantages are designed into civil recovery for the purpose of more efficiently targeting property *suspected* to have been acquired through criminal activity.[5]

The contention that the *in rem* nature of the proceedings determines their classification as civil is indicative. Evidently relying on the assumption that there is no good title to the assets in question, the court in effect attenuates the owner/owned legal relationship constitutive of property (and property rights) and purports to hold *the property itself* to be at fault. There are several points here worth noting. First, the artificiality of the property being liable: the very basis of proceedings *in rem*, the notion that the property itself is liable, is fundamentally contrived, not least because property lacks the capacity to act in its own right. Second, the presumption that the property bears the brunt of its

[3] John Locke, *Two Treatises of Government* (Peter Laslett ed, Cambridge University Press [1689] 1988).

[4] *Murphy v GM, PB, PC Ltd, GH and Gilligan v CAB* [2001] 4 IR 113; *Walsh v Director of the Assets Recovery Agency* [2005] NICA 6. We address the punitive/non-punitive question later in this chapter; see also Chapter 4 on 'Punishment'.

[5] 'Suspicion' is explored in more detail both in the next section and in Chapter 7.

forfeiture: far more likely is that the situation of being forfeit is of no consequence to the property, but its deprivation is likely to be of significance to the individual affected. Ownership is primarily a legal relation between persons in respect of things,[6] so any material reduction in or denial of that legal relationship can be expected detrimentally to affect the owner. Indeed, the disincentive effect is a central motivation underpinning civil recovery legislation, the idea of removing the profit incentive from serious and organized criminal activity.[7] Our third point concerns the role played by suspicion. It is the enforcement agency's *suspicion* of the individual's criminal activity that causes their property rights to be thrown into question and triggers the subsequent civil recovery proceedings,[8] but suspicion permeates the action yet further. Even though the court is not necessarily interested in a finding of guilt on the part of the individual, civil recovery proceedings *do* involve allegations of unlawful conduct, which need only be proven to the civil standard, with this proof deemed sufficient to *dissolve* any existing rights the individual had in that property. We take the position that the deprivation of property—to which an individual may have good and legitimate title—is a serious enough sanction to demand the satisfaction of proof to the criminal standard.[9]

Contemporary civil recovery powers are not the first time that property has been held as either liable or guilty and thus subject to confiscation/forfeiture. Historically there existed provisions such as forfeiture of the deodand and forfeiture in the admiralty jurisdiction, both of which turned similarly on an *in rem* construction, and both of which focused on the materiality of property as a means of bringing legal processes to bear, albeit tenuously, against owners who would otherwise escape sanction.[10] Prior to 1846,[11] a deodand was any piece of personal chattel property that directly occasioned the death of an adult human being and which was subsequently forfeit to the sovereign.[12] The underlying idea was that if an animal or inanimate object caused an accidental death, then it was declared at inquest to be *responsible* for that death and thus an accursed

[6] Lisa M Austin, 'The Public Nature of Private Property', in James Penner and Michael Otsuka (eds), *Property Theory: Legal and Political Perspectives* (Cambridge University Press 2018) 2.

[7] See generally Chapter 2, and specifically, Chapter 3.

[8] See also Chapter 7 on 'Explaining Unexplained Wealth'.

[9] The position we take here is influenced by liberal legal theory and, as such, adopts a liberal conception of property. For further consideration of the standard of proof, see Chapter 5.

[10] Anthony Gray, 'Forfeiture Provisions and the Criminal/Civil Divide' (2012) 15(1) *New Criminal Law Review* 32, 36–40.

[11] The Deodands Act 1846 abolished the deodand. For wider consideration, see Anna Pervukhin, 'Deodands: A Study in the Creation of Common Law Rules' (2005) 47 *American Journal of Legal History* 237.

[12] Ed Kirkton-Darling, 'Searching for Pigeons in the Belfry: The Inquest, the Abolition of the Deodand and the Rise of the Family' (2018) 14(3) *Law, Culture and the Humanities* 439, 440.

thing, something that must be *deo dandum,* 'given to God', for whom the sovereign was an earthly proxy.[13] Mawani explains this common law approach, whereby:

> inanimate and animate nonhuman entities such as animals, carts, locomotives and ships were granted a legal liveliness that was to be taken only by the Crown. Nonhuman animals and objects that caused injury or death could be arrested, condemned, and forfeited to the sovereign, who would determine the ascribed value of the offending thing and apply its equivalent in the interests of the public good.[14]

The fiction at play here is that the thing, the property, the deodand *itself* is the wrongdoer, with proceedings being brought specifically against *it*—as the perpetrator—irrespective of any fault on the part of its owner.[15] As Trabsky outlines: 'The deodand was both a material object, a thing in itself that caused the death of a person, and a juridical device, deployed by coroners to cultivate a monetary relationship between the living and the dead.'[16] Kirkton-Darling makes a similar point concerning the contingency of the object made deodand, that it is 'a chattel which through the jury's shaping of the narratives of death became linked to that death.'[17] Interestingly, although the property was forfeit to the Crown, prior to its 1846 abolition the legal technology of the deodand was being increasingly employed as a means through which financial relief could be provided to the family of the deceased.[18]

The legal technology of the deodand can be said to have persisted beyond its abolition by statute, however, as a 'recurrent juridical form' predicated on the idea of the offending *res* (or thing).[19] The historic admiralty jurisdiction was

[13] William Pietz, 'Death of the Deodand: Accursed Objects and the Money Value of Human Life' (1997) 31 *Res: Anthropology and Aesthetics* 97. See also Teresa Sutton, 'The Deodand and Responsibility for Death' (1997) 18(3) *Journal of Legal History* 44.

[14] Renisa Mawani, *Across Oceans of Law* (Duke University Press 2018), p.82. See also Jacob J Finkelstein, 'The Goring Ox: Some Historical Perspectives on Deodands, Forfeitures, Wrongful Death and the Western Notion of Sovereignty' (1973) 46 *Temple Law Quarterly* 169, 185.

[15] On legal fictions, see Douglas Lind, 'The Pragmatic Value of Legal Fictions', in Maksymilian del Mar and William Twining (eds), *Legal Fictions in Theory and Practice* (Springer 2015).

[16] Marc Trabsky, *Law and the Dead: Technology, Relations and Institutions* (Routledge 2019) 4.

[17] Ed Kirkton-Darling, 'Searching for Pigeons in the Belfry: The Inquest, the Abolition of the Deodand and the Rise of the Family' (2018) 14(3) *Law, Culture and the Humanities* 439, 441.

[18] Anna Pervukhin, 'Deodands: A Study in the Creation of Common Law Rules' (2005) 47 *American Journal of Legal History* 237, 248–9.

[19] Renisa Mawani, *Across Oceans of Law* (Duke University Press 2018) 83. A similar point is made by Finkelstein: 'The deodand therefore never died, and what we observe now to be in force is not a resurrection of that institution but its transfiguration into a form which may accurately, if inelegantly be described as the *reipublicaedand*.' Jacob J Finkelstein, 'The Goring Ox: Some Historical Perspectives on Deodands, Forfeitures, Wrongful Death and the Western Notion of Sovereignty' (1973) 46 *Temple Law Quarterly* 169, 251.

one arena where such *in rem* forfeiture proceedings took place: a breach of law on the part of a vessel, regardless of that ship's status as legal person, could result in forfeiture.[20] That said, although admiralty law provided for the seizure of vessels under proceedings that were procedurally *in rem*, the actions were purposively *in personam*: the elusiveness of the global owners of the seafaring property made such proceedings a useful means of reaching them. As Mawani explains, 'legal actions against a ship were used to secure the appearance of a ship's owners or representatives in court'.[21] This is hardly surprising: as we have already illustrated in terms of civil recovery, the instrumental reliance upon procedures *in rem* to achieve alternative ends to the ones stated appears to be a central feature of this juridical form.

In his comprehensive study of the deodand, Finkelstein draws attention to how the English common law adopted the idea of 'expiation', that is, atonement or reparation—'biblical in origin and "objective" in application'—inherent in the deodand, and recast it as 'a forfeiture of the "offending thing" or things to the sovereign *without regard for the interests of the owners* of these "things" '.[22] The critical consideration in terms of justifying the forfeiture of the offending *res* is that an evident threat it posed to the public welfare necessitated its destruction. In this regard, Finkelstein's explanation of the development of the modern doctrine is worth quoting at length:

> The [deodand] procedure was the natural consequence of a bona fide concern about a human life and not a subterfuge by means of which the authorities were aiming to penalize the owner of the beast. The modern doctrine of the offending res, on the other hand, is a deliberate subterfuge—a judicial fiction, by resort to which the sovereign, with the sanction of the courts, can impose a punishment on a blameless individual who is thereby deliberately left without recourse to his constitutional rights of due process.[23]

The issue of punishment is particularly salient. Finkelstein's criticism is levelled directly against misuse of the concept of the offending (and thus liable) *res*—as a disguise for the dissolution of individual property rights in that thing—and the *de facto* punishment, via the forfeiture of their property, of the

[20] James M Turner, 'Admiralty in rem Claims and Insolvency Law' (2016) 13(5) *International Corporate Rescue* 334. A classic example can be seen in the US case of *The Palmyra* 25 US 1 (1827).

[21] Renisa Mawani, *Across Oceans of Law* (Duke University Press 2018) 82.

[22] Jacob J Finkelstein, 'The Goring Ox: Some Historical Perspectives on Deodands, Forfeitures, Wrongful Death and the Western Notion of Sovereignty' (1973) 46 *Temple Law Quarterly* 169, 249, emphasis added.

[23] Ibid, 252.

otherwise blameless owner.[24] In her discussion of the deodand relative to this point, Mawani similarly notes that a forfeiture action *punishes* the proprietor by holding them 'responsible for the actions of her/his chattel', concluding that such forfeiture of private property 'undermine[s] individual possession and ownership'.[25] A comparable conclusion is reached by Steiker, who is categorical in her stance that this is exactly the phenomenon occurring under civil forfeiture in the United States: 'The only way to avoid the conclusion that civil forfeitures are in fact punishment is to invoke the implausible common-law fiction that the forfeiture action is really against the "guilty" property rather than against the property owner and thus is not punishment "of an offender"'.[26] Two points concerning civil recovery can be emphasized here. First, it is evident that the very design of civil recovery as a procedure *in rem* is the continuation of the juridical form first exhibited through the legal fiction of the deodand. This begs the question as to why, and also to the degree of instrumentality present in its conception. Is this a straightforward recasting of the historical 'elusive shipowner problem' for contemporary 'follow the money' times, or is it more specifically targeted at achieving a civil process categorization, with all that that entails procedurally? Is civil recovery's emphasis on the *material*—that is, the property—simply an efficient means of bringing the process to bear on individuals who otherwise prove evasive? Second, there appears to be two central purposes behind the deployment of a procedure of this design against the proceeds of crime: to render the question of property rights moot by attenuating the owner/owned relationship, and to imply that the deprivation of property—whether or not this is acknowledged as punitive—is so *significantly* different to and removed from the deprivation of liberty that it can be brought about under procedurally inferior circumstances, without the requirement for wrongdoing to be proven beyond reasonable doubt. While we do not purport to equate these two deprivations, we take the position that the 'basic security of person and property' are not only conceptually connected but can be viewed as 'instrumental to all sorts of other collective goods that are necessary to a more expansive or positive conception of human freedom'.[27] In this regard, and recognizing once again that property is 'a legally defined relationship between

[24] The lack of an innocent owner defence in US civil forfeiture law was notably evidenced in the case of Mrs Bennis whose part-ownership of a car was forfeit notwithstanding that she had not been involved in criminality of her husband: *Bennis v Michigan* 516 US 442 (1996). See Donald Boudreaux and AC Pritchard, 'Innocence Lost: Bennis v. Michigan and the Forfeiture Tradition' (1996) 61 *Missouri Law Review* 593.

[25] Renisa Mawani, *Across Oceans of Law* (Duke University Press 2018) 83–4.

[26] Carol S Steiker, 'Punishment and Procedure: Punishment Theory and the Criminal-Civil Procedural Divide' (1997) 26 *Annual Review of Criminal Procedure* 775, 815.

[27] Ian Loader and Neil Walker, *Civilising Security* (Cambridge University Press 2007) 153.

persons with respect to an object',[28] we submit that the non-conviction-based approach is unjustifiably harsh in its dissolution of this legal relationship. Both these points are particularly salient when we consider that civil recovery is a 'specific property regime'—which can be 'differentiated from a "value-based" system such as is confiscation'[29]—and that a central claim is that it is as such *restitutionary* as opposed to punitive in character. The next section interrogates this notion.

A 'Specific Property' Regime

The structure of civil recovery proceedings rests upon the perception that the proceeds of crime do not in fact *belong* to the individual *owner* but are assets to which there is no legitimate proprietary right on the part of the possessor/respondent, and which should instead be turned over to the state. Alldridge explains this, noting that civil recovery:

> confers upon a designated state official a right to bring a proprietary action to acquire property in the hands of a criminal or anyone else, not being a *bona fide* purchaser for value, and to trace it into property that 'represents' the unlawfully acquired property, without any requirement first to obtain a conviction.[30]

This approach is clearly evident from the case law in both Ireland and England & Wales. In *Walsh* Lord Kerr took the position that:

> [The proceedings] are not directed towards him in the sense that they seek to inflict punishment beyond the recovery of assets that do not lawfully belong to him. As such, while they will obviously have an impact on the appellant, these are predominantly proceedings *in rem*. They are designed to recover the proceeds of crime, rather than to establish, in the context of criminal proceedings, guilt of specific offences.[31]

[28] Margaret Davies, *Property: Meanings, Histories, Theories* (Routledge Cavendish 2007) 13.

[29] Peter Alldridge, 'Civil Recovery in England and Wales: An Appraisal' in Colin King, Clive Walker, and Jimmy Gurulé (eds), *The Palgrave Handbook of Criminal and Terrorism Financing Law* (Palgrave 2018) 515.

[30] Peter Alldridge, 'Civil Recovery in England and Wales: An Appraisal' in Colin King, Clive Walker, and Jimmy Gurulé (eds), *The Palgrave Handbook of Criminal and Terrorism Financing Law* (Palgrave 2018) 515.

[31] *Walsh v Director of the Assets Recovery Agency* [2005] NICA 6, para. 41, per Kerr LCJ.

A similar stance concerning the non-punitive nature of civil recovery was evident in the Irish courts. In *GM/Gilligan*, Keane CJ stated:

> The issue in the present case does not raise a challenge to a valid constitutional right of property. It concerns the right of the State to take, or the right of a citizen to resist the State in taking, property which is proved on the balance of probabilities to represent the proceeds of crime. In general such a forfeiture is not a punishment and its operation does not require criminal procedures. Application of such legislation must be sensitive to the actual property and other rights of citizens but in principle and subject, no doubt, to special problems which may arise in particular cases, a person in possession of the proceeds of crime can have no constitutional grievance if deprived of their use.[32]

Alongside exposing both aspects of civil recovery's label, 'civil' and 'recovery', to particular scrutiny, such dicta reveal three aspects worthy of note. The first is that, as already discussed, the action is an explicitly civil one due to it being brought *in rem* against the property; the second is that there is no good title to property resulting from criminal activity; and the third is that the purported aim of the legislation is not punishment but rather, *restitution*. We now consider these latter two points—title (including third party rights) and restitution—in turn.

No good title

The judicial dicta draw attention to how the property targeted does not in fact *belong* to the individual who is in possession of it. In other words, the individual does not have any rights to that property; their alleged wrongdoing has interrupted the passage of title, and, as the individual has no good claim to the property, it is forfeit to the state.[33] The central issue here is whether or not property rights exist in relation to *suspected* ill-gotten gains, because it is the suspicion over their origin that places title to them in question.[34] The principle that crime should not pay or, rather, that no-one has a legal right to attain

[32] *Murphy v GM, PB, PC Ltd, GH and Gilligan v CAB* [2001] 4 IR 113, 153.

[33] Forfeit to the state, incidentally, and not to the private individual or individuals from which the assets were derived, which is how the law of illegality would operate: *Patel v Mirza* [2016] UKSC 42. See Sarah Green and Alan Bogg (eds), *Illegality after Patel v Mirza* (Hart Publishing 2018).

[34] On the issue of the heavy lifting done by *suspicion* in civil recovery actions, see later in this section; see also Chapter 7 for further discussion of suspicion.

benefits which accrue to them from criminal activity,[35] is relatively uncontroversial[36] and is not disputed here.[37] What we do dispute, however, is the non-conviction-based approach to confiscating proceeds of crime on the grounds that it gives too much weight to suspicion and too little to proof, not least where the issue of title is concerned.

The courts have been robust on the question of good title in the civil recovery context. In *Gilligan* it was stated:

> While the provisions of the [Proceeds of Crime] Act may, indeed, affect the property rights of a respondent it does not appear to this Court that they constitute 'an unjust attack' under Article 40.3.2 [of the Irish Constitution], given the fact that the State must in the first place show to the satisfaction of the Court that *the property in question is the proceeds of crime and that thus, prima facie, the respondent has no good title to it* . . . .[38]

The court continued that it:

> would also accept that the exigencies of the common good would certainly include measures designed to prevent the accumulation and use of assets which directly or indirectly derive from criminal activities. *The right to private ownership cannot hold a place so high in the hierarchy of rights that it protects the position of assets illegally acquired and held.*[39]

In *Murphy*, a similarly robust approach was evident:

> Where an asset is proved to be [proceeds of crime], in accordance with the 1996 Act, the obligation to vindicate personal rights does not apply to that

[35] For consideration in the context of the forfeiture rule, see *Secretary of State for the Department of Work and Pensions v LK (RP)* [2019] UKUT 421 (AAC).

[36] The extent to which proceeds of crime legislation *should* be applicable to 'non-serious' offences is open to debate, however it suffices to note here that in both Ireland and England & Wales proceeds of crime provisions can be applied to regulatory offences. See, e.g., *R v Davey* [2013] EWCA Crim 1662. For wider discussion, see Declan O'Reilly, 'Confiscating and Forfeiting the Financial Benefit from Regulatory Offences' in Joe McGrath (ed.), *White-Collar Crime in Ireland: Law and Policy* (Clarus Press 2019).

[37] For consideration in the context of the maxim *ex turpi causa non oritur actio* (no cause of action may be founded on an immoral or illegal act), see *Cleaver v Mutual Reserve Fund Life Association* [1892] 1 QB 147, 156. Some commentators have cited this maxim as evidence that the civil forfeiture of property deriving from criminal activity is 'rooted in the common law' and thus pre-dates legislation concerning the proceeds of crime: Shane Murphy, 'Tracing the Proceeds of Crime: Legal and Constitutional Implications' (1999) 9(2) *Irish Criminal Law Journal* 160.

[38] *Gilligan v. CAB* [1998] 3 IR 185, 237 per McGuinness J. Emphasis added.

[39] *Gilligan v. CAB* [1998] 3 IR 185, 237. Emphasis added.

> asset. Refusal of an order freezing or confiscating such assets, in the face of evidence establishing provenance to the required extent, should not be seen as a means of *protecting that which does not deserve protection.*[40]

So too in *Ashton*, where the court was unequivocal on this very point:

> The fact of the matter is that the person who is in possession of the proceeds of crime has, in accordance with the purpose and intention of Parliament, *no right to hold that property*. It is not a deprivation of anything. Parliament has said that such proceeds are not the entitlement of anyone. That is not to deprive anybody of anything.[41]

The effect is that the individual concerned is deemed to have no good title, with the result that the property is forfeit to the state, which has asserted an entitlement claim over this ill-gotten gain, the 'dirty' assets. This is a position peculiar to proceeds of crime, however: as Alldridge observes, 'the law does not in general grant the State such a right, and it is difficult to see what the basis would be for a moral right.'[42] He continues: 'A system of property law that automatically made all proceeds of crime the property of state would be quite different from that which obtains, would render Part 5 of POCA unnecessary, and would very seriously undermine security of transactions and of property.'[43] Civil recovery proceedings thus appear to allow for differential treatment when compared with other situations of wrongdoing relative to property, for example, whereby proprietary rights can still vest in stolen goods,[44] or where property passes even though the contract under which it does so is illegal.[45] The key issue in civil recovery proceedings appears to be the provenance of the assets, that is, whether they derive either directly or indirectly from criminal conduct. This emphasis was captured well by an enforcement official in interview, who—on the issue of legitimate title to assets deemed to derive from the proceeds of crime—concluded that the '[c]ourts have gone through that and taken the view that it wasn't yours in the first place.'[46] Or, as a former enforcement official stressed,

[40] *CAB v Murphy* [2018] IR 640, para. 132. Emphasis added.

[41] *R (Director of the Assets Recovery Agency) v Ashton* [2006] EWHC 1064, para. 43. Emphasis added.

[42] Peter Alldridge, 'Civil Recovery in England and Wales: An Appraisal' in Colin King, Clive Walker, and Jimmy Gurulé (eds), *The Palgrave Handbook of Criminal and Terrorism Financing Law* (Palgrave 2018) 517. Cf. *CAB v JWPL* [2007] IEHC 177.

[43] Ibid, 517.

[44] *Costello v Chief Constable of Derbyshire Constabulary* [2001] 1 WLR 1437. See Graham Battersby, Acquiring Title by Theft (2002) 65(4) *Modern Law Review* 603.

[45] *Singh v Ali* [1960] AC 167.

[46] IRE12.

'you are enjoying someone else's property'.[47] Indeed, the issue of good title was referenced on several occasions by enforcement-focused interviewees, many of whom held it as effectively sacrosanct. For example, one enforcement barrister noted that '[t]here is no valid constitutional interest where property is the product of criminal activity',[48] while a former enforcement official was categorical: 'you have no legal title to [the proceeds of crime]'.[49] Such views were aptly summed up by an enforcement official as follows: 'You might lose a house, but it is a house you acquired through unlawful conduct so should not have had in the first place.'[50]

The stress on alleged criminal conduct can be attributed to a core motivation behind POCA, in both Ireland and England & Wales, that is, to deter participation in serious and organized criminal activity. If good title is held to turn on how the individual came to possess the property, as we have noted that it appears to be, then proof of wrongdoing will interfere with the passage of property and preclude good title.[51] One former enforcement official illustrated this point using an example: 'if I steal your watch, the watch does not belong to me; rather, it remains your property and you can bring proceedings to ensure its return.'[52] But this is the salient point: *you*, the owner, should get the watch back, not the state. While in practice there might be difficulties in tracing the original owner or they might not be inclined, for whatever reason, to pursue the matter in civil proceedings—there is no question about the original owner's title. It is only where property cannot be returned to its original owner that the default becomes for it to revert to the state.[53] Our interviews showed that provenance was a central consideration: 'property rights should be legitimate and should be based on a legitimate basis. So I just don't see the argument there, really. "Oh its unfair", well then you should have got it from a legal source.'[54] What we can point to here, yet again, is the *assumption* that the individual has obtained the

[47] EW11.
[48] IRE04.
[49] IRE11.
[50] EW14.
[51] This was put succinctly by one interviewee: 'If you receive something as the proceeds of crime, then you don't actually get to keep it.' IRE05.
[52] IRE11.
[53] A further issue here is whether property rights actually vested in the individual concerned or whether they are extinguished only upon the making of the civil recovery order. According to an enforcement official, the individual 'had no right to hold it [the property concerned] in the first place', but went on to say that '[i]t is not quashing the title from the outset'. EW14. An enforcement barrister agreed with this latter stance: 'I think it takes away good title,' continuing '[t]ake it away, rather than mess around in that quagmire'. EW09.
[54] EW09.

property from criminal conduct, and that this assumption performs a justificatory role in terms of the state *taking* the property.

Herein lies the problem. As discussed in earlier chapters, the non-conviction-based civil, *in rem* approach does not require that guilt of specific offences on the part of the respondent be established. The focus instead rests on the *recovery* of those proceeds of crime to which the individual, so the reasoning goes, has no good title. But at no point is the state required to *prove* to the criminal standard the actual commission of the alleged iniquity, that is, the criminal conduct that has jeopardized the title to the property in question. Not only is the *in rem* action formally against the property and not the individual but the suspected wrongdoing needs only to be proven on a balance of probabilities. Bearing in mind that there are already serious concerns surrounding both the presumption of innocence and requirements to disclose within civil recovery proceedings,[55] having the eventual deprivation of property rely so significantly on suspicion of criminal activity, instead of upon proof to the criminal standard, seems—at least to us—a bridge too far.

Our key point here is that *suspicion* as to the property's provenance seems to be doing a lot of heavy lifting in terms of undermining the individual's title to it. Indeed, on this reasoning, it is irrefutable that the procedural hybridity of civil recovery is intended to justify the deprivation of property unhindered by inconvenient considerations of either property rights or due process rights. As to the procedure's instrumentality concerning good title, Alldridge arrives at a similar conclusion, noting that such proceedings are intended 'to deprive criminals and others of the proceeds of crime, *notwithstanding that the property is theirs*'.[56]

Title and third-party rights

Issues concerning good title (or otherwise) are also evident in the context of third-party rights, particularly as concerns the family home.[57] The policy rationale here is clear: it should not be possible to avoid proceeds of crime

[55] On the presumption of innocence under civil recovery, see Chapter 5; on disclosure and financial privacy see Chapter 7.

[56] Peter Alldridge, 'Civil Recovery in England and Wales: An Appraisal' in Colin King, Clive Walker, and Jimmy Gurulé (eds), *The Palgrave Handbook of Criminal and Terrorism Financing Law* (Palgrave 2018) 518. Emphasis added.

[57] While there is extensive case law on post-conviction confiscation and third-party rights, case law in the civil recovery context is comparatively scant. This issue was raised by interview proponents as an area of practical concern, and as such was explored in these discussions.

proceedings simply by transferring property to a spouse or to another third party.[58] The Irish Supreme Court in *Kelly* explained that:

> [t]here is a strong public policy dimension to this legislation. That policy is to ensure that persons do not benefit from assets which were obtained with the proceeds of crime irrespective of whether the person benefiting actually knew how such property was obtained with the proceeds of crime but subject to whether or not such person may have been a bona fide purchaser for value, where different considerations may arise.[59]

Furthermore: 'Property purchased with the proceeds of crime cannot be transferred to a spouse through family law proceedings simply as a means to defeat the legitimate objectives of the legislation. To allow for such a situation would be to negate the purpose and policy of the Acts.'[60] Similarly in England & Wales, in *Sanam*, the Court of Appeal said: 'The policy underlying Part 5 of POCA would be frustrated if a [civil recovery order] were not to be made in a case such as this.'[61] In essence, that the property in question is a family home will not prevent a civil recovery order being granted, although it is a factor that can be taken into consideration.[62]

It is our contention here that the issues already discussed above concerning the civil recovery of assets on a non-conviction basis are amplified where there are also (innocent) third parties involved. The extent of this amplification 'depends really on exactly what the situation is':[63] two scenarios illustrate our point in this regard. In scenario one, a married couple purchase a house, with both spouses contributing equally to the purchase price. If civil recovery proceedings are subsequently initiated against one spouse, then the other retains their right to one-half of the property. In the second scenario, however, the entire purchase price is provided by one spouse. If civil recovery proceedings are initiated, then the enforcement agency's standard approach is often to seek an

[58] In the context of post-conviction confiscation, see HM Government, *Serious and Organised Crime Strategy* (Cm.8715, 2013) para. 4.48, and subsequently the Serious Crime Act 2015, s. 1 ('Determination of extent of defendant's interest in property').

[59] *CAB v Kelly* [2012] IESC 64, para. 32. See also *CAB v H* [2011] IESC 10.

[60] *CAB v Kelly* [2012] IESC 64, para. 43.

[61] *Sanam v NCA* [2015] EWCA Civ 1234, para. 295.

[62] *CAB v Kelly* [2012] IESC 64. In *Sanam v NCA* [2015] EWCA Civ 1234, para. 22 the Court of Appeal referred to the views of the trial judge, who had suggested: 'if the court had an unfettered discretion as to what should happen to [the property] registered in Mrs Sanam's name, there would be much to be said in favour of allowing her to keep it, but the court does not have an unfettered discretion or indeed any discretion at all. She said that section 266 provides the only statutory defence once a finding has been made that the property is recoverable.'

[63] EW05. Also IRE03.

order over the entire property.[64] *Sanam* is a perfect example of such a situation, one where the spouse was '"a complete innocent" caught up in the web of [her husband's] conduct'.[65] The Court of Appeal referred to the trial judge's description as follows:

> She has done nothing to deserve the situation in which she has found herself. This is not a case of a wife who was happy to live "high on the hog" from the proceeds of crime with no questions asked, turning a blind eye to where the money was coming from.[66]

The emphasis placed on the awareness or knowledge, or lack thereof, of a spouse is notable here, and similarly evident in the Irish courts. In *Kelly* it was established that '[a] court will have regard to the extent of a person's knowledge or notice (either express or implied) that property was acquired by or through the proceeds of crime. Actual knowledge of criminal wrongdoing will be a substantial factor in the balance'.[67] This centrality of knowledge was further demonstrated by one of our interviewees, an enforcement barrister, who explained its influence as follows: '[M]ost of the wives in that situation have been part of the arrangements... in the Soprano sense, they haven't done anything but they have known exactly what was happening.'[68] That interviewee acknowledged that different considerations might apply 'in the case of somebody who was absolutely taken for a ride', but noted in qualification that such cases would be 'very rare'.[69] Similarly, an enforcement official was dismissive of third-party arguments run by spouses or extended family: 'A lot of these people have quite enjoyed living a particular lifestyle and have often wilfully turned a blind eye as to what hubby or father or uncle have been doing.'[70] Even if a person was simply unaware of their spouse's criminality, an enforcement barrister stated that that 'would not be an answer to the state's claim for civil recovery of the

[64] A defence solicitor in England & Wales expressed concern as to an overly rigid approach in this regard: 'the law is very restrictive, and that is where I believe that POCA has gone wrong—they have written down almost everything and given very little discretion to judges. And once you have written it down, there is little allowance for judges to give something.' EW08.

[65] *Sanam v NCA* [2015] EWCA Civ 1234, para. 15.

[66] *Sanam v NCA* [2015] EWCA Civ 1234, para. 15.

[67] *CAB v Kelly* [2012] IESC 64, para. 34. The court continued: 'The fact that an applicant was allegedly unaware of the source of funds for the acquisition of property does not act as a bar to the making of an order under the Act' para. 34.

[68] IRE07.

[69] IRE07.

[70] EW14.

house', although did acknowledge that such a situation 'could lead to significant unfairness'.[71] The same interviewee continued:

> [I]n certain circumstances, the court might look at the situation and make some sort of other order or provision. The difficulty would be, if I were acting for the state I would say that the legislature has made it clear what they want to happen and, as unfortunate as the situation is, the wife cannot always hold a legitimate claim notwithstanding that it might lead to personal hardship.[72]

By contrast, on the same point a defence solicitor stressed the following: 'I feel very strongly, morally, that there has to be some sort of protection for innocent third parties who may or may not have any knowledge of the crime, but who were not involved in the crime.' This solicitor gave the example of a spouse who either 'did not have the courage' to leave their partner or 'who stayed in the family for the purpose of bringing up the children under one roof and now becomes part of a broken family', with accommodation and assets all being taken away.[73]

The theme of innocent parties was a recurring one in our interviews. While some enforcement officials took a hard line in this regard—for example, this stance that there is 'no issue with a family home when it is the proceeds of crime; constitutional protections do not apply when it is deemed to be proceeds of crime. So that is just not an issue'[74]—others recognized both practical and compassionate considerations: '[W]hilst I think criminal proceeds should be taken, what we can't be doing is putting children, families out on the streets. The kids didn't commit the crime. It's a difficult issue.'[75] This former enforcement official clearly struggled with the competing concerns, stating that '[t]here isn't an entitlement to it, and we do have a reasonably good welfare state', before subsequently showing a degree of internal conflict through the

[71] EW05. A defence solicitor emphasized the potential for unfairness: 'if you haven't got the money to instruct lawyers and then probably High Court proceedings as well, you're in real difficulties if you're an innocent third party. Real difficulties. It costs a lot of money.' EW02. Also EW08.

[72] EW05.

[73] EW08. Another interviewee, an enforcement barrister, stated: 'The fact that the wife knows, I think, is questionable—they might know or they might have a suspicion, but does that really matter if they know or not? As long as they are not involved. If they are involved, then its slightly different. But even so, it misses the point—it's destroying the family home. And it's the children is what would particularly concern me because you are taking that away from them.' EW09.

[74] IRE12. Another enforcement official stated: 'The Supreme Court in this country has decided that if the family home is the proceeds of crime, and the wife is living there mortgage free—unlike the rest of society who have had to pay their own way . . . The point that the Supreme Court has made is that if it is a home that was purchased with proceeds of crime, then no constitutional protection arises.' IRE05.

[75] EW10.

observation that putting people—that is, innocent family members—out on the streets is 'pretty brutal'.[76] In contrast, there was no such internal conflict for the following interviewee: 'The state has obligations to provide people with a roof over their head and there are of course state benefits. That's what the State is there to step in for. It's not like defendants are ever literally put out on the street.'[77] They continued: 'In any case involving vulnerable people, then the state will provide in some shape or form and maybe the defendant should have thought more about this themselves in terms of the risks that they bring to their own family.'[78]

The inclusion of children in the repercussions of civil recovery proceedings seemed to pose a particular conundrum for some of our interviewees though. One defence solicitor said:

> I suppose one argument would be that no wife of a bank robber is under any illusions about what her husband does for a living, and so why should they enjoy the protection of the Family Law Protection Act when they know perfectly well that it's all paid for with dirty money. The same argument really doesn't extend to the children.[79]

This reality was acknowledged by enforcement practitioners also,[80] with one enforcement barrister encapsulating the problem as follows: '[Y]ou have to balance between the family home, children, and the benefit to the child; and this area, the rights of the child, has not really been thought of.'[81] This is an evident understatement, not least when we emphasize, once again, that civil recovery proceedings *do not require a criminal conviction*. While it can be argued that the confiscation of a family home is justified under circumstances where a post-conviction confiscation order follows from a criminal conviction, where guilt has been established beyond reasonable doubt,[82] such a significant

[76] EW10.

[77] EW14.

[78] EW14.

[79] IRE08.

[80] IRE05; IRE07; IRE13; EW05; EW10.

[81] EW09. That interviewee also stated that the civil recovery legislation 'doesn't really care, and I don't think you can care necessarily because if not you can use family as a human shield but I think it's a massive area of contention'. Although this can be contrasted with their stance in n.73 above.

[82] For wider discussion of policy considerations, and application in caselaw, see Sarah Wood, 'What Happens When Assets Are Tainted: Financial Remedies v Confiscation Proceedings Revisited' [2021] *Family Law Journal* 1064. For consideration of the impact upon innocent family members, however, see Craig Fletcher, 'Social Value or Social Harm? The Impact of the Proceeds of Crime Act 2002 upon the Defendant and their Families' in Katie Benson, Colin King, and Clive Walker (eds), *Assets, Crimes, and the State: Innovations in 21st Century Legal Approaches* (Routledge 2020).

deprivation of property with potentially wide-ranging implications for the family in question is unjustifiable where wrongdoing has only been established to the civil standard.

Restitution

Evident in policy and judicial discourse is an emphasis on civil recovery as 'restitution'. In other words, the deprivation of property is not punishment of the individual but rather an entitlement claim based upon a(n ill-gotten) gain.[83] The suitability of such a gain-based recovery approach within this context is debatable but the primary issue concerns the parties to the action. The entitlement claim does not come from a person deprived of their property, but rather from the state. What the state stands to gain is not, nor ever was, its own property; the property was not taken from the state, nor has the state been deprived of its possession or use. All of this calls into question the restitution label. Indeed, nothing discussed thus far provides any justification as to why recovery should be on the part of the state or why there should be, as Alldridge puts it, such 'state appropriation of property'. He continues:

> It might be property that the possessor should never have had, or only had because s/he acted illegally, but it was never the State's property, so the State is not getting something back: it is *getting* something, and arguments about the legitimacy of the procedure should start from that basis.[84]

If, as we contend, there is a question mark over the state's entitlement to 'recover' property that never belonged to it, does that not push this state appropriation of property closer to constituting punishment? Controversially, no—at least, not according to the English & Welsh and Irish courts, whose interpretation of this point has been, as noted above, especially lenient. The European Court of Human Rights has been similarly accommodating, taking the consistent position that forfeiture of property cases do not come under the

[83] Birks uses the term 'gain-based recovery' in relation to restitution as a legal response. Peter Birks, *Unjust Enrichment* (2nd edn, Oxford University Press 2005) 11. Giglio prefers the term 'gain-related recovery' in the context of restitution. For wider consideration of terminological difficulty, see Francesco Giglio, 'Gain-Related Recovery' (2008) 28(3) *Oxford Journal of Legal Studies* 501.

[84] Peter Alldridge, 'Civil Recovery in England and Wales: An Appraisal' in Colin King, Clive Walker, and Jimmy Gurulé (eds), *The Palgrave Handbook of Criminal and Terrorism Financing Law* (Palgrave 2018) 516.

criminal limb of Article 6.[85] This determination downplays the seriousness of the deprivation of one's property, not least considering that the determinative wrongdoing need only be established on the balance of probabilities. The 'impact on the appellant',[86] to use Lord Kerr's words, is, we argue, seriously understated. We return to this argument in the final section of this chapter.

In Chapter 4, we examined the courts' approach to civil recovery as punishment. More specifically, we discussed how the courts determined that civil recovery is not punishment but rather *something else*: preventive, reparative, and/or compensatory. We dispute that determination on the grounds that the characterization of civil recovery as any or all of these does not preclude it having punitive character also.[87] Building upon the above discussion concerning 'no good title', we pick up on this point again here. In *Walsh*, it was said that civil recovery proceedings are 'not directed towards [the appellant] in the sense that they seek to inflict punishment *beyond the recovery of assets that do not lawfully belong to him*',[88] which suggests that, for Lord Kerr, actual punishment for the wrongdoing would be *over and above* the deprivation of assets in civil recovery proceedings.[89] This is worth highlighting, not least because it reminds us, in the specific context of punishment, of the overlap between the criminal law and private law wrongs—many courses of conduct punishable as crimes are also tortious[90]—but also because it exposes the private law influences upon Lord Kerr's reasoning here. In private law, when punitive damages are awarded, they are awarded *in addition* to compensation. Tort law, for example, places the defendant under the obligation to restore the claimant to the position they would have been in had the wrong not been committed, to the extent such is possible,[91] while the inclusion of punitive damages goes beyond this corrective *restorative* duty and sanction *in excess* of the claimant's loss.[92]

[85] See, e.g., *M v Italy*, App. No. 12386/86, 15 April 1991; *Air Canada v UK* [1995] 20 EHRR 150; *Dassa Foundation v Liechtenstein*, App. No. 696/05, 10 July 2007; *Gogitidze v Georgia* [2015] ECHR 475.

[86] *Walsh v Director of the Assets Recovery Agency* [2005] NICA 6, para. 41

[87] See Chapter 4, 'Punishment'.

[88] *Walsh v Director of the Assets Recovery Agency* [2005] NICA 6, para. 41, per Kerr LCJ. Emphasis added.

[89] This broadly coheres with the conceptual claims about punishment in *inter alia*: Matthew H Kramer, 'John Austin on Punishment', *University of Cambridge Faculty of Law Research Paper* No. 45/2011; HLA Hart, *The Concept of Law* (2nd edn, Oxford University Press 1994) 38–42; Joel Feinberg, *Doing and Deserving* (Princeton University Press 1970) 95–118, 'The Expressive Function of Punishment'.

[90] See generally Matthew Dyson (ed.), *Unravelling Tort and Crime* (Cambridge University Press 2014).

[91] Goudkamp and Katsampouka give the following contract law example: if X hires contractor C to build a swimming pool 10 feet deep, but it turns out to be only 9.5 feet deep, it would be inappropriate to repudiate the contract but C can be required to compensate X. See James Goudkamp and Eleni Katsampouka, 'Punitive Damages and the Place of Punishment in Private Law' (2021) 84(6) *Modern Law Review* 1257.

[92] For wider consideration of punitive damages, see Ernest J Weinrib, *The Idea of Private Law* (Oxford University Press 2012) 135; James Goudkamp and Eleni Katsampouka, 'Punitive Damages and the

If we follow this line of reasoning then the judicial designation of civil recovery as non-punitive is easier to understand: not only does punishment comprise the censure and hard treatment, but it must also—importantly—have the effect of bringing the wrongdoer *below* their starting position, of rendering them materially worse off (be that in liberty or property) than they were before the wrongdoing took place.[93] Under this rubric, Lord Kerr's reasoning, as well as Keane CJ's position that 'a forfeiture is not a punishment',[94] is more plausible: the seizure of the proceeds of crime—assuming we know them to be such—is arguably not punishment.

We reject that position, however. Commenting on the case of *Attorney General v Blake*,[95] concerning an account of profits, Goudkamp and Katsampouka dismiss contentions that such an account cannot constitute punishment simply because it restores a defendant to their prior position by removing profit. They contend that such an assertion—and it is only an assertion—is wrong: first, being deprived of a gain is 'unpleasant' and thus capable of constituting punishment; second, an account will not necessarily restore the defendant to their earlier position if, for example, it does not factor in time and effort expended towards that gain; and, third, even if an account does restore the *status quo ante* the absence of punishment from the remedy's goals is a *non sequitur*.[96] They continue:

> The fact that a given act may not be punitive in terms of its effects does not mean that the act concerned was not done for the purpose of punishment but, rather, simply that that goal (if pursued) was not realised in the instant case. Because, as we have seen, the courts have made it explicit that an account is sometimes awarded in order to punish, it is irrelevant for present purposes that an account may not, on occasion, be punitive in terms of its outcome.[97]

Place of Punishment in Private Law' (2021) 84(6) *Modern Law Review* 1257. On punitive damages and punishment, see Benjamin C Zipursky, Theory of Punitive Damages (2005) 84 *Texas Law Review* 105.

[93] Such a view has support in literature: 'profit stripping cannot be explained on punitive grounds. This is because stripping profits never punishes. A defendant who has the profit he made from a wrong taken from him does not benefit from the commission of the wrong, but that is far from saying that he is thereby punished for it. Imagine that I start with assets worth $100,000 and then commit a wrong that brings me a further $10,000. A court then takes this $10,000 from me and hence I am left with what I started with: $100,000. It is not possible to regard this as punishment, as I am no worse off than I was before.' Allan Beever, 'Justice and Punishment in Tort: A Comparative Theoretical Analysis' in Charles Rickett (ed.), *Justifying Private Law Remedies* (Hart 2008) 296.

[94] *Murphy v GM, PB, PC Ltd, GH and Gilligan v CAB* [2001] 4 IR 113, 153.

[95] [2001] 1 AC 268.

[96] James Goudkamp and Eleni Katsampouka, 'Punitive Damages and the Place of Punishment in Private Law' (2021) 84(6) *Modern Law Review* 1257, 1281–2.

[97] Ibid, 1282.

Such arguments equally apply to civil recovery. This non-conviction-based process removes the assets and thus any gain, but its dissolution of the owner/owned legal relationship is certainly punitive in a situation of good title. The stigma and censure dimension of both the proceedings themselves and the deprivation are, we argue, sufficiently unpleasant as to constitute punishment.[98]

A further consideration is the role of the state. In *Blake*, the state was a party to the undertaking at issue.[99] By contrast, in civil recovery proceedings, the state's role is similar to a prosecutor in criminal proceedings, acting in the public interest. Civil recovery can thus be viewed as a state response to serious and organized criminal activity. In this regard, the distinction between state responses to alleged criminal activity and state responses to other things, notably private law wrongs,[100] is a moral distinction that turns, vitally, on the fact that it is a *state* response that imposes a potentially harmful effect. In a private law context, the state will often be a neutral arbiter between two parties of identical normative status, and the symmetry of the parties thereby justifies the use of the balance of probabilities as the standard of proof. In some instances, the state might even be one of the parties in private law proceedings, such as where it sues for breach of contract, as in *Blake*, or where it is sued by an individual for its negligent actions. The private law nature of the proceedings is again salient here though. As noted above, in criminal proceedings the state acts as the *prosecutor* on behalf of the public at large. Leaving aside the thorny issue of where the seized assets eventually end up,[101] our contention is that, in civil recovery proceedings, the state is not a neutral party as in private law proceedings, or even a wronged party seeking the return of *its* property. Rather, its role is more akin to an investigator and/or prosecutor in criminal proceedings. We have already discussed the significant power asymmetry between the state and the individual in the context of procedural protections and the criminal process[102] but it bears repeating here. The state, the Leviathan, as the superior beast, must acknowledge its moral responsibility in criminal proceedings to the defendant—to the citizen—and offer *more* procedural protection, not less,

[98] See Chapter 4, 'Punishment'.

[99] Prior to being employed by the intelligence service, Blake had signed an Official Secrets Act declaration not to divulge information, an undertaking that was deemed to be contractually binding.

[100] We are grateful to Alex Green for this insight.

[101] In England & Wales, recovered proceeds are split between the Home Office and relevant enforcement agencies: Home Office, *Asset Recovery Incentivisation Scheme—Review* (February 2015) 2. In Ireland, recovered proceeds are sent to the Central Fund, however there are plans 'to establish a Community Safety Innovation Fund to allow the money seized from criminal activity to be more directly utilised in communities affected by crime'. Parliamentary Questions, 25 January 2022, PQ.478, per Minister McEntee.

[102] See Chapter 2; see also Antony Duff, Lindsay Farmer, Sandra Marshall, and Victor Tadros, *The Trial on Trial, Volume 3: Towards a Normative Theory of the Criminal Trial* (Hart 2007) 287–8.

if its response to their alleged wrongdoing is to be considered just. Therefore, when the state responds to alleged criminal activity by imposing something that *might* be harmful, *whether or not it is, in the technical sense, punitive*, it has a moral obligation to offer the protections of criminal law.[103]

Civil recovery is a state response to criminal activity—a response that is undertaken on behalf of the public at large. Proceedings are weighted in favour of the state, with the *burden* of proof being relatively easy to satisfy and the *standard* of proof being the civil standard, and the deprivation of property suffered by a respondent being presented neither as punishment nor even as harm, but as *recovery* or *restitution* of proceeds of crime to the state. This is a fallacy: as argued earlier, the state is *taking*—not recovering/restituting—the property in question. This notwithstanding, restitutionary justifications were strongly evident throughout our proponent interviews. For example, when asked whether civil recovery involves punishment, one official responded in the negative and continued: 'If you steal this book from me, the state might prosecute you for theft. But me taking the book back off you is not a punishment.'[104] This analogy does not quite hold, however, as the obvious distinction to be drawn between it and the operation of civil recovery is that the wronged party is taking *their* book back. Even if it were the state taking the book, the analogy is still on shaky foundations: the state is not taking back *its* book but is instead taking a book that allegedly belongs to another person—the supposed lawful owner. Pressed on this point, this enforcement official stated 'yes, but it is not a punishment', continuing to underscore that 'the person of last resort, to ensure that the person does not benefit from it, is the state'.[105] The emphasis here is solidly one of state intervention on public security grounds: the problem of uncertainty is ignored, the state shelves the procedural safeguards that would usually inhere in the law, and the risk passes from the community at large to the individual under suspicion.[106]

Such a state interventionist inclination also permeated views of other enforcement-focused interviewees, specifically the idea that civil recovery is in the public interest. Indeed, the perceived affront caused by serious and organized crime to public security, public welfare, and public conscience came to the fore.[107] As one barrister noted, 'if the court is satisfied on the balance

[103] This emphasis on the liberty of the subject has a long history: see, e.g., Quentin Skinner, *Liberty Before Liberalism* (Cambridge University Press 1998).
[104] IRE05.
[105] IRE05.
[106] See Richard V Ericson, *Crime in an Insecure World* (Polity Press 2007) 204–6.
[107] See *CAB v JWPL* [2007] IEHC 177.

of probabilities that the property is a proceeds of crime, then the state is empowered by a statute *to deprive the individual of those property rights* and that is a proportionate use of a statutory power'.[108] Another barrister emphasized: 'the public interest in defeating crime is very profound.'[109] A former enforcement official described civil recovery as a statutory tort on behalf of the people.[110] The 'public good' argument is unsubtle but evidently effective: in light of the limitations of conventional criminal law mechanisms, civil recovery purports to reduce the attractiveness and profitability of criminal conduct by depriving criminals of their criminal proceeds.[111] As we have argued throughout this book, however, civil recovery achieves its goals by means of its hybrid character and non-conviction-based operation, which combine to circumvent those elevated criminal law procedural safeguards intended to protect the individual from the abuses of state power.[112]

In this regard, and to return to the central issue of restitution, it is also worth highlighting what appears to be, on the part of both the legislature and the judiciary, a strategic downplaying of the *seriousness* of 'recovery'. Whether or not the deprivation of property is undertaken explicitly as a sanction or to remove a benefit, the outcome is the same. The next section presents a liberal theoretical account of property that supports our two-pronged claim that the deprivation of property—and its impact upon individual liberty—is more detrimental and thus problematic than currently allowed and that, in any event, suspicion is an unworthy and unreliable trigger for non-conviction-based proceedings.

'Life, Liberty, and Estate'

Although 'much contemporary theorising about criminal law is conducted against a backdrop of liberal ideals, values and assumptions which are seldom fully articulated, much less systematically explored',[113] the importance of a liberal orientation to our central argument is such that specific explanation of it is vital. These liberal theoretical underpinnings can be seen in our discussion of preventive justice,[114] our overt focus on due

[108] EW03. Emphasis added.
[109] IRE07.
[110] IRE11.
[111] See Chapter 3.
[112] See Chapter 5.
[113] Paul Roberts, 'Criminal Law Theory and the Limits of Liberalism', in AP Simester, Antje du Bois-Pedain, and Ulfrid Neumann (eds), *Liberal Criminal Theory: Essays for Andreas von Hirsch* (Hart 2014) 327–8.
[114] See Chapter 2.

process,[115] our emphasis on proportionality,[116] and in our liberal conception of property and property rights, upon which we will now elaborate.

A secular political morality, liberalism centres on the unit of the individual rather than 'aggregated abstract welfare', and prioritizes 'embodied individual wellbeing'.[117] It does so in a manner consistent with the deontological injunction that humans—as rational actors—be treated as ends in themselves instead of mere instrumental means;[118] indeed, to do otherwise would undermine the situation whereby the equal status of all is guaranteed by all. Fundamentally, therefore, liberal legal theory can be said to concern itself with prioritizing individual liberty and autonomy in a way that treats every human being as worthy of equal concern and respect.[119] A liberal theory of *property*, therefore, is one that introduces into the mix the idea of resources, both tangible and intangible, and articulates the myriad ways in which property contributes to individual autonomy: by demarcating the private sphere, for example, and by protecting citizens from state interference and intrusion.[120] By conceptualizing how our individual relations with *things* are constituted, regulated, delimited, and prohibited, liberal theories of property engage with issues of right, authority, and—perhaps most centrally—self-determination.[121]

Property, for liberal theorists, is thus the primary means through which individuals secure liberty, its central role as an instrument of liberty and equal rights. As Dagan explains, the 'right to property is often understood as one of the necessary implications of the status of individual natural persons as free and equal, which may explain its inclusion in the Universal Declaration of Human Rights'.[122] Indeed, it has been argued that *both* human rights and property rights are rights *in rem*, which is to say that 'they create corresponding obligations of non-interference on a very large and unspecified mass of dutyholders'.[123] Perhaps the most well-known liberal conception of property

[115] See Chapter 5.

[116] See Chapter 7.

[117] Paul Roberts, 'Criminal Law Theory and the Limits of Liberalism', in AP Simester, Antje du Bois-Pedain, and Ulfrid Neumann (eds), *Liberal Criminal Theory: Essays for Andreas von Hirsch* (Hart 2014) 333.

[118] 'All rational beings stand under the law that each of them is to treat himself and all others never merely as means but always at the same time as ends in themselves.' Immanuel Kant, *Groundwork of the Metaphysics of Morals* (Mary Gregor, transl. & ed.) (Cambridge University Press 1998) 41

[119] Ronald Dworkin, *Law's Empire* (Fontana Press 1986) 213.

[120] Margaret Davies, *Property: Meanings, Histories, Theories* (Routledge Cavendish 2007) 10.

[121] For a different perspective on the deon-telos of property, see David Lametti, 'Property and (Perhaps) Justice. A Review Article of James W Harris, Property and Justice and James E. Penner, The Idea of Property in Law' (1998) 43 *McGill Law Journal* 663.

[122] Hanoch Dagan, *A Liberal Theory of Property* (Cambridge University Press 2021) 1.

[123] Thomas W Merrill and Henry E Smith, 'The Morality of Property' (2007) 48(5) *William & Mary Law Review* 1849, 1851; see also James Penner, *The Idea of Property Law* (Oxford University Press 1997) 29–30.

comes from Locke, whose seventeenth-century writings 'signalled his desire to use the term in a broad sense, encompassing life and liberty as well as a specific interest in ... estate'.[124] Underkuffler explains this further by noting that, at this point in history, 'property included not only external objects and people's relationships to them, but also all of those human rights, liberties, powers, and immunities that are important for human well-being, including: freedom of expression, freedom of conscience, freedom from bodily harm, and free and equal opportunities to use personal faculties'.[125] In this sense, not only do we see the clear operative *function* of property, namely, to provide 'individuals with security and a stable horizon for their expectations',[126] but also the robust connections and interplays between property and other individual rights and freedoms. Indeed, in its instrumental necessity for autonomy, property can be considered no less a resource for individual liberty than physical liberty.[127] Arguably this point also sees cursory articulation in Dicey, where it is stated that 'no man is punishable or can be lawfully made to suffer *in body or goods* except for a distinct breach of law established in the ordinary legal manner before the ordinary Courts of the land'.[128] Moreover—and although the difficulties with both 'labour desert' and realism within Lockean property theory are well-documented[129]—it is useful to highlight the 'bottom-up' quality of Lockean property rights, that is, their 'pre-political' nature as individual entitlements that exist separate from the state.[130] It is this 'private authority' of property, as Dagan puts it, that 'advances the autonomy of owners', who can then 'justifiably expect others to respect it', while 'the law rightly vindicates this expectation'.[131]

The law is integral, therefore, in facilitating and maintaining individual autonomy in relation to property. Penner's explanation of this is particularly useful:

[124] Jeremy Waldron, *The Rule of Law & the Measure of Property* (Cambridge University Press 2012) 61.

[125] Laura S Underkuffler, 'On Property: An Essay' (1990) 100 (1) *Yale Law Journal* 127, 129.

[126] Jeremy Waldron, *The Rule of Law and the Measure of Property* (Cambridge University Press 2012) 61.

[127] On 'equality of resources', see Ronald Dworkin, *Sovereign Virtue* (Harvard University Press 2000), ch.2.

[128] Albert Venn Dicey, *Lectures Introductory to the Study of the Law of the Constitution*, (2nd edn, MacMillan 1886) Lecture V, 110 (emphasis added).

[129] James E Penner and Henry E Smith, 'Introduction', in James E Penner and Henry E Smith, *The Philosophical Foundations of Property Law* (Oxford University Press 2013) xix. The 'labour desert' or 'value-added' theory is a consequentialist argument which holds that, when labour produces something of value to others—that is, social value—then the labourer deserves to benefit from it on the grounds that it is the production of social value that deserves reward, not the labour that produced it.

[130] Richard A Epstein, *Design for Liberty: Private Property, Public Administration, and the Rule of Law* (Harvard University Press 2011) 63.

[131] Hanoch Dagan, *A Liberal Theory of Property* (Cambridge University Press 2021) 5.

> The interest in property is the interest in exclusively determining the use of things... But the freedom to determine the use of things is an interest of ours in part because of the freedom it provides to shape our lives... The interest in property is an interest in *exclusively* determining the use of things... The claim is that a right to a thing is a property right only to the extent that some others are excluded from the determination of its use....[132]

Penner further clarifies that property rights can be bifurcated into two types, the general and the specific. In terms of the latter, he notes that:

> [w]e have special rights to those items of property we own. Here the law protects our particular interest in the specific items of property we have ... [W]e see that these special rights *in rem* correlate to a general duty *in rem* upon all others not to interfere with property.[133]

This *exclusion* thesis of property rights, that is, that the right to property should be conceived as the right of exclusive use, construes property as an *in rem* co-ordination device.[134] Importantly, it is the duty *in rem* that gives shape to the property right *in rem*, a duty that is incumbent upon *all others* to exclude themselves from interference with another's property. Property thus construed is a 'private counterweight to state power',[135] a legal relationship that provides protection for the individual against the state.

What bearing does this brief theoretical excursus have upon our analysis of civil recovery? There are two points that we want to raise in this regard. First, and in reference to our earlier contention that the label *restitutionary* downplays the seriousness of civil recovery, this liberal theoretical account bolsters our standpoint that the deprivation of property—and its impact *upon* individual liberty—is far too quickly accepted as *significantly* less than the deprivation of physical liberty. We reiterate that it is not our intention to equate these two deprivations but, instead, to highlight the ready acceptance of civil recovery as unproblematic when it has the capacity to dissolve an owner/owned relationship on the balance of probabilities.

Although our criticism so far has been trained on the judicial response to this issue, our enforcement-focused interviewees exhibit similar views concerning

132 James E Penner, *The Idea of Property in Law* (Clarendon Press 1997) 49. Emphasis in original.
133 Ibid 50.
134 Thomas W Merrill and Henry E Smith, *The Morality of Property* (2007) 48 *William & Mary Law Review* 1849.
135 Margaret Davies, *Property: Meanings, Histories, Theories* (Routledge Cavendish 2007) 11.

property and property rights. For example, one enforcement official argued, 'In no civil case will you end up in jail. It's not a loss of liberty, it's only money at the end of the day. It's as simple as that.'[136] A former enforcement official in fact drew this very distinction:

> [I]t's almost philosophical—do we value life and a person's liberty different than we value hard commodities, cash and assets, things like that? And, actually taking away somebody's liberty, I would very firmly be in the camp that it's absolutely critical that you reach that high burden [i.e. beyond reasonable doubt]. *But this is not the same.*[137]

Another interviewee problematized this very issue from the other perspective:

> I get the impression that, for criminals, doing a spell in prison is seen by them as an occupational hazard or as something that they should take on the chin when it happens as it is recognized as a risk that they run. When it comes to civil recovery, the impression I get is that there is a real shock that their 'stuff' can be taken by the state in a way in which they have very little to do as an alternative (in contrast to, say, confiscation where they can choose to go to prison if they don't want to pay up), but with civil recovery the action is in respect of the property itself so that will be forfeited. In a way, that really gets to criminals.[138]

It is certainly arguable that many people might prefer a custodial sentence over the seizure of, for example, large sums of money or the family home.[139] On this reasoning, the assumption that the deprivation of physical liberty is *necessarily* the more draconian punishment, and that the deprivation of property under the rubric of restitution is not as serious, is open to dispute.

Our second theoretical point concerns the exclusion thesis of property, as discussed. This thesis, and the idea of property as an *in rem* coordination device, are useful foundations for our argument that civil recovery conveniently denies the relationship between owner and owned. Neither the property law

[136] IRE05.

[137] EW10, our emphasis.

[138] EW05. As another barrister stated: 'Hit them in the pockets. If you send them to prison, they'll get out of prison but they'll come back to their properties.' EW03.

[139] Samuel Sittlington and Jackie Harvey, 'Prevention of Money Laundering and the Role of Asset Recovery' (2018) 70 *Crime Law & Social Change* 421. Compare Petrus van Duyne, Wouter de Zanger, and Francois Kristen, 'Greedy of Crime-Money: The Reality and Ethics of Asset Recovery' in Petrus van Duyne et al. (eds), *Corruption, Greed and Crime Money. Sleaze and Shady Economy in Europe and Beyond* (Wolf Legal Publishers 2014).

of Ireland nor that of England & Wales automatically makes the proceeds of crime the property of state, and yet—as discussed above—in our interviews proponents were quick to reject the idea that property rights subsisted in assets suspected to be the proceeds of crime. For example, when asked whether the state had better title to proceeds of crime, one enforcement official answered in the affirmative, '[f]or the common good and for the benefit of the taxpayer'.[140] Others rejected outright any criticism of civil recovery on the basis of property rights.[141] An enforcement barrister was categorical: 'You don't have a property right in something which was gained unlawfully', and: 'There is no valid constitutional interest where property is the product of criminal activity'.[142] More concerning was the speculative dimension that came to the fore, as illustrated by this exchange:

> *Interviewer*: If I have a house, have paid all relevant tax, etc, it is registered properly in my name, and then CAB [Criminal Assets Bureau] come after that property. I have evidence to show my title. Why do I then have to do more?
>
> *Respondent*: It might not be yours. It might be proceeds of crime. It may be money laundered and the laundered money is now in that house. The money used to buy the house is directly from a crime, money laundering, and you haven't spent a penny of your own money. You might say 'it is my money put into the house', but it is still not yours. We say that money made from drug dealing is wrong. The community aspect of it is that if you can show that that money came from an honest source ... [*trails off*].[143]

In our interviews there was very little pushback on this issue, although one defence barrister did acknowledge the problem. When asked about the enforcement agency stance on property rights, that civil recovery respondents have no rights to the proceeds of crime, this barrister noted that this was 'a typical prosecutor's answer,' continuing to say: 'If they're right, then of course its correct, but if they're wrong ... [*trails off*].'[144]

This goes to the heart of the matter, and to the central issue with civil recovery as a hybrid civil/criminal procedure. Mere suspicion as to criminal wrongdoing is insufficient to justify confiscating property, and the proof that

140 IRE12.
141 EW10; EW11.
142 IRE04.
143 IRE05.
144 EW07.

would justify such an interference with property rights is not necessarily forthcoming in a civil recovery action.[145] Considering civil recovery is an action *in rem*, a logical assumption would be that the proprietary right would follow the *res*, but this does not actually appear to be the case—the state instead asserts a *personal* restitutionary right against the respondent in response to the alleged benefit received by that respondent. Alldridge is clear on this point: the state combines both this proprietary claim and the civil recovery proceedings within an instrumental scheme, which is to say, as 'part of a crime control strategy directed to deprive criminals and others of the proceeds of crime, notwithstanding that the property is theirs'.[146]

In light of the foregoing, the tactical aspect of civil recovery is increasingly apparent and—from a liberal perspective—far from appealing. As Waldron has noted, 'it may be thought to be no accident that those who assault private property rights tend to use methods of governance at odds with the formal and procedural principles of the Rule of Law'.[147] The next chapter will critically discuss this instrumentality and the various attempts to justify it under the rubric of pragmatism. It will also lead the argument that, where undertaken erroneously, civil recovery not only constitutes a threat to individual property rights but also has the potential to comprise the moral harm of a serious miscarriage of justice.

[145] See Chapter 7 on suspicion.

[146] Peter Alldridge, 'Civil Recovery in England and Wales: An Appraisal' in Colin King, Clive Walker, and Jimmy Gurulé (eds), *The Palgrave Handbook of Criminal and Terrorism Financing Law* (Palgrave 2018) 518.

[147] Jeremy Waldron, *The Rule of Law and the Measure of Property* (Cambridge University Press 2012) 21.

7

A Pragmatic Response?

Introduction

Commenting on the English & Welsh civil recovery provisions, Rees et al. describe Part 5 of the Proceeds of Crime Act (POCA) as 'a statement of law enforcement at its most pragmatic'.[1] Pragmatism is a recurring theme amongst proponents of civil recovery, to the extent that the non-conviction-based (NCB) approach might be described as a form of 'practical justice'.[2] Having teased the idea of civil recovery as a pragmatic response to serious and organized crime for several chapters, we will now pay it dedicated attention. We chose to discuss pragmatism separately from other issues because it comprises the most substantial disconnect between academia and law enforcement: while academic literature to date has largely focused more on the importance of ostensibly liberal legal principles,[3] enforcement-focused practitioners tend to concern themselves with the 'reality' of civil recovery measures and the effective operation of the law in practice.[4] It is our contention that this schism is problematically misleading about the importance that enforcement-focused practitioners place on due process protections. We base this contention on information drawn from our practitioner interviews in Ireland and in England & Wales, and introduce the view that even self-professed proponents, in favour of civil recovery's expediency and categorical about its rule of law compliance, acknowledge that there are tensions within the process. Notwithstanding such tensions, proponents are adamant in their defence of civil recovery as a viable

[1] Edward Rees, Richard Fisher, and Richard Thomas, *Blackstone's Guide to The Proceeds of Crime Act 2002* (5th edn, Oxford University Press 2015) 172.

[2] For consideration of 'practical justice' in the context of international criminal justice, see Mark Findlay and Joanna Chuah Hui Ying, *Principled International Criminal Justice: Lessons from Tort Law* (Routledge 2019) 104 et seq.

[3] For consideration of the 'gap' between academic normatively-oriented critique and 'the positive conditions of the political order' in the context of civil preventative orders, see Peter Ramsay, 'The Theory of Vulnerable Autonomy and the Legitimacy of Civil Preventative Orders' in Bernadette McSherry, Alan Norrie, and Simon Bronitt (eds), *Regulating Deviance: The Redirection of Criminalisation and the Futures of Criminal Law* (Hart 2009).

[4] This can arguably also be cast in terms of the requirement for practitioners to work with the law as it is as opposed to how it ought to be, while academic commentators may take a more expansive and/or critical view.

Civil Recovery of Criminal Property. Colin King and Jennifer Hendry, Oxford University Press.
 DOI: 10.1093/oso/9780198824251.003.0007

practical approach to the well-charted criminal justice shortcomings in effectively tackling serious and organized crime, a stance that mirrors the 'tough on crime' justificatory rhetoric coming from political actors.[5]

A note here on terminology before we progress. Although we have previously used the term *expediency* to discuss the motivations behind outcome-driven proceeds of crime legislation,[6] throughout our practitioner interviews it became clear that the term featuring most prominently was its semantic relation, *pragmatism*. This term was used in its everyday sense[7] to describe civil recovery as a realistic and practical approach to addressing the enduring conundrum of bringing the justice system to bear upon the career criminal. Our use of the term 'pragmatism' is not intended to denote either a particular school of thought or to present a political-philosophical position,[8] nor do we propose to offer either a defence or a critique of 'pragmatism' as a theoretical concept.[9] Our aim is rather more modest: to consider, within the context of civil recovery, the idea of 'pragmatism' as colloquially understood, its influence in terms of the alleged clash between outcomes and due process, and its role in the balancing act between expediency and legitimacy.

To these ends, this chapter proceeds in three main parts. First, we interrogate the idea that there is no inherent problem in confiscation without conviction and that it is an appropriate means to a specific end. Here, we draw upon our interview data to explore issues of necessity, fairness, and proportionality. Second, we reject the flawed rhetoric, raised frequently by proponent interviewees, that the innocent have nothing to fear. Third and finally, having

[5] For consideration of political discourse in relation to civil recovery, see Chapter 3.

[6] Jennifer Hendry and Colin King, 'Expediency, Legitimacy, and the Rule of Law: A Systems Perspective on Civil/ Criminal Procedural Hybrids' (2017) 11(4) *Criminal Law and Philosophy* 733.

[7] Pragmatism is defined as 'the quality of dealing with a problem in a sensible way that suits the conditions that really exist, rather than following fixed theories or rules'. *Cambridge Dictionary*, available at: <https://dictionary.cambridge.org/dictionary/english/pragmatism>.

[8] The term 'pragmatism' is open to interpretation. For wider discussion, see Morris Dickstein, 'Introduction: Pragmatism Then and Now' in Morris Dickstein (ed.), *The Revival of Pragmatism: New Essays in Social Thought, Law, and Culture* (Duke University Press 1998).

[9] There is an extensive literature that encompasses *pragmatic* considerations in the criminal justice system and beyond, however the terms 'pragmatic' or 'pragmatism' are used in different senses across such literature. It is important then to set out how the term is used or interpreted. See, e.g., Asher Flynn and Arie Freiberg, *Plea Negotiations: Pragmatic Justice in an Imperfect World* (Palgrave 2018); Sian Elias, *Fairness in Criminal Justice: Golden Threads and Pragmatic Patches* (Cambridge University Press 2017); Susan Dieleman, David Rondel, and Christopher Voparil (eds), *Pragmatism and Justice* (Oxford University Press 2017); John Jackson and Yassin Brunger, 'Witness Preparation in the ICC: An Opportunity for Principled Pragmatism' (2015) 13(3) *Journal of International Criminal Justice* 601; Megan O'Neill and Daniel McCarthy, '(Re)negotiating Police Culture through Partnership Working: Trust, Compromise and the 'New' Pragmatism' (2014) 14(2) *Criminology and Criminal Justice* 143.

exposed these issues and flagged the potential for miscarriages of justice[10] in civil recovery actions, we argue that this constitutes moral harm. Relying on the Dworkinian distinction between bare harm and moral harm,[11] we lead the argument that the circumvention of criminal law's procedural protections, facilitated by and justified through its civil/criminal hybridity, downplays both the increased likelihood and extent of the moral harm of erroneous deprivation of property.

An Academia/Law Enforcement Divide?

Before commencing with our tripartite analysis, it is worth considering the apparent disconnect between the academic literature, on the one hand, and the views of enforcement-focused practitioners on the other, not least to explore whether or not this disconnect is in fact as entrenched as has been supposed. One prominent view concerning this supposed schism has been that policymakers and enforcement officials have focused less on arguments from principle and due process considerations, prioritizing instead the goals of the legislation and practical outcomes.[12] In this regard, the central issues are efficiency and expediency, as discussed in Chapter 3. The corollary has been how scholarly discussions about serious and organized crime focus too much on issues of fairness, due process rights, and procedural protections, all to the detriment of efficiency and expediency.[13] Indeed, much of the critical literature in this field has in fact queried the legitimacy of the non-conviction-based approach, as well as expressing concern that civil recovery deliberately bypasses the criminal law's elevated procedural safeguards and, by that token, those important guiding principles that comprise the rule of law.[14]

[10] For a broad taxonomy of 'miscarriages of justice', see Clive Walker, 'Miscarriages of Justice in Principle and Practice' in Clive Walker and Keir Starmer (eds), *Miscarriages of Justice: A Review of Justice in Error* (Blackstone Press 1999).

[11] Bare harm is where an individual suffers as a result of punishment, while moral harm is the harm suffered by an individual when punishment is unjust. See Ronald Dworkin, *A Matter of Principle* (Harvard University Press 1985) 80.

[12] In considering philosophical pragmatism, Kenny outlines: 'It requires you to set your highest goals, and to do whatever you need to do to bring them about, calculating the worth of particular actions not by principled accounts of their rightness but by their effects. Principles, on this view, are meaningless abstractions that get in the way, muddy the water, and distract you from your goals.' David Kenny, 'The Human Pared Away: Hilary Mantel's Thomas Cromwell as an Archetype of Legal Pragmatism' (2022) 34(1) *Law and Literature* 109.

[13] For wider discussion of fairness-based and efficiency-based arguments, see Shi-Ling Hsu, 'Fairness versus Efficiency in Environmental Law' (2004) 31 *Ecology Law Quarterly* 303. For consideration of efficiency in the criminal justice system, see Luke Marsh, 'Leveson's Narrow Pursuit of Justice: Efficiency and Outcomes in the Criminal Process' (2016) 45(1) *Common Law World Review* 51.

[14] See Chapter 5 for criticism of civil recovery on due process grounds.

As our empirical data demonstrates, however, the reality of the situation is far more nuanced. While there was a not-unexpected focus by proponents on efficiency and expediency, this was not the only emphasis. Several interviewees took a fundamentally contractarian position, giving precedence to the idea of being a good citizen.[15] Others adopted an overtly utilitarian view, stressing the policy objectives of civil recovery and articulating them in terms of increasing the overall welfare of society.[16] Most interviewees in favour of civil recovery were of the perspective that civil recovery constitutes a reorientation of efforts to tackle organized crime away from individual guilt and towards property, that is, what Ryan describes as 'a framework of justice that is apersonal, non-moral, regulatory and administrative in nature'.[17]

In exploring this seeming disconnect, a deceptively simple initial question can be posed: what is the problem with confiscation without conviction?[18] As we discuss in Chapter 3, where we examine civil recovery's various justifications, the standard criminal law approach of investigation, prosecution, conviction, and imprisonment was deemed inadequate in dealing with organized crime-related cases, which impacted negatively on the use of post-conviction confiscation powers in both Ireland and England & Wales.[19] The introduction of the alternative, *non*-conviction-based approach to seizing property deemed to be the proceeds of crime was in response to demands for a more effective and advantageous strategy. This is not to say that its introduction was not controversial—it most certainly was—but this controversy featured predominantly within academic debate; until now there has been little to no information as to its reception by practitioners. In this regard the insights gleaned from our interviews are genuinely illuminating.

Prevalent amongst civil recovery's proponents is the idea that, in non-conviction-based proceedings, the due process protections afforded by the criminal law are not undermined because they are not applicable. In essence,

[15] Alan Norrie, 'Citizenship, Authoritarianism and the Changing Shape of the Criminal Law' in Bernadette McSherry, Alan Norrie, and Simon Bronitt (eds), *Regulating Deviance: The Redirection of Criminalisation and the Futures of Criminal Law* (Hart 2009).

[16] Jeremy Bentham, *An Introduction to the Principles of Morals and Legislation* (T. Payne and Sons 1780) 1–6, 'Of the Principle of Utility'.

[17] Patrick Ryan, *An Examination of How the Methods Employed by the Criminal Assets Bureau Move Ireland in a New Direction of Crime Control* (PhD Thesis, University of Limerick 2019) 24.

[18] This question is posed by Michele Panzavolta in 'Confiscation and the Concept of Punishment: Can There Be a Confiscation Without a Conviction?' in Katalin Ligeti and Michele Simonato (eds), *Chasing Criminal Money: Challenges and Perspective On Asset Recovery in the EU* (Hart Publishing 2017) 26. Panzavolta is in favour of non-conviction-based confiscation, though 'only so long as certain conditions are in place' 27.

[19] IRE03; IRE07; IRE09; EW03; EW05; EW10; EW11. See also Mike Levi and Lisa Osofsky, *Investigating, Seizing and Confiscating the Proceeds of Crime* (Home Office 1995).

civil recovery proponents are accepting of the label 'civil', seeing it as determinative of procedure to be followed. The academic position in this regard is well charted, but the practitioner one far less so,[20] and the juxtaposition here is worth noting. Despite acknowledging that the criminal law's heightened procedural standards do not apply in civil recovery proceedings, proponents nonetheless express clear commitments to core safeguards of the criminal justice system, such as, the presumption of innocence. This begs the question as to how these commitments align with civil recovery, which—as critics have argued—specifically *undermines* safeguards that would otherwise apply in criminal proceedings?[21] This ambiguity suggests, at minimum, a degree of cognitive dissonance. The next two sections explain how proponents justify civil recovery as a pragmatic response.

A Means to an End?

Across our proponent interviews, one recurring theme was that civil recovery 'may be a necessary evil'.[22] Expanding on this view, this official explained:

> NCB [non-conviction-based] may be like chemotherapy: imprecise, destructive, but in many circumstances, it is the only treatment available and, if a better solution came along tomorrow, I would 100% endorse it. It is tackling a cancer in society, to continue the metaphor. But I don't know of a better treatment. Post-conviction based? No, that has been shown definitively not to work, because you can't get convictions... It is perhaps like chemotherapy; it is not a pretty treatment. It has the potential to cause harm and difficulty, but it's the only thing that gets results.[23]

[20] There is some literature on civil recovery from the perspective of law enforcement officials, that purports to justify the civil approach. See, e.g., Stef Cassella, 'The Case for Civil Forfeiture: Why In Rem Proceedings are an Essential Tool for Recovering the Proceeds of Crime' (2008) 11(1) *Journal of Money Laundering Control* 8; Anthony Kennedy, 'Justifying the Civil Recovery of Criminal Proceeds' (2005) 12(1) *Journal of Financial Crime* 8.

[21] Similar questions can be asked in relation to other aspects of the criminal justice system, such as the daily practice of prosecutors or defence lawyers. See, respectively, Marianne Wade, 'Meeting the Demands of Justice Whilst Coping with Crushing Caseloads? How Sykes and Matza help us understand prosecutors across Europe' (2018) *Journal of Criminal Justice and Security* 1; Daniel Newman and Lucy Welsh, 'The Practices of Modern Criminal Defence Lawyers: Alienation and its Implications for Access to Justice' (2019) 48 *Common Law World Review* 64.

[22] IRE05. Even civil liberty organizations recognize pragmatic considerations: 'There are a lot of benefits to it when you are thinking of protecting communities and victims of crime.' IRE10. A crucial consideration for that interviewee, however, was the lack of an alternative given inadequate resourcing of the criminal justice system.

[23] IRE05.

Two points are worth flagging here. First, while this official acknowledges the *bluntness* of civil recovery, they nonetheless consider it to be necessary. Second, in the implicit cost-benefit analysis being undertaken, the official—like many proponent interviewees—prioritizes the aim of the legislation, the core rationale that crime should not pay, and the fundamental issue of *fairness* over respect for due process rights and safeguards. These can be cast in terms of competing values: it is unfair that an individual benefits from their criminal activity, so any effective interference with this benefit should necessarily *trump* the operation of those criminal process protections to which that individual should otherwise be entitled. The following three sub-sections will explore this reasoning in relation to (i) fairness, (ii) proportionality, and (iii) the standard, and burden, of proof.

Fair response or necessary evil?

Civil recovery has been described by its proponents as 'a rational response',[24] a 'really ground-breaking' power,[25] 'an increasingly powerful weapon',[26] 'a success',[27] and an 'appropriate policy response'.[28] Interviewees emphasized the inadequacy of conventional criminal law approaches to tackling serious and organized crime, alongside the need for a genuine, practical alternative. As one practitioner described, 'we had a build-up of certain criminal groups that had become particularly strong and had effectively begun to act with impunity really and build up power bases. In one way or another it required to be addressed by the legislature'.[29] Another interviewee stressed: 'It's the basic idea that crime shouldn't pay and, you know, if law enforcement aren't given some tool to address that, then the reality is that people will run rings around it.'[30] Similarly, it was stressed that '[t]here has to be a way of tackling these people up the chain'.[31]

While such views mirror the commonly-held academic view that there was—and is—a need for appropriate powers to tackle criminal activities, they start to diverge when it comes to the substance and extent of these powers.

24 EW13.
25 EW03.
26 EW05.
27 IRE03.
28 IRE09.
29 IRE03. Also IRE07, who emphasized the nature of crime in Ireland at the time and the need for action.
30 EW12.
31 EW14.

Critics of civil recovery maintain that any such powers should be proportionate and justified, and consider the non-conviction-based approach to fall short of these requirements. This position can readily be contrasted with *post*-conviction confiscation, which follows a criminal trial where a defendant's guilt has been established beyond reasonable doubt and which, notwithstanding some practical concerns,[32] is much less objectionable.[33] One interviewee, a criminal defence solicitor very critical of civil recovery, took the position that allegations of criminality by a state body merit the enhanced procedural protections of the criminal process. They further stated that:

> We don't have such an extreme criminal problem that you can really say anything goes. And I would prefer, if we're dealing with the question of criminal assets, I would prefer that asset seizure is more related to proven offending.[34]

Another defence solicitor echoed this stance: 'It should be that you prove that someone is guilty, then you forfeit their assets.'[35]

By contrast, proponents not only emphasize the *need* for the non-conviction-based approach but also contend that it is both fair and proportionate. Consequently, the 'fair and proportionate' fault line can be said to run through practitioner debates on civil recovery, even where there is awareness of and sensitivity to the extent of the changes it provokes. During our interviews proponents of civil recovery acknowledged that it constitutes a significant move away from conventional criminal law and that there is a need to tread carefully in relation to the procedure's hybridity: one interviewee noted that 'one has got to be very aware of the nature of the claim that's being made and the fact that its underlying aspect is a criminal allegation',[36] while another was of the opinion that judges 'need to be careful about maintaining the difference between the criminal finding and the civil finding'.[37]

[32] Craig Fletcher, 'Social Value or Social Harm? The Impact of the Proceeds of Crime Act 2002 upon the Defendant and their Families' in Katie Benson, Colin King, and Clive Walker (eds), *Assets, Crimes, and the State: Innovations in 21st Century Legal Approaches* (Routledge 2020); Karen Bullock, 'Criminal Benefit, the Confiscation Order and the Post-Conviction Confiscation Regime' (2014) *Crime, Law and Social Change* 45. At the time of writing, the post-conviction scheme is under review in England & Wales: Law Commission, *Confiscation of the Proceeds of Crime after Conviction: A Consultation Paper* (CP 249) (2020).

[33] Though for consideration of controversies, see Peter Alldridge, 'Proceeds of Crime Since 2003—Two Key Areas' [2014] *Criminal Law Review* 171.

[34] IRE08.

[35] EW08.

[36] EW03.

[37] EW05.

The proponent perspective on civil recovery's procedural hybridity, and the extent to which it blurs the lines between the civil law and the criminal law, are worth highlighting here. In our interviews, proponents repeatedly stressed that civil recovery proceedings simply are not *criminal* in character: 'But you're *not* a criminal. Because the law says, to get to that stage, you have to have a criminal trial, and that's meaningful.'[38] In the words of one enforcement barrister, 'you can draw a distinction between this and criminal proceedings, and that is a perfectly adequate distinction to draw'.[39] In the same vein, another participant stated that, 'determining an issue of criminality but not applying the sanction is not a criminal trial'.[40] When pushed on the issue of civil recovery proceedings involving the state making allegations of criminality on the part of the respondent, an official responded:

> But that is all it is—an allegation. And you are able to rebut that. The determination is made not by CAB [Criminal Assets Bureau], but by an independent court. It doesn't matter what I think about a person, it is only when an independent court makes a finding of fact that you are holding the proceeds of crime as a result of your conduct.[41]

These standpoints inform the proponents' position on the fairness of civil recovery: there is nothing inherently unfair with this *civil* process, as there is no determination of guilt. In support of this stance, the *in rem* (against the property) character of civil recovery proceedings was underscored, with interviewees noting that, if there is a concern of 'someone's name being dragged through the mud, they could look for an order of anonymity.... This is a case against the property.'[42] Further to this: 'It doesn't strike at the individual, it strikes at the property, no one is in fear of going to prison.'[43] Another

[38] IRE07. They continued: 'if it's to be a crime, that's the criminal courts. So, that division has always existed, still exists at the moment, and I don't see anything alien or strange about it.'

[39] EW05.

[40] IRE11.

[41] IRE05. As for the making of criminal allegations, many proponents dismissed criticism on the basis that other processes also involve serious allegations outside the criminal process (e.g. health and safety, bullying, sexual harassment): 'There are lots of allegations out there that would affect my character more than a proceeds of crime application.' IRE05. Also IRE07. Another interviewee gave the example of one person assaulting another; the attacker can be sued in civil proceedings even though there is an allegation of criminality. In relation to arguments about inequality of arms and the State making allegations of criminality, that interviewee said that in civil proceedings a wealthy individual might have more resources, and that the beyond reasonable doubt standard would not (and should not) apply in such instances. For them, the same rationale applies where the state might allege criminal wrong (e.g. where it is defrauded and sues for return of the money). IRE04.

[42] IRE06. For further defence of the *in rem* nature, see Mark Sutherland Williams and Thomas Jaggar, 'Civil Recovery: Then and Now' [2010] *Criminal Bar Quarterly* 5, 6.

[43] EW13.

interviewee highlighted the indirect quality of such *in rem* proceedings, noting that 'the focus is on the items, that they are directly or indirectly the proceeds of criminal activity. So the "indirectly" is an important provision too, because that means I don't have to prove that you have committed a criminal offence'.[44] Although it was conceded that respondents in civil recovery proceedings do suffer 'civil consequences, to vindicate the rights of the public',[45] these were considered to be specifically civil, non-punitive, and proportionate to the situation taken as a whole: 'So the judge can say "look, it's you, you've got it, I can't be sure of everything you've ever done in the past but, looking at this cumulative situation, this is what it seems to me to be, on the balance of probabilities"'.[46] A former enforcement official emphasized this point: 'It's the same as any civil case. Civil liability flows. It is not criminal liability, even if the point is the judge is making a civil finding that it is the proceeds of crime.'[47]

A proportionate response?

Not only did our interviews indicate that proponents of civil recovery viewed it as fair, but also that they considered it to be a proportionate legislative response to tackling crime. It is useful here to establish what we mean by the term proportionality, not least given the lack of consistency in the concept's use.[48] Adopting the four-stage analysis by Goold et al., listed below, we apply each in turn to civil recovery:

- Does the purpose of any rights restriction serve a legitimate democratic purpose?
- Is the measure in question suitable to attaining the identified purpose?
- Is the measure necessary for that purpose (specifically, is it the least restrictive measure available)?
- Is the measure proportionate in the strict sense (i.e. does it strike a proper balance between the purpose and individual rights in question)?[49]

[44] IRE07.
[45] IRE07.
[46] IRE07.
[47] EW12.
[48] See, e.g., Ian Dennis, 'The Human Rights Act and the Law of Criminal Evidence: Ten Years On' (2011) 33 *Sydney Law Review* 333, 346, where it is said that 'the European Court of Human Rights has not deployed the concept with any consistency in the context of art.6'.
[49] Benjamin Goold, Liora Lazarus, and Gabriel Swiney, *Public Protection, Proportionality, and the Search for Balance* (Ministry of Justice 2007) 1–2. See also *Huang v Secretary of State for the Home Department* [2007] UKHL 11. Goold et al. distinguish 'proportionality' from 'balancing', which 'involves a broad brush, and sometimes opaque, analysis aimed at a resolution of the interests at stake and

Passing the first stage is fairly straightforward. Efforts to tackle criminal activity, particularly organized crime, certainly serve a legitimate democratic purpose.[50] Here it suffices to note that organized crime is seen as a priority for national governments in both Ireland and England & Wales.[51]

The second stage, the suitability of the measure for attaining its stated aim, is more difficult. Our interview data points towards the widespread assumption that money is a key motivator for criminal activity,[52] with proponents concluding that 'the best way in which to make somebody feel that they have paid for their crimes is actually to take their money away'.[53] This stance is reinforced by the idea that state removal of assets suspected to be the proceeds of crime is fair; as one proponent states, effectively in as many words: 'the concept of taking benefit out of crime is fair'.[54] Another emphasized: 'I am unequivocal in my belief that NCB asset recovery is fair, as it is an *in rem* process, where we are seeking to recover property from people who should not have had it in the first place.'[55] In terms of the non-conviction-based approach, this demands some unpacking. The principle that individuals should not benefit from their own wrongdoing—that is, that crime should not pay—is well established, not to mention further supported by authority that rights do not result from a person's crimes.[56] These are not in dispute. Indeed, it is worth here reiterating

the rights involved. Unlike proportionality, it does not operate from a presumption that public interest goals must be restricted by rights, or that rights take precedence over public interest goals which are not suitable and necessary to their purpose. Rather, when balancing, courts are effectively applying a utilitarian analysis of the rights and public interest goals in question, giving no significantly greater weight to rights than to security measures. The balancing which takes place at the fourth stage of the proportionality test—proportionality strictu sensu—must also be distinguished here. It is one thing to ask at the outset whether the rights and measures are 'balanced' in a broad utilitarian sense, it is another to ask this question after the first three stages of the proportionality test have been fully satisfied' (2).

[50] See our in-depth discussion of this consideration in Chapter 3.See also *M v Italy*, App. No. 12386/86, 15 April 1991.

[51] A separate matter concerns the extent and impact of organized crime, but that is an empirical question beyond the scope of this book. For a law enforcement perspective, see National Crime Agency, *National Strategic Assessment of Serious and Organised Crime 2020*. Available at: <https://www.nationalcrimeagency.gov.uk/news/nsa2020>. See also Ruth Crocker et al., *The Impact of Organised Crime in Local Communities* (Police Foundation 2017). See also HM Government, *Serious and Organised Crime Strategy (Cm 9718)* (November 2018); Department of Justice and Law Reform, *White Paper on Crime: Discussion Document No. 3—Organised and White Collar Crime* (October 2010). For wider discussion, see Liz Campbell, *Organised Crime and the Law: A Comparative Analysis* (Hart 2013).

[52] Of course, money is not the only motivator. For consideration in the context of fraud and motivations, see Matthew Hollow, 'Money, Morals and Motives: An Exploratory Study into Why Bank Managers and Employees Commit Fraud at Work' (2014) 21(2) *Journal of Financial Crime* 174.

[53] EW03. According to an enforcement official, 'My experience is that some of the people involved in criminality will do time in prison standing on their head, that's not what actually worries them, but attack their property which will invariably impact their family, that has a significant impact.' EW14.

[54] IRE11.

[55] EW14.

[56] *Cleaver v Mutual Reserve Fund Life Association* [1892] 1 QB 147. See also Chapter 6.

our position as not being opposed to the idea that those committing crimes should be denied the benefit of any such resultant criminal proceeds: proceeds of crime powers are an important tool in the pursuit of the legitimate democratic purpose of tackling serious and organized criminal activity. What we do dispute—and where we disagree with civil recovery's proponents—is the confiscation of proceeds of crime outside of a criminal process.[57] Our position on this has been established and explained in earlier chapters, but can be stated as follows: we have strong concerns that the non-conviction-based approach undermines due process and rule of law safeguards.

These concerns lead to the third stage of the proportionality test, which involves both the necessity and scope of the measure in terms of achieving its intended objective. This goes to the crux of the matter, with proponents insisting that civil recovery is *necessary* for the purpose of tackling organized crime. Indeed, for our enforcement official proponents, civil recovery recognizes 'the reality of the occupational criminal, which the criminal justice system is simply unsuited to do'.[58] The infamy of reputed Mr Bigs, or Godfathers of organized crime,[59] is significant here: with explicit reference to such characters, one interviewee made the case that '[t]hey've just not had their hand in the till. They've been operating at a level that's one step back, and have others do the work. Very seldom do you catch a big person nowadays'.[60] One enforcement barrister explained that the majority of their cases concerned either drugs or organized crime, noting that the UK National Crime Agency (NCA) are 'dealing with very high-level organised crime who have unexplained assets'.[61] True to its 'follow the money' roots, the appeal of civil recovery lies in its applicability where authorities *know* that a particular person is involved in criminal activity but cannot prove that to the criminal standard. In the words of a former enforcement official:

[57] Our focus in this book is on civil recovery powers. Different considerations might apply with so-called 'classic' non-conviction-based models where a criminal conviction is not possible on specific grounds (e.g. the defendant has died, absconded, or cannot be brought before the court), given that this model is tied to criminal proceedings. See discussion of terminology in Chapter 1.

[58] EW11.

[59] See Chapter 3. Political and law enforcement discourse on organized crime is often overly dependent on the idea of a hierarchical organized crime structure (such as that of the Corleone family in the Godfather films), whereas the reality is often very different. For in-depth discussion of structures of organized crime groups, see Klaus von Lampe, *Organized Crime: Analyzing Illegal Activities, Criminal Structures, and Extra-legal Governance* (Sage 2016), particularly Chapter 5, 'Criminal Structures—An Overview'.

[60] IRE12.

[61] EW09.

> It's unexplained wealth. We know this person is a career criminal. We know they don't have any form of legitimate income. None of their financials show any form of legitimate income. The only income they have—despite living this extravagant lifestyle, with a beautiful house and Range Rovers and all that – is they still get benefits. Everything else in there doesn't have a legitimate explanation. However, we just cannot prove it.[62]

This sense of frustration,[63] of *helplessness* in being unable to prosecute, permeated many of our proponent interviews.[64] Indeed, it appears to be this sense of being hamstrung by conventional processes that underpins the emphasis on outcome over process in terms of civil recovery.[65] On its face, civil recovery empowers enforcement agencies to target property that they *know* constitutes or derives from criminal proceeds, even where criminal conviction is not possible. This is justified as follows: 'It's fundamental really, how are you supposed to target people who keep themselves away from the predicate offence on the ground, but are taking the profits? How else can you do it if you don't have this confiscation system?'[66] While these are the words of an enforcement official, it would be misleading to suggest that this view is confined to enforcement officials, as it was also echoed by some barristers:

> If it walks like a duck and it quacks like a duck, then it often invariably is. There's no point in society blinding itself to obvious problems, and I don't think any fair-minded person would believe that it's appropriate that people should be able to hold onto the proceeds of crime.[67]

[62] EW10.

[63] For consideration in the context of the right of silence, see Hannah Quirk, *The Rise and Fall of the Right of Silence* (Routledge 2016) 55–6.

[64] One interviewee extended this sense of frustration to those in the local community: 'If the law can't respond, then the law becomes ridiculous, because everybody in the community knows . . . that he is the kingpin, and he's living in a bling-filled mansion laughing at law enforcement. The law then looks pathetic. That is what is so difficult.' EW12.

[65] However, for consideration of confirmation bias and expectations of guilt, see Carole Hill, Amina Memon, and Peter McGeorge, 'The Role of Confirmation Bias in Suspect Interviews: A Systematic Evaluation' (2008) 13 *Legal and Criminological Psychology* 357.

[66] IRE03. Another enforcement official stated: 'NCB is a response that would have been unavailable previously, it delivers to LEA [law enforcement agencies] an ability to target organised criminals who have managed to keep themselves up the food chain so-to-speak, those who don't get their hands dirty, so in terms of protecting society these are the people that we really do want to target. These are the ones causing the mayhem with the public, but confidently sitting back and enjoying profits from their criminality in the form of assets in the knowledge that the criminal justice system is not going to be able to touch them. I don't like the phrase iconic untouchables but it serves to illustrate the point.' EW14.

[67] IRE09.

The assertion that civil recovery is the only viable weapon in the criminal justice arsenal for combatting serious and organized crime is a bold one, however, not least given the existence of post-conviction confiscation measures. Once more, it appears that proponents are quick to prioritize the objective—tackling organized crime by impacting upon its profit incentive—over due process, although in fairness this is an avenue made convenient by the legislation that created this hybrid procedure. As discussed in Chapter 2, a central feature of civil recovery is how it instrumentally sidesteps the extra prosecutorial obstacles generated by the criminal law's heightened procedural standards. As one enforcement official acknowledged: 'The reality is that this has allowed us to look at people who haven't been made subject to the criminal justice system, because of the very exacting levels of evidential proof and hurdles to be crossed.'[68] It will come as no surprise at this point that we dispute the specific necessity of the non-conviction-based approach to seizing criminal assets.

The fourth and final stage of the proportionality test—its ability to strike a balance between a measure's objective and relevant individual rights—raises similar considerations of civil recovery's civil/criminal procedural hybridity. Proponents roundly reject claims that it undermines procedural protections, pointing towards clear and repeated judicial decisions where civil recovery has been held to be a civil process.[69] While our position is that civil recovery fails another proportionality test here on the grounds that it goes 'too far in its assault on procedural rights protections',[70] this stance is disputed by proponents. One enforcement official stated, 'I think it is fair... I say fair, but everyone knows how draconian the legislation is, but ... I think it is the right thing to be doing'.[71] Indeed, an enforcement barrister was indignant at the suggestion that procedural rights are undermined:

> I think it's a bit glib at times to say these people's rights aren't being respected. You have to ask the question 'what rights are you talking about?'. So yes, of course, it would be arguably very dangerous if people were being convicted of crimes on the basis of hearsay evidence, on the balance of proof, without a jury trial, but they are not being convicted of crimes; they are being asked to hand over property which they can't legitimately account for. What's wrong with that?[72]

[68] EW14.

[69] See Chapter 4.

[70] Jennifer Hendry and Colin King, 'How Far Is Too Far? Theorising Non-Conviction-Based Asset Forfeiture' (2015) 11(4) *International Journal of Law in Context* 398, 399.

[71] EW13.

[72] IRE09.

The standard and the burden of proof

The next issue for analysis is the civil standard of proof. It was unmistakable from our interviews with proponents that this is considered a crucial aspect of civil recovery. This is hardly surprising: as one enforcement-focused barrister pointed out, 'having the onus to establish something on the balance of probabilities is rightly recognized as much less burdensome than having to prove it beyond reasonable doubt. That is being seen for the advantage that it is'.[73] This point is widely made in academic literature on the standard of proof in civil recovery, specifically that it is easier for the state to prove criminal allegations on a civil standard,[74] but any criticism concerning use of the civil standard of proof was roundly rejected by proponents. A former CAB official dismissed criticism as 'a red herring',[75] while an enforcement barrister was unequivocal in their position: 'If anyone thinks that the balance of probability is wrong, we should then apply beyond reasonable doubt to every case, every civil case.'[76] This was a common theme: '[i]f you insist on a beyond all reasonable doubt, well then you're unlikely to achieve your objectives.'[77]

This statement goes to the heart of the matter. The perception on the part of this interviewee, rightly or wrongly, is that the success of civil recovery is wholly dependent upon use of the civil standard of proof, and that the civil standard—and civil rules, more widely—are essential, otherwise efforts to confiscate criminal assets would be doomed to fail. Again, we can identify a clear focus on desired outcomes over considerations of due process. It would be unfair of us, however, to allege that proponents do not consider issues of procedure and principle to be important: contrary to suggestions in some critical academic literature, proponent interviewees expressed the highest regard for procedural protections. It is more that, in the case of civil recovery, they believe that such protections do not, and should not, apply. As the interview quotes below demonstrate, the views held are that civil recovery is neither an exceptional nor an illegitimate procedure but rather represents a necessary alternative approach to tackling serious and organized crime, an alternative that strikes an entirely appropriate balance between considerations of security and of individual protections.[78]

[73] EW05.

[74] Michelle Gallant, *Money Laundering and the Proceeds of Crime: Economic Crime and Civil Remedies* (Edward Elgar 2005) 19.

[75] IRE11.

[76] IRE04.

[77] IRE09.

[78] See Chapter 2 for a discussion of, in the context of procedurally hybrid forms, crime as a security risk.

One CAB official, for example, noting that people often refer to the balance of probabilities as a lesser standard of proof, argued that this was an erroneous position. 'It's not a lesser standard', they argued, 'it's an *alternative* standard of proof'.[79] The same official continued:

> People often think that balance of probability is an exception when it comes to proceeds of crime. It's not an exception. It's the beyond reasonable doubt standard that's the exception, because it involves potential loss of liberty. In no civil case will you end up in jail. It's not a loss of liberty, it's only money at the end of the day. It's as simple as that. So, if it just involves money then balance of probability is your appropriate test.[80]

These sentiments were echoed by an enforcement official in England & Wales: '[y]ou are required to make out a case, just because it is civil doesn't mean that there is not a heavy burden.'[81] The same interviewee continued: 'It's not about guilt or innocence. Civil cases are not about guilt or innocence. It's about being able to satisfy that something is the fruits of unlawful conduct, albeit to a lesser standard. Innocence is about someone being found guilty or not guilty.'[82]

The *in rem* nature of civil recovery was yet again stressed,[83] as was the instrumental distinction between liberty and property.[84] Indeed, our interviews showed that it was common for proponents to draw this distinction, although there was variety in the extent to which they were categorical in their position. For example, one enforcement barrister acknowledged that:

> [I]t seems odd, certainly coming from a criminal perspective, that you can have quasi-findings being made about criminal conduct that do not require the most stringent standard of proof, but the flipside to that is to say that in that type of situation you are potentially depriving somebody of their liberty, hence the elevated standard, whereas in civil recovery the state is taking away

[79] IRE05.

[80] IRE05. Similarly, IRE07 stressed the legitimacy of the balance of probabilities standard: '[i]t's *the* standard burden of proof for all civil cases' (emphasis in original). It is also worth noting, apropos the discussion of *preventive* procedural hybrids in Chapter 2, that the escalatory model of the two-step process *does*—for several civil preventive orders—provide for a custodial sentence on breach.

[81] EW13.

[82] EW13.

[83] As one enforcement official emphasized, 'These are *in rem* proceedings. The issue therefore is whether the property has been acquired through unlawful conduct, not whether a person has been involved in unlawful conduct. There is the criminal process for that.' EW14.

[84] EW10.

> somebody's property where there is not the same type of threat to somebody's autonomy as in taking away their liberty.[85]

The same barrister continued: 'I think there is an argument to be had there, but ultimately it is one where the legislature has decided that this is where they want to draw the line. I think it is defensible, just about, though I can see that there are some concerns there.'[86]
Giving voice to some of those concerns, a former enforcement official actually mused that: 'I think if it was my money, I might feel different (*laughs*).'[87] We take the view that a great many people would feel quite differently were it *their* money, *their* car, or *their* house that was subject to seizure by the state without a finding of guilt.[88] The deprivation of property is downplayed relative to the deprivation of liberty, and perhaps strategically so, but its significance to the individual deprived should not be overlooked. Once again, the instrumental reliance on the *in rem* nature of the proceedings is used to justify both the civil label and the use of the lower standard of proof. Such a finding aligns with research undertaken in the wider criminal justice system: Wade notes that 'prosecutorial decision-making and actions are principled in nature'[89] but goes on to say that '[d]espite the persuasiveness of such principled thinking, one need not look far to find evidence of prosecutors thinking very pragmatically on such points'.[90] This is our experience also: such pragmatic thinking was pervasive throughout our interviews with proponents of civil recovery.

A comparably instrumentalized approach is evident in relation to the burden of proof. As we will explain later in this chapter, while the initial burden falls on the applicant enforcement agency, concerns persist as to there being a *reverse* burden of proof. Such concerns have gained more traction with the introduction in England & Wales of unexplained wealth orders (UWOs), an investigative tool that can ultimately lead to a civil recovery order.[91] Barristers who represent enforcement authorities acknowledge the reverse burden argument in this context:

[85] EW05.
[86] EW05.
[87] EW10.
[88] See Chapter 6 for a comprehensive account of the liberal property-theoretical position that this very much downplays the importance of property *as a dimension of liberty*.
[89] Marianne Wade, 'Meeting the Demands of Justice Whilst Coping with Crushing Caseloads? How Sykes and Matza help us understand prosecutors across Europe' (2018) (5–6) *Journal of Criminal Justice and Security* 1, 11.
[90] Ibid, 12.
[91] For consideration of UWOs, see Anton Moiseienko, 'The Limitations of Unexplained Wealth Orders' [2022] *Criminal Law Review* 230.

> UWOs, from a purely academic perspective, I find more problematic in the sense that it is not only the lower standard of proof but you are also sort of reversing the burden of proof a bit. You are saying that you, the respondent, need to explain how you have obtained these assets from the evidence that you have. It really is a leap from the state having to prove its case in many respects. This is a real step in the direction of conferring significant power on the state.[92]

That said, the same frustration that came through in interview conversations about suspected career criminality was also evident on the part of enforcement officials discussing unexplained assets, especially when faced with requiring engagement from suspects. In the context of the adoption of UWOs, one former official grumbled: 'Nobody is going to tell you where the money came from, it's just not going to happen, so therefore if we could turn around and say the guy is on thirty grand a year, can we please change the jurisprudence or whatever and make the defendant explain first.'[93] While we are sympathetic to this sense of dissatisfaction with the failure of criminal law effectively to combat serious and organized crime,[94] considering the repeated declaration from interviewees that civil recovery *simply would not work* if the criminal standard of proof were required, it is hard to escape the conclusion that the intent behind the use of the civil standard is the reduction of the evidentiary burden. The next section will criticize the standpoint that, this reduced standard notwithstanding, people not involved in criminal activity should have no concerns about civil recovery.

Disclosure Requirements ('The Innocent Have Nothing to Fear')

The suggestion that innocent people have nothing to fear from particular laws or powers is not a new one. In Ireland, such arguments have been particularly prominent in political discourse in the context of anti-terrorism[95] and

[92] EW05. As a former enforcement official acknowledged: 'Plainly the UWO is a massive intrusion on financial privacy, but it was introduced because the Home Office felt that law enforcement were not doing enough. And despite the introduction of the power, there hasn't been a slew of them.' EW12.

[93] EW10.

[94] Jennifer Hendry and Colin King, 'How Far Is Too Far? Theorising Non-Conviction-Based Asset Forfeiture' (2015) 11(4) *International Journal of Law in Context* 398.

[95] 'There are concerns about this legislation. Civil liberties are important, and that includes the civil liberties of the majority of the Irish people. Nobody wants to see innocent people jailed—there are too many examples of that—but I hope the people who explain their position have nothing to fear.' Dáil Éireann, Offences Against the State (Amendment) Bill, 1998, Second Stage, 2 September 1998, vol. 494, col. 90, per Deputy Browne.

anti-organized crime[96] law reform, while in England & Wales similar arguments have been voiced in relation to the right to silence,[97] DNA evidence,[98] and intelligence-gathering,[99] to name but a few. These arguments are underpinned by a logic of securitization, whereby civil liberties are marginalized in favour of steps taken either to safeguard or actively enhance public security.[100] Effective law enforcement is the order of the day, according to this security logic, with this rationale used to justify not only a clear disregard for civil liberties, human rights, and due process, but also to prioritize state interventionism, increased social control, reduced restraints on state authorities, and the exercise of arbitrary power. Why worry about procedural protections if you are not involved in any wrongdoing, is the line—don't you know that it's only *criminals* who need to concern themselves with things as base as their rights against the state?

The notion that only *bad people* will be affected and that *good people*—well-behaved, law-abiding, innocent people—have nothing to be concerned about is, of course, nonsense. Reality bears this out: numerous examples of innocent people being wrongly convicted of crimes that they did not commit demonstrates conclusively the fallacy of the notion that innocent people have nothing to fear.[101] Furthermore, there are many instances of innocent groups

[96] 'Laws are in place to protect the law abiding citizens of the State, not to shield the guilty... A person who commits a crime must serve the time but I do not see how this affects an innocent person.' Dáil Éireann, Criminal Justice Bill, 2007, Second Stage, 22 March 2007, vol. 634, col. 683, per Deputy Dennehy.

[97] 'The so-called right to silence is ruthlessly exploited by terrorists. What fools they must think we are. It's time to call a halt to this charade. The so-called right to silence will be abolished. The innocent have nothing to hide and that is exactly the point the prosecution will be able to make in future.' Michael Howard at the 1993 Conservative Party conference, quoted in Hannah Quirk, *The Rise and Fall of the Right of Silence* (Routledge 2016) 44.

[98] 'the advances we have made in DNA and fingerprinting are significant. We have the ability to use the data not just as a sword with which to pierce the criminality of those who would hide from us, but the opportunity to use the data as a shield to protect those who are innocent of any offence and are often wrongly accused. It is easy to alight on only the examples which have enabled us to convict and bring to justice those who are guilty of crime, but not to highlight sufficiently the large number of people who have been set free as a result of the data being available and capable of being utilised to their benefit and that of the public.... I very much hope that when noble Lords consider what I have to say they bear in mind that this is not simply a sword, but also a shield, and also that all those who have nothing to fear from having their fingerprints and DNA samples retained may come to find that it is of benefit.' HL Deb, Criminal Justice Bill, 7 July 2003, vol 651, cols 17–18, per Baroness Scotland of Asthal.

[99] 'The net effect is that if you are a law-abiding citizen of this country going about your business and personal life, you have nothing to fear about the British state or intelligence agencies listening to the content of your phone calls or anything like that.' William Hague, quoted in *BBC News*, 'Hague: Law-abiding Britons have Nothing to Fear from GCHQ', 9 June 2013.

[100] See Chapter 2 for a discussion of security considerations relative to the design of civil/criminal procedural hybrids.

[101] Notable examples in England & Wales include the Birmingham Six, Guildford Four, and Maguire Seven and, in Ireland, Nora Wall and Frank Shortt. For a personal insight, see Paddy Armstrong, *Life After Life* (Gill Books 2017).

or communities being unfairly targeted,[102] or of abuse of powers by police officials.[103] But it is not only in political discourse[104] that wrongheaded notions such as 'the innocent have nothing to fear' have been aired: these ideas are also evident in judicial discourse in both Ireland[105] and England & Wales.[106] Contentions that the innocent have nothing to fear are also evident in the civil recovery context, particularly in respect of disclosure requirements. In both jurisdictions, a respondent in civil recovery proceedings can be asked to account for their property,[107] a point that came through particularly strongly in our interview data. Before presenting this data, however, it is worthwhile first to establish the general approach to this issue taken in civil recovery proceedings by courts in Ireland and in England & Wales and also to state our own position.

In *M v D*, a discovery order was granted on the facts of the case. The court suggested, however, that while the present case was relatively straightforward, other cases might not be (e.g. an application based on hearsay proof of suspicion, particularly if substantiated by a plea of privilege). Moriarty J hinted that, were the Criminal Assets Bureau to contend, in any such future case, that the innocent have nothing to fear, such a contention would be insufficient: 'a generalised advertence to "the innocent who have nothing to fear" would not appear to in any realistic sense satisfy the requirements of ss.2 or 3 of the Act of

[102] David Lammy (Chair), *The Lammy Review An independent review into the treatment of, and outcomes for, Black, Asian and Minority Ethnic individuals in the Criminal Justice System* (2017); Irish Network Against Racism, *Alternative Report on Racial Discrimination in Ireland* (2019), Issue 10, Racial Profiling by Police and Other Law Enforcement Personnel.

[103] Digital Rights Ireland, 'Garda Who Abused Phone Records to Spy on Ex Will Not Be Prosecuted, Will Keep Job', *Digital Rights Ireland Blog* (2 September 2011), available at:< https://www.digitalrights.ie/garda-who-abused-phone-records-to-spy-on-ex-will-not-be-prosecuted-will-keep-job/>, where a Garda in the intelligence division abused her position by accessing phone records of her former boyfriend; ITV News, Met Police officer who murdered Sarah Everard sentenced to life behind bars (30 September 2021), available at: <https://www.itv.com/news/2021-09-30/officer-who-murdered-sarah-everard-after-fake-arrest-faces-whole-life-sentence>, where a police officer used his warrant card and handcuffs to kidnap, rape, and murder a woman walking home alone.

[104] See also *Review of the Criminal Courts of England and Wales* (2001) (Auld Review), ch.10, para. 5: 'Those fundamental principles [i.e. the burden of proof and the right of silence] are there to protect the innocent defendant from wrongful conviction, not to enable the guilty defendant to engage in tactical manoeuvres designed to frustrate a fair hearing and just outcome on the issues he intends to take.'

[105] In *Heaney and McGuiness v Ireland* [1996] 1 IR 580, 590 O'Flaherty J stated: 'the innocent person has nothing to fear from giving an account of his or her movements, even though on grounds of principle, or in the assertion of constitutional rights, such a person may wish to take a stand. However, the Court holds that the *prima facie* entitlement of citizens to take such a stand must yield to the right of the State to protect itself.'

[106] In *Istel Ltd v Tully* [1993] AC 45, 50, Lord Templeman stated: 'All the allegations made by the plaintiffs are denied by Mr. and Mrs. Tully but, of course, if there has been no fraud, the disclosure by Mr. and Mrs. Tully of their dealings and correspondence will not cause any harm but will on the contrary demonstrate that the suspicions of the plaintiffs are ill-founded.' He went on to claim that the exercise of the right to silence protects the guilty while being unnecessary to safeguard the innocent (53).

[107] POCA (Ire), s. 9(1); POCA (E + W), s. 357.

1996.'[108] This decision was emphatically supported by McGuinness J in *Gilligan v CAB*, in which several contentions concerning self-incrimination were roundly rejected:[109]

> The [Bureau's] argument here seems to me to tend towards a sophisticated version of "the innocent have nothing to fear", which I would not accept as being sufficient in itself to offset a threat to the privilege against self-incrimination. There have been sufficient miscarriages of justice in the history of crime in this and in other jurisdictions to indicate that a belief that 'the innocent have nothing to fear' is not necessarily the whole answer. The defendants' argument also rather blithely passes by the fact that a failure to give evidence by the respondent will in all probability result in the disposal of the respondent's assets.[110]

McGuinness J continued:

> It is certainly arguable that any encroachment on that privilege contained in Sections 2, 3 and 9 of the 1996 Act is in pursuit of the State's entitlement 'to maintain public peace and order'. However, this is qualified by the caveat that 'the constitutional rights of the citizen must be affected as little as possible'. In order to minimise any encroachment on the citizen's rights and in order to operate the procedures under the Act in a way which in accordance with constitutional justice, it seems to me that the court would need to take particular care in deciding whether to make an order under s.9 requiring disclosure. This is especially so when one bears in mind the wide scope of the discovery which may be ordered.[111]

[108] [1998] 3 IR 175, 179.

[109] In *Gilligan*, the Criminal Assets Bureau had contended that a respondent to proceedings under the Proceeds of Crime Act is not forced to give evidence that might be self-incriminating. The respondent can, so it was contended, give evidence freely in an attempt to realize his assets or he can decline to say anything that might incriminate himself. Alternatively, he can give evidence while omitting anything that might incriminate himself. Moreover, it was further contended that, while the onus of proof might well shift to the respondent, there is no obligation on him to give evidence. He can discharge the onus on him by means of cross-examination, third party evidence, or independent 'real' evidence. These contentions were all rejected.

[110] [1998] 3 IR 185, 230.

[111] [1998] 3 IR 185, 233. Subsequent to this decision, in fact, a new provision was inserted into the Irish legislation to regulate the use of information disclosed under compulsion, specifically that its use is limited in criminal proceedings; see POCA 1996, s. 9(2) as inserted by POC(A)A 2005, s. 11.

A very different approach was evident in *SOCA v Namli*, however. In that instance, the Serious Organised Crime Agency (SOCA) had sought information on the ultimate source of funds, which was not forthcoming:

> SOCA contends that there is no reliable evidence of any legitimate source of the funds which were loaned by the two BVI companies; that if there were any legitimate source of these funds Mr Namli would have provided a proper explanation of it but that he has failed to do so; that Mr Namli repeatedly failed to explain the source of the funds; and that the probability is that they represent proceeds of the illegitimate business conducted by FMB. Mr Namli on the other hand relies on his acquittal in the Turkish proceedings and maintains that he has provided a proper explanation. SOCA made repeated requests to Mr Namli in correspondence and in Requests for Information that he should identify the ultimate source of the funds concerned, but Mr Namli steadfastly refused to provide this information, insisting that SOCA had failed to plead a sufficient case to require him to do so. I agree with SOCA that Mr Namli's responses can accurately be characterised as stonewalling.[112]

The High Court accepted SOCA's submission 'that an honest man with nothing to hide would have been able and willing to provide this information'.[113]

Considering the overtly liberal position we have adopted throughout the book, it will be unsurprising that we have strong reservations about the notion that innocent people have nothing to fear from civil recovery powers. Not only is this 'nothing to fear' rhetoric motivated by security rationales, but it also—inescapably—relies upon the flawed premise that enforcement agencies *know* who is guilty and who is not. As one defence solicitor emphasized: 'There's one thing to say what you know and another to say what you can prove. How do you *know* that these people are guilty?'[114] Indeed, the wide literature on confirmation bias in criminal investigations reinforces these concerns,[115] while such rhetoric, moreover, ignores the possibility of mistake or abuse of power. The possibility that wholly innocent people might get caught in the net should,

[112] *SOCA v Namli* [2013] EWHC 1200 (QB), paras 139–140.

[113] *SOCA v Namli* [2013] EWHC 1200 (QB), para. 140.

[114] EW08.

[115] In the context of investigative interviewing, for example, Hill et al. demonstrate that expectations of guilt lead interviewers to ask more guilt-presumptive questions and to be more confident in their judgments of guilt/innocence. The same study further highlighted that the mock suspects responded to guilt-presumptive questions in a manner that appeared to confirm the expectation of guilt, even where that person was innocent. See Carole Hill, Amina Memon, and Peter McGeorge, 'The Role of Confirmation Bias in Suspect Interviews: A Systematic Evaluation' (2008) 13 *Legal and Criminological Psychology* 357.

give serious pause for thought, even if one is of the view that civil recovery is justified in all other respects.

Our position is, however, not shared by the civil recovery proponents interviewed; on the contrary, the prevalent view was that it is both a key policy for and a pragmatic response to the problem of serious and organized crime. As one Irish interviewee explained:

> The finding that they happened to be in possession or in control of property representing the proceeds of crime is not, *a fortiori*, a finding that they have been guilty of crime, just that they have in their possession property of that type. And the difficulty, I think, in the absence of that is that you have an untenable policy position where people, and often in more deprived communities at that, are clearly living the high life with no provable legitimate source of income, which is clearly coming from crime, and that needs to be tackled as well.[116]

Proponents emphasized that there are safeguards in place before property is ultimately forfeit: 'And you're giving the people the due process to come back and challenge all that, and years go by before you can actually forfeit.'[117] Similar points were put forward by proponent interviewees in England & Wales;[118] according to one former enforcement official: 'Procedurally, there is no reason why it should be unfair. And it gives the opportunity for agencies ... to do something where the unpalatable alternative might be that they can't do anything. And I think that that was the original intention of the Act.'[119] As justifications go, these are both tepid in tone and unpersuasive in reality. Notwithstanding our views on this, however, the next section will pay some attention to the argument that respondents are given adequate opportunity to explain themselves.

Explaining unexplained wealth

An issue antecedent to the requirement for a respondent to explain their wealth is that of the role of enforcement agencies as gatekeepers, that is, as a supposed safeguard against speculative cases being brought. In our interviews,

[116] IRE09.
[117] IRE07.
[118] EW09; EW12; EW13; EW14.
[119] EW12.

enforcement officials highlighted their gatekeeper role, specifically that potential cases are scrutinized thoroughly before a decision is made to initiate proceedings:

> many more cases are rejected each year before we bring it to court. I think there's a good solid reason for that and that is that we shouldn't properly, in any circumstances, bring a section 2 application [for an interim order] to court about which we have the slightest doubt.[120]

Indeed, it was suggested by enforcement officials that they 'probably overcover'.[121] The same interviewee elaborated on this point: 'We probably would get away with less, but we do have high standards in our files.'[122] An analogous approach is evident in England & Wales, with one former enforcement official stating: 'I think we have been too cautious, we've probably only pursued ones where we've had a very very good chance of winning.'[123] A current enforcement official took a similar view: 'Any NCB proceedings brought will have been subject to rigorous consideration on both its merits and its litigation risk. I don't think that anyone ever brings a civil recovery case just because the case gets over the magical 50% mark.'[124]

When deciding whether or not to initiate proceedings, officials *self-apply* a higher standard than the balance of probabilities:

> Well, that's just the reality, because, you see, we're crime investigators, we're saying it's the proceeds of crime, so in reality the standard of evidence will equate to the criminal standard ... the balance of probability test included in the legislation, I think, was included because of the difficulties at the time that were experienced by the lack of evidence against particular individuals.[125]

As one former enforcement official pointed out in relation to the early years of civil recovery in England & Wales, particularly where solicitors involved had backgrounds in criminal confiscation, 'they tended to be trying to prove things beyond all reasonable doubt, and they just didn't need to'.[126] Another former enforcement official concurred: 'all of the people who end up doing civil

[120] IRE03.
[121] IRE12.
[122] IRE12.
[123] EW12.
[124] EW14.
[125] IRE03.
[126] EW11.

recovery inevitably have come from a criminal background because they've just gravitated towards it and they tend to be risk-averse.'[127] For enforcement officials, therefore, there is a degree of confidence in the pre-trial decision making—that is, that the evidence backs up their case—such that there is no fear that a decision 'could go either way'[128] or that an innocent person could be made subject to an erroneous decision. For proponents, therefore, not only does the burden of proof rest with the agency bringing the application,[129] but a further safeguard is this gatekeeper role of enforcement officials, whereby they 'weed out' the weak cases. It was evident across interviews that proponents believe these to constitute sufficient safeguards such that innocent people ought not be afraid of civil recovery proceedings.

The view that the innocent have nothing to fear is notably widespread in relation to unexplained wealth. For many proponents, unexplained wealth *demands* explanation: as one former CAB official asserted, when the prosecutorial threshold is reached then 'something calls for an explanation' and the respondent is 'best placed to provide that explanation.'[130] Another official stated: 'if you are alleged to be a criminal in possession of money, then you should be able to show where you got the money to buy, for example, a house—that should be relatively easy to do.'[131] To state this position succinctly: 'if you can't explain it, why should you have it?'[132] For some proponents, not only was there a sense that a respondent is ideally positioned to account for their possession of property and should therefore *have* to do so, there was also a sense that it is entirely legitimate to require that respondents provide an account of wealth: 'I think it is legitimate. If someone cannot explain the legitimacy of their income, it is right and proper that we should be using the powers that makes enquiries into it.'[133] One barrister was categorical: 'I do not understand the objection to people being asked to explain the source of their income',[134] while

[127] EW12.

[128] IRE13.

[129] As one enforcement barrister emphasized, from POCA's inception: 'A conscious decision, I think, was taken by the Attorney General, and by the powers that be. It was better to have a system where the police were put on proof, for good or ill. And I think that's a very interesting point too, because it demonstrates that, contrary to what some people have tried to say in the past, this wasn't a kind of knee-jerk, flash in the pan reaction. There was a lot of thought that went into this and I think that it proves the strength of the system here because it had to be tested. If we'd gone for the other type of situation, I think that our system could well have been challenged, could have fallen down, would have developed lazy policing, you know, sloppy approaches. It would have been far less effective.' IRE07. The burden of proof is considered further above at the text to n. 91 et seq.

[130] IRE11.

[131] IRE13.

[132] EW13.

[133] EW13. An enforcement barrister opined: '[A]ccounting for your wealth seems to be just a matter that has to be done.' EW09.

[134] IRE04.

another posed the rhetorical question: '[i]s there anything wrong with calling upon people to demonstrate the legitimate provenance of their income?'[135] Yet another barrister opined that 'There is no problem in principle—so long as it is sufficiently protected—to the state being allowed to obtain disclosure of information.'[136] Similarly, an enforcement official declared that: 'I don't perceive a difficulty with someone being asked about assets in their possession, they should have some sort of way of explaining.'[137] This thinking is redolent of the securitized logic discussed at the outset, whereby the good citizen in effect proves their virtue by relinquishing their rights, their privileges, and the duties owed to them by the state.[138]

In practice, it appears that enforcement agencies do act as 'gatekeepers' in the simple sense that they will afford opportunity for explanation during their investigation and will only initiate court proceedings in the event that they do not receive a satisfactory answer.[139] It is important to note here that this gatekeeping approach depends upon *cooperation* from a suspect: cooperate with us and prove that your property is legitimate, *or else* we will bring proceedings against you.[140] Presenting such investigations as offering individuals an opportunity to justify and, implicitly, to defend their financial circumstances has the effect of masking the central issue here, however, which is 'the extent to which a person needs to explain him/herself, specifically his/her ownership of and dealings in property, to the State'.[141] During our interviews this idea of financial

[135] IRE09.

[136] EW05.

[137] EW14.

[138] Alan Norrie, 'Citizenship, Authoritarianism and the Changing Shape of the Criminal Law' in Bernadette McSherry, Alan Norrie, and Simon Bronitt (eds), *Regulating Deviance: The Redirection of Criminalisation and the Futures of Criminal Law* (Hart 2009). See also Jennifer Hendry, '"The Usual Suspects": Knife Crime Prevention Orders and the "Difficult" Regulatory Subject' (2022) 62(2) *British Journal of Criminology* 378.

[139] IRE03; IRE05; IRE11; EW14.

[140] This view also appears to be implicit in judicial thinking: 'Mr Atkinson further says that he has not been unwilling to attend interview. Previously he had taken the position that he should not attend the interview unless he had a legal representative with him, but he no longer maintains that position and there is an interview arranged for tomorrow. He has told me that he will attend the interview, that he has nothing to hide and that he is willing to answer questions and provide explanations in relation to whatever questions the applicant may have about his assets and the source of those assets. That seems to me to be an important breakthrough because Mr and Mrs Atkinson need to understand—and to understand very clearly—that this freezing order is not simply going to go away, and that it is very strongly in their interests to cooperate in answering questions and providing the information which SOCA are seeking. Unless and until an interview takes place and the information requested at that interview is provided, the freezing order is likely to remain in place, and there is not going to be a conclusion to the investigation which SOCA is carrying out.' *SOCA v Atkinson* [2013] EWHC 676 (Admin), paras 8–9.

[141] Peter Alldridge, 'Civil Recovery in England and Wales: An Appraisal' in Colin King, Clive Walker, and Jimmy Gurulé (eds), *The Palgrave Handbook of Criminal and Terrorism Financing Law* (Palgrave 2018) 534.

privacy[142] was explored with proponents of civil recovery: while they acknowledged the existence of financial privacy, several took pains to stress that there 'are certain circumstances where you lose it',[143] with both taxation proceedings and public policy considerations being widely cited as grounds:[144]

> like with all rights, these are not absolute, and while information does need to be protected, the legislature is allowed to draw a line where it sees fit as between peoples' right to privacy and the state's right to investigate unlawful activity. So, to a certain extent that has been answered by Parliament and there is that balance to be struck there.[145]

In a similar vein, an enforcement official stated:

> On a pragmatic basis, this is, and always was, aimed at top end fraudsters and organised criminals who by definition are likely to be adept at squirrelling money away and making money look like its legitimate when it isn't. So, if you do not weigh the scales somewhat in favour of law enforcement, you're declaring these people untouchable. And the law was an attempt to redress that balance.[146]

Across proponent interviewees the general consensus was that it is perfectly valid to require disclosure in civil recovery cases as long as appropriate protections are in place.[147] Not only are respondents afforded the opportunity to explain the legitimate source of property,[148] as already discussed—because 'most people don't have assets the source of which they cannot explain'[149]—but it was also stressed that there is also a threshold below which no information will be required.[150] Establishing lawful provenance, and doing so with comparative

[142] Sharman defines financial privacy as the right to determine what financial information about the individual concerned should be known to others (including to the state): Jason Sharman, 'Privacy as Roguery: Personal Financial Information in an Age of Transparency' (2009) 87(4) *Public Administration* 717.

[143] IRE04. Also IRE09; EW05; EW07; EW10. One interviewee went so far as to ponder: 'With things like STRs [suspicious transaction reports], to what extent do any of us have financial privacy nowadays. Everything is subject to somebody looking at it.' IRE12.

[144] IRE07; EW03; EW09; EW10; EW11; EW12.

[145] EW05.

[146] EW12. Another enforcement official stated: 'The powers of a Disclosure Order have been described as draconian even by the Courts, no doubt about it, but Parliament intended POCA to provide law enforcement with the tools to effectively recover the proceeds of crime, it takes a certain amount of hard power to crack certain nuts.' EW14.

[147] IRE07; EW03; EW05; EW09; EW13.

[148] IRE05; IRE09; EW07.

[149] IRE04. Also IRE11; IRE12; EW07; EW09

[150] IRE04; IRE11.

ease, was emphasized as particularly important,[151] on the basis that failure to provide an *adequate* response is likely to compel authorities into assuming that the property in question is the proceeds of crime.[152] Notably, this is in spite of the privilege against self-incrimination being in operation in terms of the requirement to disclose,[153] once again raising concerns as to the practical value of this particular safeguard.[154]

Strong themes running through these proponent responses were the idea of fighting organized crime and the overt rhetoric of efficiency, expediency, and pragmatism. Indeed, it quickly became apparent to us that this rhetoric has been adopted by some respondent-focused practitioners. Before moving on to discuss such views in the next sub-section, however, we first explore the enforcement emphasis on requiring respondents to cooperate.

One enforcement official highlighted what they identified as the 'paternalistic role of the state', and continued in a staunchly state-interventionist and public security-oriented vein:

> There is a sense of social protection… There is a social contract. The state has an obligation to protect, but protection comes with responsibilities as well… So, what we are saying is that there is a social protection that goes on and we have to be able to say, 'where did you get it?' We are protecting it, we are willing to go to war over this [*laughs*]. That's the absolute fall-back position. What we have to be able to say is, 'is it yours?'[155]

When pressed on this position, the same interviewee acknowledged that it is, 'in a way, draconian for the state to say, "where did you get it?" [but] it doesn't happen in a gulag-type of approach, everyone is not going to be subject to a Proceeds of Crime application'.[156]

They elaborated on this position as follows: 'It would be improper if it was being run on a daily basis on every citizen of the country, saying you have to justify everything you do. There's nothing wrong with saying to a person "where did you get that car, how did you pay for it?" '[157] Another enforcement official stated: 'The legislation has built into it requirements that protect the

151 IRE13; EW09.
152 EW05.
153 IRE11; EW05.
154 A concern expressed by respondent-focused practitioners: EW01.
155 IRE05.
156 IRE05.
157 IRE05. Similarly, one barrister suggested that disclosure only applies in 'strong cases', for example where a person has significant convictions and/or inferential evidence that a person is engaged in criminality: IRE04.

individual or the suspect. Before you get to a point where someone can be required to explain, you'd have to satisfy the court of something. It's not simply a matter of going to court and saying "I want them to explain", there are criteria there.'[158] Once again, there is a sense amongst proponents of civil recovery that innocent people have nothing to fear, whether from recovery investigations or proceedings: providing you have done nothing wrong, then you are unlikely to be targeted. Even in the event that you are targeted, so the argument goes, if your finances are legitimate then you should experience no difficulty in proving that this is the case. Innocent citizens apparently need not concern themselves with such niceties as safeguards, because good people will never have to avail themselves of such protections; the fact that such safeguards even exist should further assuage people that *they* have nothing to fear. Our position is that this should be exposed as a worrisome and problematically pervasive notion.

The requirement to disclose is seen as a key tool for law enforcement. Again, the view that innocent people have nothing to fear is to the fore:

> In the modern world—one looks at Al Qaeda, or ISIS, or any other criminal investigation—intelligence is key. And if you have nothing to hide, people are entitled to be challenged on that basis. I think a zone of privacy as complete as the one you have suggested, would play into the hands of organised crime.[159]

The expectation—now a common theme across the criminal justice system more broadly—of active participation on the part of the individual under investigation is thus *so* presumed that it becomes *de facto* mandatory and serves effectively to diminish the initial burden of proof upon the enforcement agency. In the event that the individual does not cooperate, this is likely to bolster any existing suspicion against them: what could they be hiding? Moreover, this indicates a clear sense of Us versus Them, a situation whereby only cooperation can dispel suspicion.

There are several points that can be teased out of this apparent bifurcation of people into two categories: on the one hand, the innocent and good, on the other, those who are—at best—worthy of suspicion. The first point is that little or no pretence of a presumption of innocence is being maintained here. Instead, the enforcement agency starts from a position of suspicion and demands that the individual concerned provides evidence to dispel the agency's preconception. Second, when twinned with the lower standard of proof used

[158] EW13.
[159] IRE07.

in civil recovery proceedings, this suspicion-first approach—alongside the idea that, if one objects to disclosure, this 'is prima facie evidence of roguery of one kind or another'[160]—is liable to generate errors while also leading to potential confirmation bias. Third, not only is this approach indicative of the changing nature of both the criminal justice system and the relationship between the individual and the state that we discussed in Chapter 5,[161] it can also readily be described as exhibiting at least some of the features of Jakobs' conceptualization of enemy criminal law.[162] '[E]ssentially a police power which treats its objects as dangers to be managed, as distinct from citizen criminal law, which responds to subjects invested with rights',[163] the three elements of 'enemy criminal law' are that (i) punishment occurs in advance of any harm, (ii) sanctions are disproportionate, and (iii) procedural rights are restricted or circumvented.[164] Manifestation of *any* of these features should, we argue, be a red flag that such practices are problematic in terms of their compliance with the egalitarian values of the rule of law. Whether or not this is conceded, it is undeniable that enforcement agencies in both Ireland and England & Wales have adopted overtly pragmatic approaches to civil recovery proceedings; our interview data certainly supports the contention that such crime fighting measures are being allowed to supersede individual privacy rights.

Defending civil recovery proceedings

This is not to say that pragmatic considerations were the sole preserve of enforcement practitioners and officials. On the contrary, several practitioners who generally act on behalf of civil recovery respondents also recognized the

[160] Jason Sharman, 'Privacy as Roguery: Personal Financial Information in an Age of Transparency' (2009) 87(4) *Public Administration* 717, 717. Thus we see conflict between privacy as an abstract good juxtaposed against values of efficiency and public security. For wider discussion, see James Rule, 'The Limits of Privacy Protection' in Benjamin Goold and Daniel Neyland (eds), *New Directions in Surveillance and Privacy* (Routledge 2009).

[161] See Chapter 5 on the Non-Conviction-Based Approach, specifically the Presumption of Innocence. For wider discussion see, generally, Antony Duff, Lindsay Farmer, Sandra Marshall, and Victor Tadros, *The Trial on Trial, Volume 3: Towards a Normative Theory of the Criminal Trial* (Hart Publishing 2007); Shane Kilcommins and Barry Vaughan, 'Reconfiguring State-Accused Relations in Ireland' (2006) 41 *Irish Jurist* 90.

[162] Günther Jakobs 'Kriminalisierung im Vorfeld einer Rechtsgutsverletzung' (1985) 97(4) *Zeitschrift für die gesamte Strafrechtswissenschaft* 751.

[163] Nicola Lacey, *In Search of Criminal Responsibility. Ideas, Interests and Institutions* (Oxford University Press 2016) 158.

[164] Günther Jakobs 'Kriminalisierung im Vorfeld einer Rechtsgutsverletzung' (1985) 97(4) *Zeitschrift für die gesamte Strafrechtswissenschaft* 751. See also Daniel Ohan, 'Trust, Distrust and Reassurance: Diversion and Preventive Orders Through the Prism of *Feindstrafrecht*' (2010) 73(5) *Modern Law Review* 721.

influence of this approach in their advice to clients. Some did this with a sober sense of resignation—pragmatic in its own way—that the disclosure expectation is now so entrenched in enforcement agency practice that failure to engage is tactically unwise.[165] One defence solicitor explained:

> We're just so used to it. You know, we just go 'Okay, fine. You've got to tell them where it all comes from' and, I mean, it's part of the reversal of proof paradigm, really. They [clients] resent it and you'll probably never get the truth out of them really, but [*laughs*].[166]

Other defence practitioners emphasized the policy rationale underpinning the proceeds of crime legislation: 'The upshot is that you have to disclose, so tough luck. And, that's fine, I haven't any problems with it in principle—the whole point is to recover the proceeds of crime and, guess what, criminals will pretend that they don't have money.'[167] This was not an uncommon stance. Other interviewees were similarly adamant that disclosure orders are not at all problematic: 'Absolutely, I have no issue with those orders',[168] stated one defence practitioner, on the basis that many cases will primarily be reliant on the respondent's knowledge. The same interviewee continued: 'Most of this comes on the basis of a criminal offence, and that is where my belief is that your privacy is gone out of the window.'[169] Another defence solicitor referred to the 'sniff test', and opined that where something smells off, then a person should be able to account for their money to the court.[170]

Not only do these interview quotes highlight that individuals subject to a disclosure order will, in all likelihood, find themselves in the position of simply *having* to engage with the authorities, they also reveal that many respondent-focused practitioners hold suspicions about their own clients. This is not limited to civil recovery proceedings, of course. Viewing one's own clients through lenses of suspicion and mistrust is an increasingly prevalent feature of a contemporary criminal justice system that has seen the rise of neoliberal, managerial systems oriented towards encouraging defence solicitors—already under significant caseload pressures—in the direction of guilty pleas,

[165] EW02; EW04.
[166] EW02.
[167] EW04. That interviewee did, however, criticize obstacles put up by enforcement authorities to prevent individuals accessing money.
[168] EW08.
[169] EW08.
[170] EW06.

settlements, and otherwise speedy resolutions.[171] And although such views were expressed by only a few interviewees in this study, unfortunately this does not inspire confidence in a client-centred approach to legal representation, a theme consistent with wider research on legal aid solicitors in the criminal process.[172] This is not to say that respondent-focused practitioners were completely unaware of this problem, as definite attempts were made to justify this initial viewpoint of suspicion. Some even referred to placing their faith in the authorities, claiming for example that the courts would not grant an order without justification: 'My starting point is to have some faith that the application and the order has been correctly made and that the request in and of itself is founded on there being some form of case to answer, and that it is not completely without any merit.'[173] The same interviewee further noted that, where an order is granted, the option to challenge that order is open to the individual.[174] One barrister summed up their view of financial privacy and disclosure requirements as follows:

> In principle, you should have financial privacy but, if there is major discordance between what you're enjoying and what it's known you've earned, I don't think it's particularly objectionable to require somebody to explain that. I think the key is, it turns on the evidential requirements that need to be satisfied before one of these orders is made.[175]

However balanced these views appear on their face, they reveal an inclination towards the acceptance of the case against their client, instead of a client-centred approach. They furthermore also align with McConville and Marsh's argument that there is a risk of 'succumb[ing] to the impression that police evidence is shrouded in infallibility'.[176] Considering that McConville and Marsh

[171] Daniel Newman and Lucy Welsh, 'The Practices of Modern Criminal Defence Lawyers: Alienation and its Implications for Access to Justice' (2019) 48 *Common Law World Review* 64.

[172] Daniel Newman, 'Are Lawyers Neurotic?' (2018) 25(1) *International Journal of the Legal Profession* 3.

[173] EW06.

[174] EW06. In practice, however, it is difficult to challenge such an order, as this interviewee readily acknowledged: 'the witness statement and the basis for the accompanying order is almost always sufficient for the advice to be "it will be a waste of money trying to make a challenge to the court, and remember that if you are unsuccessful you will be paying for the other side's costs". The cost/benefit analysis is such that it is simplest to reply and focus on that, rather than going back to court and trying to challenge a disclosure request. Also, there is a more pragmatic attitude, which would be rather than antagonising the investigators too soon, it is more prudent to play a longer game and try and be perceived as more cooperative; so not jumping to rush back to court but rather working with the investigators to manage the problem—if the problem can be managed.' EW06.

[175] EW07.

[176] Mike McConville and Luke Marsh, *Criminal Judges: Legitimacy, Courts and State-Induced Guilty Pleas in Britain* (Edward Elgar 2014) 50.

made that argument in relation to what they described as 'more vulnerable agents', specifically defendants and jurors in a criminal trial,[177] it is particularly concerning that comparable views are held by some respondent-focused practitioners.

Not all respondent-focused practitioners agreed with these views as discussed, however. When asked whether a respondent should have to explain provenance of property, one defence solicitor retorted, 'This person shouldn't [pointing at themself]. And what's different about me, a citizen?'[178] Some interviewees were generally sceptical, noting that the obligation to account for property represents 'an interesting inroad into the right to remain silent',[179] while others took more issue with the extent to which financial information provides a detailed picture of a person's lifestyle and behaviour. Rejecting the idea that it is only those involved in criminal activity who need financial privacy, a few interviewees suggested that an individual might have a perfectly good and legitimate reason for not wishing to disclose their financial history.[180] For example:

> Your bank reveals that you've had a particular peculiar interest which may be highly embarrassing, which you may keep very, very secret from everybody, but you then have to disclose it. Now, you may well subscribe to various things which are not illegal, which are not of themselves against any law, but for personal preferences, you may well have a very private element of your private life that you want to stay private, but you get catched up [sic] in this and that all comes out because obviously your bank statements show that you're paying for bondage or S+M or whatever it is, which you've kept quiet from everybody for years. There's no secrets once it's out.[181]

The same interviewee gave another example of a case where, following a raid, an individual was asked to account for £20,000 cash. That individual had to disclose that she had a 'gentleman friend who used to provide her with cash and various other items', an explanation that was confirmed at the court

177 Mike McConville and Luke Marsh, *Criminal Judges: Legitimacy, Courts and State-Induced Guilty Pleas in Britain* (Edward Elgar 2014) 50.

178 IRE08.

179 EW04. But see text to n.167 above where the same interviewee expresses a contradictory view on disclosure.

180 A point also made by Sharman, who notes that financial information might disclose, for example, maintenance to an unacknowledged child; adultery; or favoured family members expressed in a will. Jason Sharman, 'Privacy as Roguery: Personal Financial Information in an Age of Transparency' (2009) 87(4) *Public Administration* 717.

181 EW01.

proceedings. This was 'highly embarrassing' for her, and ultimately led to her divorce.[182]

While these bawdier examples show the potential for disclosures to cause embarrassment and disruption in people's private lives, it is worth noting that '[r]egardless of any wrongdoing, the knowledge that governmental institutions and transnational bodies are accessing this data can have far-reaching consequences'.[183] This point is important in the context of restrictions upon information disclosed pursuant to POCA provisions being used in, for example, a criminal case, leading some defence solicitors to question whether the privilege against self-incrimination actually applies in practice:

> The fear is that you're in a civil procedure, you'll have an obligation to disclose, if you don't disclose you're in contempt, you can go to jail for that. You disclose material, 'Oh, thank you' basically. We'll go off and now nick you, because you disclosed this is a tax offence, a regulatory offence. That's the problem.[184]

A further criticism of civil recovery's disclosure requirements is that, unlike in criminal proceedings, where—at least in theory—a solicitor can advise a client not to say anything and to wait for disclosure by the police, a person subject to civil recovery investigation cannot simply remain silent. When this issue was raised with interviewees, a CAB official conceded the point while explaining that 'what we do, on day one, is we go with an order and we go with a folder and say "here's an order and here are the lever-arch folders; here is our ultimate case", on day one'.[185] They continued:

> We say your asset has been frozen, your house has been frozen on the basis of the following, and we give them the five folders, for example. That goes to the person, and they know what we are saying, on day one, about them. It's not as if we go in and get an *ex parte* order and ... [trails off]. What will happen then is that people will then bring discovery applications against us, and we would always resist them on the basis that we've given everything. What we are saying at the very start is that there's no harm in having your asset frozen

182 EW01.

183 Kathleen Lotmore, 'The Decline of Financial Privacy and its Costs to Society' (2017) 23(9) *Trusts & Trustees* 944, 946.

184 EW01. That interviewee further implied that 'screens', or restrictions on use of disclosed information, 'exist on paper alone'.

185 IRE05.

> because we aren't taking it. We can put it in a bank account, have an argument about it, and freeze it.[186]

The position taken by some defence solicitors on this silence point is also illuminating. While it was acknowledged that a defendant in a criminal trial can theoretically sit back and require the prosecution to prove the case against that person, such a tactic is not necessarily advisable.[187] In an illustration that indicates a degree of pragmatism, one defence solicitor spoke of a criminal fraud trial where money was coming into the defendant's bank account:

> There has to be an answer about where this cash is coming from. If you sit back and say, "I have no obligation to tell you", so be it, but you know the score and the jury is very likely to come back and convict you. You know what is going to happen and any lawyer will be able to tell his client: 'You're not going to win this by staying quiet. On the other hand, if you come forward and give an explanation, supported by proof, you have an equal chance of walking away with a not guilty verdict.' I think the same applies here [in civil recovery proceedings].[188]

This defence solicitor continued in this matter-of-fact vein: 'If you have been under suspicion of crime, or where there have been convictions, then sitting behind that "why should I tell you?" is not justified. *Being very practical about it*, you have to come forward and tell where this has come from.'[189] In terms of solicitor strategies, therefore, it appears the tactic of simply remaining silent is invariably a poor option for a respondent. Importantly, however, this is based wholly on the adverse inferences that solicitors—from experience—*expect* to be drawn on the part of the enforcement agencies. The determining factor is, once more, *suspicion*—the default starting position of enforcement agent suspicion of criminal wrongdoing gives rise, problematically, to a degree of strategizing by the more practically minded practitioners in the form of client

186 IRE05.

187 Indeed, it is increasingly untenable given demands for active participation and increased efficiency. For wider consideration, see Abenaa Owusu-Bempah, *Defendant Participation in the Criminal Process* (Routledge 2017).

188 EW08.

189 EW08. Our emphasis. Another defence solicitor noted that pragmatic behaviour along these lines is exhibited even by respondents themselves: 'Often my clients feel particularly put out that they have to form a response and they have to go to the time and trouble of replying, but they do tend to accept that it is part of the process. And at the back of their minds they will have other concerns, and filling out a questionnaire about their financial circumstances tends in reality to be the least of their problems.' EW06.

advice to engage with the disclosure process. Under these circumstances, as a safeguard, the right of an individual to remain silent when questioned by an agent of the state, becomes entirely ineffectual.

The role of the courts

In our interviews, the courts were repeatedly emphasized as being a crucial safeguard in civil recovery actions.[190] In Ireland, these proceedings are dealt with in the High Court, which was described as 'utterly independent' and as providing 'huge protection',[191] not least because, as one official stated, 'we don't get everything our own way'.[192] An enforcement barrister summed up the idea of the courts operating as a safeguarding mechanism as follows:

> [B]oth the Gardaí [the Irish Police] and the lawyers knew that everything they did was going to be tested. There was no question of an easy administrative fix here. This all was going to be subject to minute-by-minute scrutiny by experienced High Court judges, and I think that is a critical part of any system with assets seizure—the court involvement. It's actually good for the prosecution, it's good for the authorities. It prevents them from having cushy administrative processes that they don't test properly; it sets a proper evidential threshold; it's the right way to proceed.[193]

They provided further elaboration on their positive outlook:

> [Y]ou should welcome judicial supervision. You should welcome the thing being incorporated into the mainstream system. You should welcome the presence of independent lawyers working for you, and you should probably welcome the presence of lawyers acting for the other side... if your system is good enough and your evidence is good enough, then if there's a contest then you should win it.[194]

190 IRE05; IRE06; IRE07; IRE11; IRE12; IRE13; EW03; EW09; EW12; EW13.

191 IRE11.

192 IRE12, although the same interviewee acknowledged that 'ultimately, most cases do go our way'. Also IRE13.

193 IRE07. That same interviewee continued on to say that, within two years, civil recovery in Ireland 'became a normal part of the High Court. That was also very important, because it then wasn't somehow weird and wonderful; it was normal. And the impact on the defendants, I think, was very powerful as well because, once they realised they were being treated fairly, that it wasn't just the guards dealing with it, the court was there. I think that that calms the whole thing down and I also think that the Gardaí were extremely good at dealing with the defendants.'

194 IRE07.

In England & Wales, proponents also expressed positive views about the High Court as a safeguard. Interviewees spoke about having to satisfy the court in relation to specific orders (disclosure orders and unexplained wealth orders were mentioned),[195] about having to 'make out a case',[196] and about 'all the challenges of the High Court, all the risks of the High Court, likely to be resisted pretty fully'.[197] As an enforcement official contended: 'There is an exacting examination by the courts. NCB has judicial scrutiny at its core.'[198] A former enforcement official expressed a preference for doing more civil recovery work and to do so 'more aggressively, but we don't because there is an inevitable caution about taking High Court action and losing'.[199] Thus the High Court location acts as a restraint on decisions whether or not to initiate proceedings, which reinforces the previously discussed gatekeeper role of enforcement agencies.[200]

By contrast, several respondent-focused practitioners expressed scepticism about this purported safeguard. One defence solicitor referred to early Irish case law,[201] stating that this was 'really the first indication that I had that it was not going to be a level playing field'.[202] That same interviewee opined that 'the High Court has made a clear policy decision, and the Supreme Court as well, a clear policy decision, that CAB is to be supported'.[203] Equally, other respondent-focused interviewees referred to judges being case-hardened[204] and overly inclined to grant an order, particularly an order *ex parte*.[205] One barrister voiced their suspicion that the High Court has a tendency to be 'quite conservative', with the result that 'there's hardly any cases that have been lost that have gone to trial'.[206]

When we put such scepticism concerning the courts' safeguarding role to proponents of civil recovery, however, it was firmly rejected:

> There tends to be this fiction that judicial decision making, and the approach to case law on the part of judges, ignores the policy implications of what they're doing, and fundamentally the Oireachtas [i.e. National Parliament],

195 EW13; EW14.
196 EW13.
197 EW12.
198 EW14.
199 EW12.
200 See text associated with n.121 and n.139.
201 *M v D* [1998] 3 IR 175.
202 IRE08.
203 IRE08.
204 EW01. Indeed, even enforcement barristers acknowledged the risk of judges being case-hardened: EW03; EW09.
205 EW02; EW04.
206 EW04.

> on behalf of the people, passes a particular statutory regime. The first question for the courts is: is this compatible with the constitution? If it's compatible with the constitution then, whether the judges like it or not, that's the regime they have to apply. So, you can say that the judges, as a matter of policy, were going to make sure that they upheld the regime but, in doing so, they applied the jurisprudence on property rights, on constitutional safeguards, and were satisfied it met it. I haven't read any particularly convincing critique of that which would suggest that it was wholly wrong, you know. And the Supreme Court have said that the powers are draconian and, in my view, they undoubtedly are and, therefore, one has to be extra careful in how you go about applying them but, as I say, I think the judges have generally been astute to ensure that there isn't any injustice in these cases.[207]

While the rank and calibre of the High Court provides important safeguards for civil recovery proceedings, we should be careful not to overstate this in terms of circumstantial protections. The presence of judicial oversight alone is no guarantee against procedural errors and improprieties,[208] whereas the very fact that miscarriages of justice occur within criminal proceedings—replete with elevated procedural protections—should give pause concerning the use of civil recovery, absent those heightened procedural safeguards, to confiscate proceeds of crime.

Having scrutinized the supposed safeguards inherent in the process and highlighted the extent to which we find them wanting, our focus now turns to the kind of harm we consider civil recovery to have the potential to cause. The next section problematizes the pragmatic approach in terms of the erroneous deprivation of property facilitated by civil recovery, casting this as a particular sort of injustice.

Principle, Policy, Procedure—and Pragmatism

A prominent theme in this chapter, and indeed this book, has been the need to balance the legislative goals of civil recovery against the civil liberties of

[207] IRE09. In the context of belief evidence, the same interviewee stated: 'the judiciary have an important role not to let stuff through just on the nod'.

[208] An enforcement barrister expressed concern as to safeguards being diluted, particularly where some applications (e.g. for Account Freezing Orders) are dealt with in lower courts rather than in the High Court. They described the shift away from the High Court as 'good in that it swings the balance, but it means that there is much less oversight'. EW09. Similar concerns were expressed by respondent-focused interviewees: EW06; EW08.

respondents.[209] This idea of balance features in several respects: for example, weighing the interests of society as a whole against the interests of particular individuals, or evaluating community benefits vis-à-vis restrictions upon individual liberty. It can also be construed in terms of protection—balancing the interests of public security, on the one hand, with the human rights and due process safeguards afforded to individuals accused of undesirable or criminal behaviour, on the other. As mentioned above, we previously articulated this balancing act in terms of expediency and legitimacy and have led the argument that the non-conviction-based approach serves to privilege normatively-motivated political expediency concerning serious and organized crime over fundamental considerations of due process under the rule of law.[210] Our ongoing concern is that, by treating civil recovery as a *civil* process instead of a criminal one, the elevated procedural safeguards of the criminal process are deliberately and instrumentally circumvented, upsetting this delicate balance at the risk of injustice.

It is still useful to consider this in terms of a balancing act. Civil recovery's legislative goals are fourfold: (i) to disrupt the profit incentive of serious and organized crime; (ii) to undermine organized criminality's economic foundation; (iii) to deter further organized criminal activity; and (iv) to enable a law enforcement 'follow the money' approach.[211] These goals encapsulate the perceived benefits to society offered by civil recovery and—so the pragmatic argument goes—combine to provide justification for any subsequent infringement upon the rights and liberties of an individual who has their assets seized. As far as weighing the social advantages against individual liberties goes, the benefits that civil recovery provides for society at large are purported—certainly by proponents—to outweigh its drawbacks. This spurious balancing exercise is held as sufficient to justify the harm that civil recovery risks to individuals against whom it is employed.

Such a utilitarian calculus is hardly an unusual one for legislatures to make; if anything, it is fairly standard for the adoption of procedural or evidential rules. Our intention is not to problematize the calculation so much as to query the accounting. Indeed, our criticism of the pragmatic argument—which distills to the assertion that civil recovery is imperfect yet effective—is that too little

[209] For consideration of third parties, see Chapter 6. See also Natalie Skead and Sarah Murray, 'The Politics of Proceeds of Crime Legislation' (2015) 38 *University of New South Wales Law Journal* 455, 491.

[210] Jennifer Hendry and Colin King, 'Expediency, Legitimacy, and the Rule of Law: A Systems Perspective on Civil/ Criminal Procedural Hybrids' (2017) 11(4) *Criminal Law and Philosophy* 733.

[211] For wider consideration, see Chapter 3.

consideration has been taken of the *kind* of harm to individuals that is risked by this process. We reject this prevailing pragmatic view on the grounds that it miscategorizes the particular *moral* harm inherent to the non-conviction-based approach.

Bare harm and moral harm

Dworkin's essay 'Principle, Policy, Procedure' sets out the distinction between two types of harm, namely bare harm and moral harm. In this he argues that it is important to distinguish between:

> what we might call the bare harm a person suffers through punishment, whether that punishment is just or unjust—for example, the suffering or frustration or pain or dissatisfaction of desires that he suffers just because he loses his liberty or is beaten or killed—and the further injury that he might be said to suffer whenever his punishment is unjust, just in virtue of that injustice. I shall call the latter the 'injustice factor' in his punishment, or his 'moral' harm.[212]

This distinction can be illustrated as follows. A person that is fined or imprisoned suffers bare harm, irrespective of whether they are factually guilty. Whether a verdict is 'just' or factually correct, is irrelevant to considerations of bare harm. 'Justness' only comes into play in terms of moral harm: there is a difference between a guilty person being imprisoned and an innocent one being imprisoned, with only the latter suffering moral harm.

Compared to the subjectively experienced deprivations and frustrations suffered as bare harm, moral harm is an objective matter, and constitutes a distinct type of injury against which people should be specifically protected.[213] Difficult questions arise, however, when it comes to quantifying harm of this objective sort and, in particular, how it should be weighed against other practical considerations. As Dworkin notes, reasonable people can—and do—disagree about the relative importance of avoiding individual injustices. For this reason, he argues that decisions as to how any society should weigh or quantify moral harm should be made by majority rule, if they are to be made fairly. In practical

[212] Ronald Dworkin, *A Matter of Principle* (Harvard University Press 1985) 80.
[213] Ibid.

terms, this means that a majoritarian institution, such as a legislature, must be the one to adopt generally applicable rules of evidence and procedure. In this manner, whenever a legislature adopts a procedural or evidential rule, it weighs the intended benefits to society (general interest, common good, increased security) that result from the adoption of that rule *against* the risk and magnitude of whatever moral and bare harm that rule might give rise to. In most situations, according to Dworkin, there is no obvious balance to be struck: the rule is justified by virtue of having been taken *by* the majority institution, and fairness subsists if, in the exercise of the resultant rules, there is no discrimination against any independently distinct groups.[214] This is not the case for civil recovery, however, as the procedure's hybridity serves effectively to *hide* the relevant moral harm.

By way of explanation, let us revisit the pragmatic view of civil recovery, which can be explained as follows. As established throughout this chapter, the pragmatic view is that the problems of serious and organized crime, including the challenges these pose for criminal law enforcement, are *so important* as to constitute considerations of general welfare and security. These general welfare considerations therefore *outweigh* whatever risk and magnitude of moral and bare harm—generated by these procedural and evidential rules—that might be suffered by individuals who have had their assets seized under this process. Essentially, the pragmatic view of civil recovery is that it addresses the pressing problems of organized and career criminality in a manner that is *on balance* justified, notwithstanding the potential moral and bare harm to the individual.

While we query this weighting, we do not argue that the bare harm generated by individuals having their assets seized has been subject to miscalculation.[215] Rather, it is our contention that the misunderstanding subsists in terms of *moral* harm, in the sense that the pragmatic view characterizes such harm *purely* in terms of the erroneous seizure of assets. This is evident from the practitioner interviews, which emphasize both the civil label and the *in rem* dimension of civil recovery, highlighting the 'mere' loss of money and assets. The following quotations have already been featured in this chapter but they are worth restating here for emphasis:

[214] Ibid.

[215] For consideration of harm in the context of post-conviction confiscation, specifically the lived realities of those subject to confiscation orders and impact upon family members, see Craig Fletcher, *'Double Punishment'—The Proceeds of Crime Act 2002 (POCA): A Qualitative Examination of the Post-Conviction Confiscation Punishment in England and Wales* (PhD Thesis, Manchester Metropolitan University, 2019).

- 'In no civil case will you end up in jail. It's not a loss of liberty, it's only money at the end of the day. It's as simple as that. So, if it just involves money then balance of probability is your appropriate test.'[216]
- '[I]t seems odd, certainly coming from a criminal perspective, that you can have quasi-findings being made about criminal conduct that do not require the most stringent standard of proof, but the flipside to that is to say that in that type of situation you are potentially depriving somebody of their liberty, hence the elevated standard, whereas in civil recovery the state is taking away somebody's property where there is not the same type of threat to somebody's autonomy as in taking away their liberty'.[217]
- 'I think it's a bit glib at times to say these people's rights aren't being respected. You have to ask the question "what rights are you talking about?". So yes, of course, it would be arguably very dangerous if people were being convicted of crimes on the basis of hearsay evidence, on the balance of proof, without a jury trial, but they are not being convicted of crimes; they are being asked to hand over property which they can't legitimately account for. What's wrong with that?'[218]
- 'It needs to be the civil standard because its civil based. And, it's also about the property. It never would work otherwise.'[219]

All of the above quotations *assume* that the moral harm resulting from the erroneous seizure of assets is analogous with a wrongful civil judgment. This, we argue, is mistaken. The erroneous confiscation of assets, something that is disproportionately more likely under civil recovery proceedings, as a result of the role of suspicion in discharging the burden of proof, and the civil standard of proof, as discussed, is not comparable with a wrongful civil judgment. Rather, such erroneous confiscation de facto constitutes the unjust *punishment* of that individual as if they have been engaged in criminal or undesirable behaviour. The analogy is actually far closer to wrongful criminal judgment,[220] which is to say, a miscarriage of justice and thus a much greater moral harm.

Recast in this way, our objection to the pragmatic approach becomes clearer. Those adopting this purportedly fitting, practical, *realistic* approach are, we argue, misled by the civil label into believing that the only thing at stake for the

216 IRE05.
217 EW05.
218 IRE09.
219 EW09.
220 Blackstone's famous ratio establishes that 'the law holds that it is better that ten guilty persons escape than that one innocent suffer'. William Blackstone, *Commentaries on the Laws of England in Four Books, Volume 2* (J.B. Lippincott 1753).

individual is property—important in itself, as we have explained in Chapter 6, but not, as repeatedly emphasized by proponents, actually comparable with the loss of liberty. Since they are mistaken about the moral harm that results from the erroneous seizure of assets, pragmatists skew the all-important balance overly in favour of addressing the social problem, at the expense of adequately protecting individuals against the moral harm of wrongful punishment. Importantly, if moral harm is understood in this manner, then the civil/criminal hybrid procedural character of civil recovery ceases to provide a mask for the injustice inherent to an incorrect decision under these procedural rules.

8
Conclusion

Concluding Remarks

Our aims in writing this book have been several. Civil recovery legislation has been on the statute books in Ireland for the past twenty-five years and in the United Kingdom for the past twenty, so the time was ripe not only for a detailed and dedicated retrospective but also for a critical deep-dive investigation of this hybrid procedure's operation in practice. Employing socio-legal and comparative methods to create an original data set, we have undertaken a blended doctrinal, contextual, and conceptual analysis of civil recovery in terms of *inter alia* its procedural hybridity, its legislative justifications, its benevolent judicial reception, its compliance with the requirements of due process, its *in rem* character, and its supposed pragmatism in tackling the problem of serious and organized crime. Our conclusion, in light of this wide-ranging analysis, is that the non-conviction-based (NCB) approach employed by civil recovery is procedurally and morally problematic. These closing remarks should thus be read in light of our consternation at the widespread acceptance—in both jurisdictions—of a practice at such odds with the requirements of due process and the rule of law.

We have three final issues to reflect upon, as follows: (i) the self-legitimation strategies—exposed by our interview data—of civil recovery proponents; (ii) the worrisome international spread of NCB-type practices; and (iii) the equally disquieting proliferation of hybrid proceduralism as a regulatory technique, both nationally and internationally.

Self-Legitimation

Our motivation at the outset of this research was to explore what practitioners think about civil recovery in both Ireland and England & Wales. There is extensive academic literature that is critical of civil recovery, and yet limited argument and analysis in favour of this measure.[1] Thus, we wanted to build upon

[1] With the exception of a small number of enforcement practitioners, such as: Francis Cassidy, 'Targeting the Proceeds of Crime: An Irish Perspective' in Theodore Greenberg, Linda Samuel, Wingate

Civil Recovery of Criminal Property. Colin King and Jennifer Hendry, Oxford University Press.
 DOI: 10.1093/oso/9780198824251.003.0008

the doctrinal and theoretical literature on civil recovery to examine whether the critical academic position is reflected amongst practitioners. Our hypothesis was that enforcement-focused practitioners would reject criticisms and advocate in favour of civil recovery, whereas respondent-focused practitioners would be more critical. In many ways, this hypothesis proved to be accurate, although with some notable exceptions.

Given the limited literature advocating for civil recovery, we were keen to explore in particular the justifications of civil recovery provided by proponents, and the self-legitimation strategies they employed in relation to those justifications. We draw here on the insights of Bottoms and Tankebe, who distinguish between two type of legitimacy: audience legitimacy, which is the legitimacy of criminal justice services from the perspective of those they serve, such as the general public or convicted offenders,[2] and legitimacy from the perspective of the power-holder, or the 'voice within'.[3] The distinction here is between the perceived legitimacy of those in power from an external or citizen perspective, compared to the power-holder's internal perspective concerning their *own* legitimacy. In terms of the latter, those in power justify themselves *to* themselves, in a process described as self-legitimation.[4] In the context of criminal justice, the primary purpose for power-holders concerns 'the maintenance of a just social order';[5] indeed, self-legitimation strategies are prominent in Tuesta's analysis of prosecutorial discretion,[6] which evidences at least three justification

Grant, and Larissa Gray, *Stolen Asset Recovery: A Good Practices Guide for Non-Conviction Based Asset Forfeiture* (World Bank 2009); Stef Cassella, 'The Case for Civil Forfeiture: Why In Rem Proceedings are an Essential Tool for Recovering the Proceeds of Crime' (2008) 11(1) *Journal of Money Laundering Control* 8; Anthony Kennedy, 'Justifying the Civil Recovery of Criminal Proceeds' (2005) 12(1) *Journal of Financial Crime* 8.

[2] Audience legitimacy has spawned an extensive literature, for example on procedural justice see Jason Sunshine and Tom Tyler, 'The Role of Procedural Justice and Legitimacy in Shaping Public Support for Policing' (2003) 37 *Law & Society Review* 513; Tom Tyler, 'Procedural Justice, Legitimacy, and the Effective Rule of Law' (2003) 30 *Crime & Justice* 283; Kristina Murphy, 'Procedural Justice and Its Role in Promoting Voluntary Compliance' in Peter Drahos (ed.), *Regulatory Theory: Foundations and Applications* (ANU Press 2017)

[3] Anthony Bottoms and Justice Tankebe, '"A Voice Within": Power-holders Perspectives on Authority and Legitimacy' in Justice Tankebe and Alison Liebling (eds), *Legitimacy and Criminal Justice: An International Exploration* (Oxford University Press 2013).

[4] Rodney Barker, *Legitimating Identities: The Self-Presentations of Rulers and Subjects* (Cambridge University Press 2001).

[5] Anthony Bottoms and Justice Tankebe, '"A Voice Within": Power-holders Perspectives on Authority and Legitimacy' in Justice Tankebe and Alison Liebling (eds), *Legitimacy and Criminal Justice: An International Exploration* (Oxford University Press 2013) 71.

[6] For a different perspective, 'legitimation work' is analysed by McEvoy in the context of cause-lawyers, where he identifies three ideal types, namely 'cause lawyers as struggle lawyers; cause lawyers as human rights lawyers; and cause lawyers as "a pragmatic moral community"': Kieran McEvoy, 'Cause Lawyers, Political Violence, and Professionalism in Conflict' (2019) 46(4) *Journal of Law & Society* 529, 531.

regimes. These are: increasing the odds of rescuing victims and achieving sentencing outcomes (legal efficiency); the preservation of collegiality (including considerations of how their decisions impact on other, under-resourced, departments); and getting the job done (including considerations of the common good, in that instance the elimination of human trafficking).[7] Here, we reflect upon the self-legitimation strategies of enforcement-focused practitioners and how they justify the use of civil recovery.[8] Three themes came to the fore: civil recovery is a necessary and pragmatic power to tackle organized criminality; it is a non-criminal power; and it only concerns property, not liberty.

In terms of being *necessary* and *pragmatic*, our proponent interviewees reflected the policy stance from the enactment of civil recovery legislation, namely that organized crime is a threat to society, one that must be tackled. Proponents contended that the criminal process was ill-equipped, or inadequate, to tackle organized crime, particularly the so-called 'Mr Bigs', those apex criminals operating at significant remove from the coalface. Concern was expressed that 'criminals' were escaping prosecution and/or conviction, with the result that they were able to keep the proceeds of their criminality. Furthermore, even if an individual were to be convicted, there was unease over the limitations and weaknesses of post-conviction confiscation powers. In this regard, civil recovery was portrayed as a means of targeting proceeds of crime without the shackles of the criminal process.

The second self-legitimation strategy evident amongst proponent interviewees was a staunch view that civil recovery is not a criminal matter, instead being civil. While some conceded that a criminal allegation underpins civil recovery proceedings, the general consensus amongst proponents was that these are not criminal proceedings. This view was then used to reinforce other rationalizations, for example, as civil recovery is not criminal it is by definition not punitive, nor does it involve determination of guilt. The non-criminal nature was, in this same manner, used to excuse lesser evidential rules, such as the application of the civil standard of proof. Moreover, it was stressed that there are safeguards in place that ensure fairness within and throughout the process, with it even being suggested that innocent people have nothing to fear from civil recovery.

[7] 'Prosecutors, with the idea that the ends justify the means, outline a civil narrative that legitimizes the use of irregular mechanisms in criminal investigations.' Diego Tuesta, 'Rethinking Prosecutorial Discretion: Towards A Moral Cartography of Prosecutors' (2021) 61 *British Journal of Criminology* 1486, 1498.

[8] For wider consideration of self-legitimation, see Alexandra Cox and Camila Gripp, 'The Legitimation Strategies of "Progressive" Prosecutors' (2022) 31(5) *Social & Legal Studies* 657.

The description of civil recovery as non-criminal leads nicely into the third self-legitimation strategy evident amongst proponent interviewees, namely that it *only* concerns property: as the action is purportedly against the property itself (*in rem*), and not against the individual (*in personam*), then there is no need for criminal law safeguards. For these interviewees, civil recovery simply does not constitute punishment. Proponents stressed that the individual deprived of the property in question is not actually *deprived* of anything, on the grounds that they had no good title to the property in question. The emphasis here rested squarely on the deprivation of property, rather than liberty, a distinction which served to reinforce the *civil* nature of civil recovery in the minds of enforcement-focused interviewees. Indeed, an evidently instrumental reliance on the supposed *in rem* nature of civil recovery shone through these interviews.

These justification strategies, however, merely serve to reinforce the concerns in critical academic literature, specifically the circumvention of criminal procedural safeguards; the mislabelling of civil recovery as 'civil'; and the instrumental reliance on the *in rem* designation. Moreover, while there is a recurring emphasis on 'public interest' amongst proponents, only one perspective is stressed, namely the importance of tackling organized crime. However, criminal procedural protections, for example, are also in the public interest.[9] A related issue is the cognitive dissonance exhibited by civil recovery proponents who are ardent—both overtly and robustly—about core safeguards of the criminal justice system.[10] Throughout our analysis of the interview data, it became more and more apparent to us that in spite of their avowed commitment to criminal procedural safeguards, such as the presumption of innocence and the standard of proof, many proponents were accepting of the circumvention of such safeguards in this specific context. Moreover, they used language that belied their expressed belief that civil recovery proceedings were not criminal in character, speaking about respondents as if they were *criminals* while insisting that civil recovery was a wholly civil measure, and they emphasized the importance of hitting *criminals* in the pocket and making individuals pay for *their* crimes.

[9] See Richard V Ericson, *Crime in an Insecure World* (Polity Press 2007) 204–6.

[10] The term cognitive dissonance, coined in the 1950s by American social psychologist Leon Festinger, describes the conscious or unconscious 'discomfort' that people experience when two thoughts (cognitions) or behaviours are in contradiction with each other: for example, when someone smokes in spite of being aware of the health dangers, or when someone with professed 'green' values buys a fuel-hungry car. See Leon Festinger, *A Theory of Cognitive Dissonance* (Stanford University Press 1957).

The dissonance identified here is an inconsistency largely generated, we argue, by civil recovery's *civil* label and its expedient criminal justice aims. This is where proponents struggle to reconcile their incompatible views concerning this hybrid procedure's alleged preventive, reparative, and/or compensatory nature and its application against respondents suspected of involvement in criminal activity. While such dissonance can be unconscious, of course, the ongoing contradiction is problematic because it puts to the lie the civil classification that purports to validate the non-conviction-based approach to the deprivation of property. It is simply not plausible that the civil label is sufficient to cause practitioners to proceed uncritically as far as this process is concerned. We should note here that we reject—on the grounds that the interviews were with 'elite' experienced practitioners in Ireland and in England & Wales—any suggestions that civil/criminal hybrid procedures such as civil recovery are conceptually and terminologically challenging, and that some ambiguity in phrasing can be expected as a result. Terminological inexactitude and even conversational slippage are unedifying explanations for this charted phenomenon.

Notably, however—and somewhat contrary to our initial hypothesis—some views expressed in interviews did not neatly map the enforcement- or respondent-focused backgrounds of practitioners. While this was certainly the dominant trend, there were some anomalous views. For example, a small number of respondent-focused interviewees expressed positions that would be more readily associated with enforcement-focused interviewees, such as the view that respondents should cooperate, or that financial privacy considerations are irrelevant. Indeed, for these interviewees, there was an evident sense of suspicion or mistrust towards their own clients, although we should reiterate that such views were expressed by a very small number of respondent-focused interviewees. By the same token, a similarly small number of enforcement-focused interviewees expressed views that were commensurate with a respondent-focused position. These interviewees acknowledged that civil recovery is a blunt tool; that it is draconian; that they would feel different if it were *their* property subject to civil recovery; that it is unfair on innocent third parties; and that the *in rem*/*in personam* distinction is a legal fiction.

Comparing Civil Recovery

Our comparison has been deliberately restricted to Ireland and England & Wales, but that is not to say that the non-conviction-based approach is a feature of these jurisdictions alone. On the contrary, the past twenty-five years have seen a significant increase in the number of legal systems with equivalent practices. Whether or not we include this rise within the general context of preventive justice, as discussed in Chapter 2—and there are reasons not to, not least that civil recovery proceedings necessarily occur temporally subsequent to the alleged criminality that has generated and jeopardized the assets subject to the civil recovery order—there is no denying that such approaches have policy-maker appeal. Indeed, the appeal is evidenced by the spread of (or reform of extant) non-conviction-based confiscation legislation across the globe,[11] including in, *inter alia*, Australia,[12] some Canadian provinces,[13] New Zealand,[14] South Africa,[15] and, of course, the United States.[16] Non-conviction-based approaches have also attracted attention across civil law countries, particularly in the EU (e.g. Italy, Spain, Germany),[17] and at EU level itself.[18] There are, of course, and as has been detailed in Chapter 1, different models of non-conviction-based confiscation; as Grandi stresses:

[11] Anthony Kennedy, 'Designing a Civil Forfeiture System: An Issues List for Policymakers and Legislators' (2006) 13(2) *Journal of Financial Crime* 132; Conference of the State Parties to the United Nations Convention against Corruption, Open-ended Intergovernmental Working Group on Asset Recovery, *Procedures Allowing the Confiscation of Proceeds of Corruption Without a Criminal Conviction* (September 2021).

[12] For example, Criminal Property Confiscation Act 2000 (Western Australia); Proceeds of Crime Act 2002 (Cth). See also Lorna Bartels, *Unexplained Wealth Laws in Australia* (Australian Institute of Criminology 2010); Natalie Skead and Sarah Murray, 'The Politics of Proceeds of Crime Legislation' (2015) 38(2) *University of New South Wales Law Journal* 455.

[13] For example, Remedies for Organized Crime and Other Unlawful Activities Act 2001 (Ontario); The Seizure of Criminal Property Act 2009 (Saskatchewan). See also Peter German, *Proceeds of Crime and Money Laundering* (Carswell 2019).

[14] For example, Criminal Proceeds (Recovery) Act 2009. See also Ian Ko, '"Tainted" Assets, "Dirty" Money and the Civil-Criminal Dichotomy: A Novel Approach to the Classification of Civil Forfeiture Proceedings under the Criminal Proceeds (Recovery) Act 2009' (2015) 21 *Auckland University Law Review* 193.

[15] For example, Prevention of Organised Crime Act 1998. See also Vinesh Basdeo, 'The Legal Challenges of Criminal and Civil Asset Forfeiture in South Africa: A Comparative Analysis' (2013) 21(3) *African Journal of International and Comparative Law* 303.

[16] For example, Civil Asset Forfeiture Reform Act 2000. See also Stefan D Cassella, *Asset Forfeiture Law in the United States* (3rd edn, Juris Publishing 2022).

[17] See, *inter alia*, Andrea Planchadell Gargallo and Caty Vidales Rodríguez, 'Decomiso: Comentario Crítico Desde Una Perspectiva Constitucional' (Confiscation: Critical Comment from a Constitutional Perspective) (2018) XXXVIII *Estudios Penales y Criminológicos* 37; Francesco Mazzacuva, 'The Problematic Nature of Asset Recovery Measures: Recent Developments of the Italian Preventive Confiscation' in Katalin Ligeti and Michele Simonato (eds) *Chasing Criminal Money: Challenges and Perspective On Asset Recovery in the EU* (Hart Publishing 2017); Robert Esser, 'A Civil Asset Recovery Model—The German Perspective and European Human Rights' in Jon Petter Rui and Ulrich Sieber (eds), *Non-Conviction-Based Confiscation in Europe* (Duncker & Humblot 2015).

[18] Directive 2014/42/EU of the European Parliament and of the Council of 3 April 2014 on the freezing and confiscation of instrumentalities and proceeds of crime in the European Union; European Commission, *Commission Staff Working Document. Analysis of Non-Conviction Based Confiscation Measures in the European Union* (Brussels, 12 April 2019. SWD (2019) 1050 final); European Commission, *Proposal for a Directive of the European Parliament and of the Council on Asset Recovery and Confiscation* (Brussels, 25 May 2022. COM(2022) 245 final).

> the picture may vary from the *civil asset forfeiture* as conceived in Ireland and UK, which consist of an *action in rem* directed against the property and conducted before a civil court, to the Italian so-called 'preventive confiscation' that, though adopted by a criminal court, is not yet grounded on criminal conviction.[19]

Accordingly, it is important to be clear which model one is considering when discussing the 'NCB' approach, especially given that the different approaches across the EU are said to be 'extremely fragmented'.[20] As the European Commission acknowledges, 'important differences persist regarding non-conviction based confiscation'.[21] As stated, our focus in this book has been on the approach in both Ireland and England & Wales, which is a limitation of the study in that we focus on one model of NCB confiscation.[22] Future research might adopt a more comparative approach to different NCB models but there are sound justifications for our choice of these two jurisdictions: the pioneering and best-practice status[23] of the Irish legislation gives Ireland a certain prominence in this field, with the result that any reforms undertaken within that jurisdiction are viewed with interest from others following comparable approaches.[24] Indeed, and contrary to the usual flow of policy transfer,[25] England

[19] Ciro Grandi, 'Non-Conviction-Based Confiscation in the EU Legal Framework' in Alessandro Bernardi (ed.), *Improving Confiscation Procedures in the European Union* (Jovene Editore 2019) 34.

[20] Michele Simonato, 'Directive 2014/42/EU and Non-Conviction Based Confiscation: A Step Forward on Asset Recovery?' (2015) 6 *New Journal of European Criminal Law* 213, 217.

[21] European Commission, *Commission Staff Working Document. Analysis of non-conviction based confiscation measures in the European Union* (Brussels, 12 April 2019. SWD (2019) 1050 final) 7.

[22] Three other models are explained in Chapter 1. See also Camden Asset Recovery Inter-Agency Network, *The History, Statement of Intent, Membership and Functioning of CARIN (CARIN Manual 5th edn)* (Europol 2015).

[23] For example, Greco, *Second Evaluation Round—Evaluation Report on Ireland* (2005), 8: the evaluation team 'was impressed by the civil forfeiture scheme (*in rem*) which has provided the Criminal Assets Bureau (CAB) with effective tools to identify and seize proceeds of crime.' Also, FATF, *Ireland—Mutual Evaluation Report* (2017) 58: 'Ireland has been at the forefront of international efforts to introduce non-conviction based confiscation systems. Ireland established its multi-agency Criminal Assets Bureau (CAB) in 1996 and the country continues to enjoy a strong reputation internationally in this area.' And, Committee on Legal Affairs and Human Rights, *Fighting Organised Crime by Facilitating the Confiscation of Illegal Assets* (Doc. 14516, 26 March 2018) para. 12: 'The Irish model has been considered a real success, also at the European and international level.'

[24] For example, each year the Bureau receives a number of visitors from law enforcement agencies elsewhere who are interested in the framework and operation of the Irish approach: see Criminal Assets Bureau, *Annual Report 2021* (Stationery Office 2022) 77–9.

[25] That is, it is not unusual for criminal justice policies introduced in England & Wales (E + W) to subsequently be adopted in Ireland, a notable example in the context of civil/criminal hybrid orders being the Anti-Social Behaviour Order (ASBO) introduced in E + W by the Crime and Disorder Act 1998 followed by the Behaviour Order in Ireland by the Criminal Justice Act 2006. For wider consideration, see Claire Hamilton and Mairéad Seymour, 'ASBOs and Behaviour Orders: Institutionalised Intolerance of Youth?' (2006) 1(1) *Youth Studies Ireland* 61; Kevin Brown, 'Examining the Introduction of Legislation in Ireland to Tackle Juvenile Anti-Social Behaviour' (2007) 54(3) *Probation Journal* 239.

& Wales looked to Ireland when devising its civil recovery regime, as well as its subsequent application in practice.[26] Both jurisdictions now have over two decades of experience with NCB confiscation, thereby providing an excellent opportunity to examine their approaches empirically.

A further reason for examining both Ireland and England & Wales is that the law in both jurisdictions has over the past two decades been subject to detailed judicial review. Indeed, any future comparative analysis of different NCB models should consider the constitutionality of NCB confiscation, and how it might be received in different national courts. Notwithstanding judicial imprimatur in many countries (including Ireland and England & Wales, as detailed in Chapter 4) and in the European Court of Human Rights,[27] there continue to be reservations as to whether the NCB approach is human rights compliant:

> A key challenge to the introduction of non-conviction based confiscation legislation is the compliance with fundamental rights. The absence of a criminal conviction raises issues relating to the right to fair trial, effective judicial remedy, the presumption of innocence as well as the right to property.[28]

Although this statement reads like the sceptical academic viewpoint, it is worth noting that it in fact comes from the European Commission. Similarly, Eurojust has stated that '[t]he key impediment to the implementation of non-conviction-based confiscation systems, as suggested at various international *fora*, is the unconstitutional nature of these systems in certain Member States'.[29] What is notable, however, is that irrespective of which model is adopted in individual countries, and regardless of the significant concerns voiced by key policymakers in the field, like the EU Commission, NCB confiscation continues to be a prevalent and indeed expanding approach.

While much of the academic literature to date on NCB confiscation has adopted doctrinal and/or theoretical analyses,[30] this book offers an additional

[26] Council of Europe, *Impact Study on Civil Forfeiture* (2013) 46: 'It was the work of CAB [*the Criminal Assets Bureau*] that attracted the interest of officials in the UK and led to the passing of civil forfeiture provisions in the UK in 2002.' See also HC Deb, 30 October 2001, vol. 373, col. 764, per Mr Denham MP (Minister for Police, Courts and Drugs). Cf. HC Deb, 27 February 2002, vol. 380.

[27] For example, *M v Italy*, App. No. 12386/86, 15 April 1991; *Air Canada v UK* [1995] 20 EHRR 150; *Dassa Foundation v Liechtenstein*, App. No. 696/05, 10 July 2007; *Gogitidze v Georgia* [2015] ECHR 475.

[28] European Commission, *Commission Staff Working Document. Analysis of Non-Conviction Based Confiscation Measures in the European Union* (Brussels, 12 April 2019. SWD (2019) 1050 final) 8.

[29] Eurojust, *Report on non-conviction-based confiscation* (April 2013) 8.

[30] For example, Peter Alldridge, 'Civil Recovery in England and Wales: An Appraisal' in Colin King, Clive Walker and Jimmy Gurulé (eds), *The Palgrave Handbook of Criminal and Terrorism Financing Law* (Palgrave 2018); Jennifer Hendry and Colin King, 'Expediency, Legitimacy, and the Rule of Law: A Systems Perspective on Civil/ Criminal Procedural Hybrids' (2017) 11(4) *Criminal Law and Philosophy* 733; Anthony Gray, 'Forfeiture Provisions and the Criminal/Civil Divide' (2012) 15 *New*

perspective through qualitative interviews with leading practitioners in the field. This empirical data comprises a unique dataset that has facilitated unprecedented insight into practitioner understandings of this contentious procedure. As was expected, enforcement-focused interviewees roundly rejected any concerns that the NCB approach is not human-rights compliant and were at pains to stress its important, and pragmatic, role in tackling organized crime. Yet respondent-focused interviewees were, in general, unpersuaded by such contentions and continued to view the NCB approach with scepticism. Considering the extent of this schism, it is unsurprising that NCB confiscation continues to be a controversial approach, although it is our hope that the insights generated through this dataset will provide critical stimulus for consideration of civil recovery, alongside scrutiny of civil/criminal hybrid orders more generally. The rise of these hybrid orders is the focus of our final section.

Hybrid Proceduralism

While there has been a steady rise in the number of jurisdictions employing civil recovery-type practices, as outlined, this trend can be further contextualized by the similarly sustained increase in the use of civil/criminal hybrid procedural forms across different applications and jurisdictions. For Hendry, hybrid proceduralism is characterized *inter alia* by 'its experimental quality [and] its imaginative use of the different levers of control and compliance'.[31] Our focus in this book has been on one hybrid measure—civil recovery—but there are many others. Ireland adopted civil recovery legislation in 1996, whereas England & Wales followed in 2002. Another hybrid order is the Anti-Social Behaviour Order (ASBO), which was introduced in England & Wales in 1998,[32] and which influenced the introduction of 'civil orders' in Ireland in 2006.[33] Beyond these two discrete instances, however, Ireland has been much more reticent in the adoption of hybrid orders.[34] This is in stark contrast to

Criminal Law Review 32; Liz Campbell, 'The Recovery of "Criminal" Assets in New Zealand, Ireland and England: Fighting Organised and Serious Crime in the Civil Realm' (2010) 41 *Victoria University Wellington Law Review* 15.

[31] Jennifer Hendry, '"The Usual Suspects"': Knife Crime Prevention Orders and the "Difficult" Regulatory Subject' (2022) 62(2) *The British Journal of Criminology* 378, 387.

[32] Crime and Disorder Act 1998.

[33] Criminal Justice Act 2006.

[34] Of course, there are regulatory agencies—such as the Health and Safety Authority, Environmental Protection Agency, Office of the Director of Corporate Enforcement, and more—that also have hybrid powers: for further consideration, see Shane Kilcommins and Ursula Kilkelly (eds), *Regulatory Crime in Ireland* (First Law 2010).

England & Wales, which has firmly embraced hybrid orders across a range of diverse legal areas such as public space and community protection, domestic violence, stalking, football hooliganism, knife crime, organized crime, and more.[35]

While there might well be valid public policy considerations underpinning such orders, there remain significant concerns across both the legal profession and civil society as to the compliance of these civil/criminal hybrid orders with due process norms; the manner in which they create 'personalized penal codes' for the recipient; the ease and extent to which such orders can be challenged or appealed by those made subject to them; the apparent inconsistency of their application across different geographic regions, within different local authorities, and by different police forces; and their effectiveness.[36] In contrast to the escalation of hybrid proceduralism in England & Wales, in Ireland concerns were raised as to the value of civil orders less than three years after their introduction,[37] and these concerns persist into 2022.[38] This is perhaps unsurprising, not least given the consternation expressed in England & Wales.[39] What is notable about the proliferation of hybrid orders in England & Wales is the lack of an overarching framework for such orders. This is not down to lack of effort in this regard; many commentators have tried to identify commonalities, although the differences make this a challenging endeavour.[40] We do not propose to repeat such an exercise here. Rather, our aim is to situate civil recovery

[35] Writing in 2014, Ashworth and Zedner noted: 'Over the past decade the British state has energetically adopted civil preventive measures to tackle various forms of harm and wrongdoing, and has shown itself to be committed to ensuring that these measures are actually used.' Andrew Ashworth and Lucia Zedner, *Preventive Justice* (Oxford University Press 2014) 82.

[36] Stuart Kirby and Ann Edmondson, 'The Effectiveness of the ASBO—A Practitioner Perspective' (2012) 11(2) *Safer Communities* 96; Office of the Commissioner for Human Rights, *Report by Mr Alvaro Gil-Robles, Commissioner for Human Rights on his visit to the United Kingdom 4th – 12th November 2004 for the attention of the Committee of Ministers and the Parliamentary Assembly*. CommDH(2005)6 (8 June 2005) para.108 *et seq*.

[37] Carl O'Brien, 'Government to Review Effectiveness of ASBOS', *Irish Times* (29 June 2009).

[38] Tadhg McNally, 'The Justice Minister Wants to Know Why Asbos Are Used More in Some Areas Than in Others', *TheJournal.ie* (4 October 2022).

[39] Adam Crawford, Sam Lewis, and Peter Traynor, '"It Ain't (Just) What You Do, It's (Also) the Way That You Do It": The Role of Procedural Justice in the Implementation of Antisocial Behaviour Interventions with Young People' (2017) 23(1) *European Journal on Criminal Policy and Research* 9. Indeed, ASBOs were repealed in that jurisdiction in 2014. For consideration of this development, see Stavros Demetriou, 'From the ASBO to the Injunction: A Qualitative Review of the Anti-Social Behaviour Legislation Post-2014' [2019] *Public Law* 343.

[40] The most recent effort in this regard is Kelly's taxonomy of civil behaviour orders, hybrid behaviour orders, and executive behaviour orders: Rory Kelly, *Behaviour Orders: Preventive and/or Punitive Measures?* (PhD Thesis, University of Oxford, 2019). Cf. Andrew Ashworth and Lucia Zedner, *Preventive Justice* (Oxford University Press 2014); Andrew Simester and Andreas von Hirsch, 'Regulating Offensive Conduct through Two-Step Prohibitions' in Andrew Simester and Andreas von Hirsch (eds), *Incivilities: Regulating Offensive Behaviour* (Hart 2006).

in the context of other hybrid orders and to reiterate our due process concerns, not least given the lack of evidence as to its impact.

The earliest indication of the shift in England & Wales towards the use of hybrid orders can be seen with the Football Banning Order (FBO),[41] a supposed preventive order designed to address football hooliganism. Similar logic was evident with the introduction of ASBOs,[42] where the focus was on preventing anti-social behaviour and low-level criminality. The perception was that the criminal law was inadequate, first, due to difficulties in investigation and prosecution and, second, given the nature of the behaviour (i.e. ongoing, cumulative) particularly where it did not contravene the criminal law.[43] The emphasis on community protection again came to the fore with both the Community Protection Notice (CPN) and the Public Space Protection Order (PSPO), which target behaviour that local authorities have deemed to be problematic.[44] What can be observed here is the more and more common use of a novel civil/criminal hybrid regulatory form to pre-empt, prevent, or otherwise interrupt undesirable and potentially harmful behaviour; the focus clearly rests on the behaviour of the recipient. This regulatory form is identifiable by its operative distrust of potential perpetrators,[45] its escalatory operation (whereby a warning is followed by a sanction on breach), its creation of individualized regulatory regimes, and the manner in which it facilitates a general criminalization creep.[46]

Another area where hybrid orders are prevalent is domestic- and gender based violence, for example the Female Genital Mutilation Protection Order,[47] the initial Domestic Violence Protection Order,[48] the new Domestic Abuse Protection Order,[49] and the Stalking Protection Order.[50] One dimension that comes strongly to the fore here is the emphasis such orders place on protecting

[41] Football Spectators Act 1989.

[42] Crime and Disorder Act 1998.

[43] Labour Party, *A Quiet Life: Tough Action on Criminal Neighbours* (1995). For broader consideration, see Andrew Ashworth and Lucia Zedner, *Preventive Justice* (Oxford University Press 2014) ch.4.

[44] Anti-Social Behaviour, Crime and Policing Act 2014.

[45] Daniel Ohana, 'Trust, Distrust and Reassurance: Diversion and Preventive Orders Through the Prism of Feindstrafrecht' (2010) 73(5) *Modern Law Review* 721.

[46] The result was what Crawford et al. describe as a form of 'regulatory hyperactivity' with 'civil orders backed up by criminal penalties, whereby it is future conduct that becomes the focus of prospective regulation'. Adam Crawford, Sam Lewis, and Peter Traynor, '"It Ain't (Just) What You Do, It's (Also) the Way That You Do It": The role of Procedural Justice in the Implementation of Antisocial Behaviour Interventions with Young People' (2017) 23(1) *European Journal on Criminal Policy and Research* 9, 10-11.

[47] Female Genital Mutilation Act 2003.

[48] Crime and Security Act 2010.

[49] Domestic Abuse Act 2021.

[50] Stalking Protection Act 2019.

victims and potential victims, whether through increased responsiveness or efficiency; indeed, the Sexual Harm Prevention Order[51] extends its coverage beyond named individuals to encompass the general public, albeit only where this is judged to be necessary.[52] This procedural flexibility is double-edged, however, with concerns having been raised that the hybrid form can see such measures used as a direct alternative to prosecution, with the attendant issues this has in diminishing the seriousness of the violence against women and girls.[53]

A third area where there has been an emphasis on hybrid orders is organized crime/ terrorism, which is where we position civil recovery. One notable feature here is the reliance on situations of exception to justify either more proactive or responsive policing or regulation within a particular problem area. Quasi-criminal measures such as the control order were introduced as a response to terrorist activity,[54] while the emphasis on hybridity in the context of organized crime is exhibited by the Serious Crime Prevention Order (SCPO),[55] as well as by civil recovery. There is an evident emphasis on preventing, disrupting, and countering terrorist and/or (organized) criminal activity through 'control', which constitutes, in essence, 'executive-based risk management'.[56] As Walker states, this emphasis on 'control' 'tends to predominate and reflects more general trends in the risk society such as risk aversion, the precautionary principle, and contingency planning'.[57] The result is an emphasis on the exceptional, and the idea that exceptional problems require innovative solutions. This, however,

[51] Sexual Offences Act 2003, as amended by the Anti-social Behaviour, Crime and Policing Act 2014.

[52] Rory Kelly and Martin Picton, 'Sexual Harm Prevention Orders and Necessity' (2020) 5 *Criminal Law Review* 411.

[53] Lis Bates and Marianne Hester, 'No Longer a Civil Matter? The Design and Use of Protection Orders for Domestic Violence in England and Wales' (2020) 42(2) *Journal of Social Welfare and Family Law* 133.

[54] Prevention of Terrorism Act 2005. Control orders were ultimately replaced by Terrorism Prevention and Investigation Measures (TPIMs), however, as Tadros states: 'The differences between TPIMs and control orders are relatively marginal—the main differences are that there is a stricter limit on relocation of controlees and there is a restriction on renewing TPIMs in the absence of new evidence of terrorism related activity. Renaming control orders when claiming to abolish them is a shameful face-saving exercise by the government.' Victor Tadros, 'Controlling Risk' in Andrew Ashworth, Lucia Zedner, and Patrick Tomlin (eds), *Prevention and the Limits of the Criminal Law* (Oxford University Press 2012) 135.

[55] Serious Crime Act 2007. Unlike others, who trace the SCPO back to the ASBO 'model' (see Andrew Ashworth and Lucia Zedner, *Preventive Justice* (Oxford University Press 2014) 90), Walker contends that the precedent for the SCPO is neither the ASBO nor the FBO: 'Rather, the precedent followed here is measures addressing anticipatory risk of serious harm akin to control orders.' Clive Walker, 'Keeping Control of Terrorists Without Losing Control of Constitutionalism' (2007) 59(5) *Stanford Law Review* 1395, 1460.

[56] Clive Walker, 'Keeping Control of Terrorists Without Losing Control of Constitutionalism' (2007) 59(5) *Stanford Law Review* 1395, 1400.

[57] Clive Walker, 'Keeping Control of Terrorists Without Losing Control of Constitutionalism' (2007) 59(5) *Stanford Law Review* 1395, 1400.

has the effect of pushing the procedural limits of the criminal law in particular, masking behind the ideas of imagination, innovation, and even elegance, the instrumental blurring of procedural lines.

The instrumentality evident in civil recovery—as well as other hybrid orders—gives rise to significant due process concerns, as documented throughout this book. Our interviews offer original insights into how practitioners' view this controversial practice, both from enforcement- and respondent-focused perspectives. We reiterate our agreement with the view that *crime should not pay*, a stance that attracted general acceptance in our practitioner interviews. There is no such consensus, however, as to *how* proceeds of crime should be confiscated. Due process compliance lies at the heart of this, and questions also remain about the practical impact of civil recovery, which has to be considered in two respects: impact on the individual recipient and impact on organized crime generally. While there have been some efforts to consider the impact on recipients of other hybrid orders[58] and post-conviction confiscation,[59] such analysis of civil recovery has not yet been conducted in either Ireland or England & Wales. Its broader impact upon crime is similarly under-researched.[60] Considering the controversy that surrounds this civil/criminal hybrid procedure, clarity as to how civil recovery impacts upon the individual, as well as whether it in fact undermines organized crime, would go a long way to determining how criminal property should be confiscated.

[58] In the context of two-step preventive orders see, *inter alia*, Vicky Heap, Alex Black, and Zoe Rodgers, 'Preventive Justice: Exploring the Coercive Power of Community Protection Notices to Tackle Anti-Social Behaviour' (2022) 24(3) *Punishment & Society* 305; Kevin Brown, 'The Banishment of the Poor from Public Space: Promoting and Contesting Neo-Liberalism at the Municipal Level' (2020) 29(4) *Social and Legal Studies* 574; Sam Lewis, Adam Crawford, and Peter Traynor, 'Nipping Crime in the Bud? The Use of Anti-Social Behaviour Interventions with Young People in England and Wales' (2016) 57(5) *British Journal of Criminology* 1230.

[59] Craig Fletcher, *'Double Punishment'—The Proceeds of Crime Act 2002 (POCA): A Qualitative Examination of the Post-Conviction Confiscation Punishment in England and Wales* (PhD Thesis, Manchester Metropolitan University, 2019).

[60] In the context of post-conviction confiscation, see Colin Atkinson, Simon Mackenzie, and Niall Hamilton-Smith, *A Systematic Review of the Effectiveness of Asset-Focused Interventions Against Organised Crime* (College of Policing 2017).

Index

For the benefit of digital users, indexed terms that span two pages (e.g., 52–53) may, on occasion, appear on only one of those pages.